MANAGING FOREIGN EXCHANGE RISK

ADVANCED STRATEGIES FOR GLOBAL INVESTORS, CORPORATIONS AND FINANCIAL INSTITUTIONS

REVISED EDITION

MANAGING FOREIGN EXCHANGE RISK

ADVANCED STRATEGIES FOR GLOBAL INVESTORS, CORPORATIONS AND FINANCIAL INSTITUTIONS

DAVID F. DEROSA

IRWIN
Professional Publishing®
Chicago • London • Singapore

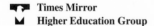
Times Mirror
Higher Education Group

Library of Congress Cataloging-in-Publication Data

DeRosa, David F.
   Managing foreign exchange risk : advanced strategies for global
investors, corporations and financial institutions / David F.
DeRosa. — 2nd ed.
    p. cm.
   Includes index.
   ISBN 0-7863-1022-7
   1. Foreign exchange. 2. Foreign exchange rates. 3. Risk.
I. Title.
HG3851.D37   1996
658.15—dc20   96–3557

Printed in the United States of America
  2 3 4 5 6 7 8 9 0 BS 3 2 1 0 9 8 7 6

For Sibylle

ACKNOWLEDGMENTS

One of the enjoyable tasks for an author is thanking friends and colleagues for their assistance. I have a long list.

Many of my colleagues at Swiss Bank have helped in the preparation of this book. I wish to especially thank Jay Greenberg, Michael Guarino, Marc Hendriks, Steve Hotopp, Bill Johnson, Judy Longman, Eila Matt, Satish Nandapurkar, David Pelleg, Ashraf Rizvi, Steve Depp, Brian Roseboro, Glenn Satty, Andy Siciliano, Carol Gary Tatti, Joe Troccolo, Ken Bercuson, Edward Pla, Stefan Hess, Hans Hsu, and John Zerolis. Special thanks go to the "G-Man" for teaching me the spot market for foreign exchange.

I wish to acknowledge the capable assistance and useful suggestions from George Constantinides, William Margrabe, Stephanie Berg, Gary Gastineau, Rainer Guidon, James O'Neill, Kevin Logan, Alan Ruskin, Fred Scala, Amy Smith, Nick Polson, Andrea Pozzi, Bruce Brittain, and Simon Smollett.

I am indebted once again to my friends Bryan Bowers and Phil Nehro for their detailed editing and inspired commentary.

I am grateful for data provided by the following companies: Greenwich Associates, InterSec, Morningstar, Goldman, Sachs & Co., Salomon Brothers, BARRA, Ferrell Capital Management, Ibbotson Associates, and Montgomery Investment Technology. Reuters Information Services has generously allowed reproduction of their exchange rate quotation screens. (Reuters shall not be liable for any loss or damage arising directly or indirectly by reason of the use or publication of any parts of the information provided.)

While preparing this edition, I had the privilege of teaching a course entitled "Foreign Exchange and Related Derivative Instruments" at the Graduate School of Business of the University of Chicago. I would like to thank two classes of students (from Spring 1995 and Autumn 1995) for diligently and patiently scrubbing errors from the early drafts of the manuscript for this book.

In 1993, the publishing company Yuuhikaku introduced a Japanese language edition of *Managing Foreign Exchange Risk* under the sponsorship of the Mitsui Marine and Fire Insurance Company. Translation was directed by Professor Gyoichi Iwata of Keio University. Naoto Akimoto, Yoji Yoshida, Yusuke Seki, and Akiko Inoue, all of Mitsui Marine, along with Professor Iwata, supplied useful ideas and criticism that have been incorporated in this revised edition.

The first edition of *Managing Foreign Exchange Risk* was published in 1990 by the Probus Publishing Company. Subsequently, Irwin Professional Publishing acquired Probus. I am grateful to Irwin for the continued interest in this book.

David F. DeRosa

CONTENTS

Chapter 8

American Exercise Currency Options and Futures Options   233

Chapter 9

Exotic Currency Options and Equity Structures with Currency Features   253

Chapter 10

Currency Overlay Programs   281

CHAPTER 1

Introduction

FOREIGN EXCHANGE RISK

In the most common context, foreign exchange risk is the risk of exchange rate translation losses associated with any economic interest that is denominated in a foreign currency. A U.S. dollar–based investor who acquires one million yen worth of shares in a Japanese company bears two risks. First, there is the risk that the shares might decline in value in their local currency. The shares might fall in value to 900,000 yen, for example. This risk is the local market risk that is borne by every investor who owns shares; it has nothing directly to do with exchange rates. The second risk to the U.S. dollar–based investor is that the yen might decline in value against the dollar. This could erode any economic benefit from a positive rate of return from the Japanese stock market. It might even create a loss for the investor despite a rise in the yen value of the shares. Ordinarily, this is what is considered foreign exchange risk; but more subtle, less direct risks can be attributed to movements in exchange rates.

Foreign exchange risk is an unavoidable consequence of international investing. Survey data show that sizable amounts of assets are at risk. In the United States, tax-exempt institutional investors, meaning pension trusts, foundations, and endowment funds, had total international assets of $300 billion

1

equivalent at the end of 1994[1] (Exhibit 1–1). Pension funds of countries other than the United States had an exposure equal to $489 billion equivalent of international assets at the end of 1994 (Exhibit 1–1). Mutual funds that specialize in international investing and that are distributed in the United States had $183 billion worth of overseas exposure at the end of 1995 (Exhibit 1–2). Given the size of the stakes, it is natural for there to be concern about currency risk.

EXHIBIT   1–1

Investments by Pension Funds in International Assets
A. U.S. Tax-Exempt Assets Invested Across Borders
Billions of U.S. Dollars

	1988	1989	1990	1991	1992	1993	1995
Total U.S. tax exempt	$2,067	$2,457	$2,410	$2,702	$3,319	$3,639	$3,760
Assets invested overseas	$62	$86	$94	$127	$156	$262	$300
Percent of total U.S. tax exempt	3.00%	3.50%	3.90%	4.70%	4.70%	7.20%	8.00%
Assets by category							
Equity	$53	$73	$74	$99	$117	$202	$241
Fixed income	$9	$13	$17	$24	$34	$49	$49
Other	—	—	$3	$4	$5	$11	$10

Source: InterSec Research Corporation.

B. Non-U.S. Pension Fund Assets Invested Across Borders, 1994
Billions of U.S. Dollars

	Japan	U.K.	Other	Total
Assets invested overseas	$85	$217	$1873	$489
Percent of total assets	7.60%	28.00%	13.40%	14.80%

Source: InterSec Research Corporation.

EXHIBIT 1-2

U.S. Foreign Mutual Fund Aggregate Net Assets, 1988–1995
Billions of U.S. Dollars

	Stock Funds					Bond Funds		
	European Stocks	Foreign Stocks	Pacific Stocks	World Stocks	Total Stocks	World Bonds	Short-Term World Income	Total Bonds
1988	0.65	5.38	1.15	10.99	18.17	4.21	0.14	4.35
1989	1.32	7.37	1.42	13.36	23.47	4.49	0.38	4.87
1990	3.77	9.07	1.36	13.38	27.58	5.35	6.73	12.08
1991	3.52	12.82	1.83	17.73	35.90	7.14	21.20	28.34
1992	3.23	16.81	2.88	19.17	42.09	10.00	14.45	24.45
1993	5.29	52.89	12.50	34.70	105.38	19.94	12.21	32.15
1994	6.08	73.52	13.40	45.38	138.38	16.25	5.54	21.79
1995	6.45	84.19	15.75	55.93	162.32	16.90	3.59	20.49

Notes: Data for mutual funds sold in the United States. European stock funds invest at least 65% in equity securities of European issuers. Foreign stock funds invest primarily in equity securities of issuers located outside of the United States. Pacific stock funds invest primarily in issuers located in countries in the Pacific Basin, including Japan, Hong Kong, Malaysia, Singapore, and Australia. World stock funds invest primarily in equity securities of issuers located throughout the world, maintaining a percentage of assets (normally 25% to 50%) in the United States. World bond funds invest in bonds denominated in currencies other than the U.S. dollar. Short-term world income funds invest primarily in various non-U.S.-currency-denominated bonds, usually with maturities of three years or less.

Source: Morningstar, Inc., 225 W. Wacker Dr., Chicago, IL 60606 (312-696-6000).

Foreign exchange risk can exert significant impact on investment performance. This can be confirmed by examination of the unhedged and currency-hedged total returns on the FT-Actuaries World Stock Market Indices (Exhibit 1–3), which are a set of popular performance benchmarks for international equity funds. Hedged returns are calculated using one-month currency forwards to hedge exchange rate risk. The returns are measured from the perspective of German mark–based, Japanese yen–based, and U.S. dollar–based investors. In each case, the stock market index excludes the investor's home market to focus the analysis on currency risk. Compound annual hedged returns are significantly different from unhedged returns. Roughly speaking, hedged returns are double or half of the corresponding unhedged returns, depending on which side of the currency the investor happened to be. Unhedged returns are more volatile than hedged returns, as can be seen by comparing the standard deviations of annual returns. Similar conclusions can be reached by examination of the data on unhedged and currency-hedged total returns on the Salomon Brothers World Government Bond Indices (Exhibit 1–4).

Some investment managers cope with foreign exchange risk by hedging with forward currency contracts. Others have developed expertise in using currency options in sophisticated strategies. Another solution is to engage the services of a specialist currency overlay manager, who assumes responsibility for the portfolio's foreign exchange risk. Whatever the means, the sheer size of the assets at risk as well as the magnitude of exchange rate movements relative to local market returns mandates that management of foreign exchange risk be made an integral part of the total investment process.

Some well-known commodity trading advisors and hedge fund managers have more aggressive attitudes towards foreign exchange. They trade positions in foreign exchange and its related derivative instruments as a high-risk asset class. Capital is put at risk in an attempt to profit from having correctly anticipated directional moves in exchange rates. In a limited number of cases, performance has been brilliant. As a rule, return profiles have been volatile, which in part can be explained by the use of substantial leverage. As such, a considerable amount of attention

EXHIBIT 1-3

Total Returns on FT-Actuaries World Stock Market Indices
Unhedged and Currency Hedged, 1986–1995

	World Ex-Germany		World Ex-Japan		World Ex–United States	
	Hedged into DEM	Unhedged DEM	Hedged into JPY	Unhedged JPY	Hedged into USD	Unhedged USD
1986	42.34%	12.82%	28.17%	0.39%	39.81%	66.55%
1987	11.35%	–2.29%	5.05%	–18.97%	–0.52%	26.25%
1988	24.05%	38.62%	13.83%	19.68%	34.50%	27.93%
1989	23.49%	11.44%	23.30%	49.03%	26.09%	12.17%
1990	–22.25%	–27.03%	–11.73%	–8.71%	–30.38%	–23.12%
1991	19.54%	21.96%	24.63%	14.84%	4.85%	13.32%
1992	1.24%	1.43%	4.22%	2.25%	–11.03%	–13.06%
1993	22.24%	30.91%	20.17%	8.84%	26.25%	32.25%
1994	0.43%	–5.47%	–7.28%	–10.26%	–0.75%	8.36%
1995	20.18%	19.73%	25.79%	28.34%	10.74%	10.45%
Compound annual return	12.92%	8.58%	11.75%	6.90%	7.83%	13.72%
Standard deviation of annual returns	17.63%	19.26%	14.33%	20.30%	21.95%	24.84%

Notes: Currency-hedged returns calculated on the basis of rolling one-month forwards and include effect of bid–ask spread.

Hedged returns for Thailand, Brazil, S. Africa, and Mexico are actually unhedged returns for lack of forwards data, but these countries are a minuscule part of the indices.

Sources: The returns are calculated by Goldman, Sachs & Co. and are derived from the FT/S&P-Actuaries World Indices which are owned by FT-SE International Limited, Goldman, Sachs & Co. and Standard & Poor's. The indices are compiled by FT-SE International and Goldman Sachs in conjunction with the Faculty of Actuaries and the Institute of Actuaries. NatWest Securities Ltd. was a co-founder of the Indices.

Compound annual return and standard deviation of annual returns calculated by author.

Total Returns on Salomon Brothers World Government Bond Indices
Unhedged and Currency Hedged, 1985–1995

	World Ex-Germany		World Ex-Japan		World Ex–United States	
	Hedged into DEM	Unhedged DEM	Hedged into JPY	Unhedged JPY	Hedged into USD	Unhedged USD
1985	12.49%	-1.98%	15.66%	-1.00%	11.14%	35.01%
1986	10.74%	-3.57%	11.18%	-6.51%	11.40%	31.35%
1987	2.17%	-3.69%	1.06%	-14.15%	9.27%	35.15%
1988	4.29%	18.63%	3.83%	8.13%	9.12%	2.34%
1989	6.55%	-0.50%	5.77%	27.58%	4.11%	-3.41%
1990	6.20%	-1.74%	5.58%	6.40%	3.32%	15.29%
1991	16.85%	18.63%	15.11%	5.29%	11.11%	16.21%
1992	14.39%	12.47%	8.50%	4.37%	8.03%	4.77%
1993	18.15%	22.19%	11.70%	-1.29%	13.42%	15.12%
1994	-2.47%	-9.43%	-6.25%	-9.77%	-4.02%	5.99%
1995	16.28%	9.18%	11.93%	25.80%	17.92%	19.55%
Compound annual return	9.41%	4.95%	7.46%	3.34%	8.47%	15.44%
Standard deviation of annual returns	6.73%	11.04%	6.53%	13.18%	5.82%	13.29%

Notes: Currency-hedged returns calculated on the basis of rolling one-month forwards.

Source: Salomon Brothers.

Compound annual return and standard deviation of annual returns calculated by author.

is now focused on monitoring and controlling the risk of trading positions in foreign exchange. Traditionally, risk control meant attempting to avoid steep capital drawdowns by concentrating on trades that have defined loss limits but are nonetheless attractive on a risk–reward basis. More recently, a new methodology based on probabilistic concepts, called dollars-at-risk, has been moving quickly towards becoming the industry standard tool for risk management.

Corporate treasurers are well versed in managing foreign exchange risk. Foreign exchange risk is also a key element of their everyday practice of doing business overseas. Corporate treasurers in the United States, continental Europe, the United Kingdom, and Japan transacted over 6.6 trillion U.S. dollars equivalent in foreign exchange in 1994.[2] Survey data show that their foremost concern is receivables and payables that derive from foreign operations. Treasurers are also concerned with the exchange rate exposure of their balance sheet when significant assets have been acquired in other countries or when financing has been obtained in overseas capital markets. Some corporations have taken foreign exchange risk management a step further with what has come to be known as economic hedging. This term refers to the management of the foreign exchange risk implied by intangible economic property rights such as market position. For example, a German manufacturer of automobiles might hedge the economic value of his share of the U.S. market by buying dollar/yen, fearing that a stronger dollar/weaker yen might enhance the competitive position of the Japanese automobile industry. But whatever the concern, corporate users tend to be hedgers rather than speculators, and their process of managing foreign exchange risk usually requires careful planning, as the entire process can be complicated by international tax, accounting, and legal considerations (see Weinrib, Driscoll, and Connors 1992).

Not to be overlooked in the grand picture are central banks. Central banks are usually the economic agents of governmental policy with regard to exchange rates, notably in the context of their periodic direct intervention into currency markets. This is why their every word and deed are scrutinized by market participants. But central banks, like all financial institutions, have an interest in managing the foreign exchange risk attributable to their holdings of international assets, including foreign currency reserves.

FOREIGN EXCHANGE AND RELATED DERIVATIVE INSTRUMENTS

Foreign exchange trading is conducted in the form of a variety of over-the-counter and exchange-listed instruments.

Spot Foreign Exchange

Spot trading in the interbank foreign exchange market is customarily for value in two bank business days after trade date (except for the Canadian dollar, which when traded against the U.S. dollar settles one bank business day later). The convention in the interbank market is that the currency designated first in the exchange rate pair is the direct object of the trade. For example, to sell 10 million dollar/mark is to sell 10 million U.S. dollars against marks. The majority of all foreign exchange transactions involve the U.S. dollar. There are two conventions in spot trading. Currencies quoted European convention are expressed as the number of units of foreign currency that are equal to one dollar. A quotation on dollar/mark of 1.5825 – 30 means that the dealer is willing to buy dollars/sell marks at 1.5825 marks per dollar or is willing to sell dollars/buy marks at 1.5830 marks per dollar. Currencies quoted American convention include the British pound, the Irish punt, the Australian dollar, the New Zealand dollar, and the European currency unit (the ECU). American convention is given in terms of the number of dollars equal to one unit of foreign currency.

Some cross rates trade directly. A cross rate is an exchange rate between two non–U.S. dollar currencies, such as the German mark/Japanese yen (mark/yen) and the British pound/German mark (sterling/mark). Cross rates, mainly involving the mark, account for most of the trading in the European Monetary System (EMS) currencies. Cross rates are linked to their component dollar exchange rates by the principle of triangular arbitrage.[3]

Forward Foreign Exchange

There are two types of forward transactions. There is the forward outright, which is no different from a spot transaction except that the value date is deferred beyond the spot value date. And there is a forward swap transaction, which is really two transactions quoted as one. A forward swap transaction consists of a spot transaction plus a companion forward outright in the opposite direction. The forward swap transaction is really a borrowing/lending transaction, meaning that it is a play on interest rates rather than a true currency transaction.

Forward transactions are quoted in two parts. First there are forward points that correspond to the value date. Forward points are indicated on dealing room screens for regular intervals of 1-, 2-, 3-, 6-, and 12-month value, but virtually any legitimate value date can be arranged. Points are added or subtracted to the second component, which is the spot level. The reason forward points are sometimes added and sometimes subtracted from the spot level has to do with the interest rate spread between the two currencies, a topic that is discussed at length in Chapter 4.

Currency Futures Contracts

Currency futures are exchange listed contracts. They work like commodity futures. The largest center for currency futures trading is the International Monetary Market (IMM) division of the Chicago Mercantile Exchange. Besides the IMM, currency futures are listed on the Philadelphia Board of Trade, the MidAmerica Commodity Exchange, and the Singapore International Monetary Exchange (SIMEX). Traders must meet the requirements of two margin calls. Initial margin represents a good faith deposit that is required when a position is opened. Variation margin is the position's mark-to-market that is debited or credited to the investor's account on the basis of daily price movements of the futures contracts.

Currency Options

Currency options are traded on organized exchanges and in the interbank over-the-counter market. A call option is a contract giving the owner ("buyer") the right, but not the obligation, to purchase from the seller ("writer") of the option a face amount of foreign exchange at a fixed strike price before or on a specified expiration date. A put option grants to the buyer the right to sell foreign exchange to the writer. The buyer pays a premium to the writer to obtain the call or the put. The Philadelphia Stock Exchange lists call and put options on foreign exchange. Calls and puts on currency futures contracts, called futures options, are listed on the IMM.

Currency Swap Transactions

Currency swap transactions are more complex forms of forward swaps. In a swap transaction, an investor exchanges the fixed or floating cash flow from a debt or asset denominated in one currency for cash flow denominated in another.

ESTIMATES OF THE SIZE
OF THE FOREIGN EXCHANGE MARKET

It is well known that foreign exchange is an extraordinarily deep market. Some estimates of the size of the trading volume are reported in parallel triennial surveys undertaken during the month of April 1995 by the Bank for International Settlements in cooperation with the New York Federal Reserve Bank.[4] Earlier surveys were undertaken in the month of April 1992 (BIS 1993) and 1989. The surveys revealed the following information.

The Overall Size of the Market

Global net turnover in the world's foreign exchange markets was estimated to have been some $1,230 billion per business day in April 1995. This figure was adjusted for virtually all double-counting, as well as for estimated gaps in reporting. (Futures and options trading was not included.) The comparable numbers were $820 billion and $590 billion, for 1992 and 1989, respectively.

A greater volume of trading took place in the form of forwards (57%) than in spot deals (43%) in the 1995 survey. Within the group of forward transactions, foreign exchange swaps continued to overshadow forward outrights by a ratio of 6 to 1.

Trading in over-the-counter currency options was estimated to be $40 billion in 1995 and $31 billion in 1992.

Trading by Currency

The U.S. dollar remained the predominant currency in the 1995 survey. It was one side of 83 percent of spot transactions. The share of the mark, the second most important currency, was 27 percent in 1995, compared to 40 percent in 1992. The share of the yen was 27 percent in 1995, up from 24 percent in 1992.

By currency pairs, dollar/mark accounted for over 25 percent of total trading in the 1992 survey. USD/JPY and GBP/USD were 20 percent and 10 percent, respectively. Direct transactions between EMS currencies were 7 percent of total turnover.

Trading by Geographical Location

London was the biggest center (30 percent), followed by the United States (16 percent) and Japan (10 percent). Next were Singapore, Hong Kong, Switzerland, Germany, France, and Australia, in respective order of importance.

THE RANDOM BEHAVIOR OF FOREIGN EXCHANGE RATES

A central question facing theoreticians and practitioners is how to model the behavior of foreign exchange rates. One school of thought is that an exchange rate can be treated as a random variable being governed by a probability distribution. In particular, the spot exchange rate might follow a random walk:

$$\tilde{S}_t = S_{t-1} + \tilde{e}_t$$

where $\tilde{S}$ and S_{t-1} represent the exchange rate in units of domestic currency per one unit of foreign currency observed at times (t) and ($t - 1$), respectively, and $\tilde{e}_t$ is a random normal white noise process. The tilde symbol ($\sim$) denotes a random variable. It is common in empirical studies to take the logarithm of the time series of spot levels and work with currency rates of return. The currency return from time $(t-1)$ to (t) is given by

$$\tilde{R}_t^C = \ln\left(\tilde{S}_t\right) - \ln\left(S_{t-1}\right) = \ln\left(\frac{\tilde{S}_t}{S_{t-1}}\right)$$

where ln is the natural logarithm. The random walk model applied to the logarithm of spot levels implies that the currency returns are white noise innovations with no tendency to run in predictable trends. More formally, one could say that the times series of currency returns is serially independent in the population.

Random walk models have had a long history in finance, dating back to the pioneering work of Bachelier (1901) on commodities markets. In the 1960s, academic thought crystallized around the theory of efficient markets. The efficient market hypothesis put forth the broad notion that market prices reflect all knowable, relevant information, including the history of prices. In that vein, any evidence that currency returns are serially random supports the hypothesis that the currency market is efficient. At the other extreme, a finding that currency returns are serially dependent might be considered a basis for the widely held belief that technical analysis, meaning the study of historical charts of currency movements, is a profitable trading strategy.

The debate as to whether currency returns are or are not serially random is not easy to settle, as the empirical evidence does not speak with one voice. Two popular statistical tests for randomness are the sample autocorrelation function and the runs test. The sample autocorrelation function estimates the correlation of a time series with its own history at various time lags. The Q-statistic tests the joint hypothesis that a group of autocorrelation coefficients (perhaps at lags 1 through 12 for monthly data) are jointly zero (Ljung and Box 1978). The runs test is a nonparametric test. It works on the serial pattern of positive and negative observations. A run is defined as a series of values with the same sign, relative to the sample mean. The expected number of runs, its standard deviation, and a t-statistic can be calculated from the observed number of positive and negative values in a sample.

Exhibit 1–5 displays sample statistics for monthly currency returns on five major exchange rates for the period January 1986 to May 1995, taken from the standpoint of a U.S. dollar investor.[5] Autocorrelation coefficients at near lags support the random walk characterization, and Q statistics fail to reject the null hypothesis of randomness at the .05 level. Runs tests also support the serial random hypothesis. Exhibit 1–6 displays empirical results on intraday currency returns (Wasserfallen 1989) and daily currency returns (Hsieh 1989). Autocorrelation and runs tests fail to reject the serial random hypothesis, although the runs test on daily returns is significant for sterling and the German mark.

Another body of tests reported by Liu and He (1991) and Kritzman (1989) rejects the serial random hypothesis with variance ratio tests. The variance ratio test compares sample variances calculated from a single sample but with differing interval lengths (e.g., variance of weekly returns compared to variance of monthly returns). Under the serial random hypothesis, variance should grow linearly with the return calculation interval. More

E X H I B I T 1–5

Summary Statistics on Monthly Currency Returns
January 1986–May 1995

	USD/DEM	USD/CHF	GBP/USD	AUD/USD	USD/JPY
Average	0.005	0.006	0.002	0.000	0.008
Std. dev.	0.036	0.039	0.036	0.028	0.035
Minimum	−0.109	−0.101	−0.124	−0.115	−0.066
Maximum	0.081	0.095	0.079	0.068	0.117
Skewness	−0.402	−0.237	−0.625	−0.877	0.260
Kurtosis	0.205	−0.189	1.237	2.633	0.031
Runs test (z)	−0.279	−0.265	−1.260	−0.794	−0.916
Autocorrelation					
Lag 1	0.015	0.064	0.140	0.031	0.014
Lag 2	0.049	0.004	−0.058	−0.012	0.027
Lag 3	−0.085	−0.056	−0.040	0.003	−0.068
SE	0.10	0.09	0.09	0.09	0.09
Q(12)	6.01	7.13	11.41	7.21	18.65

sophisticated yet is the empirical work of Hsieh, which applies ARCH models (autoregressive conditional heteroscedastic) to exchange rates. Hsieh uses a powerful statistic called the BDS statistic (see Brock, Hsieh, and LeBaron 1992) to reject nonlinear serial independence in daily foreign exchange rates on five currencies from 1974 to 1983. There is a mathematical subtlety that a time series can be linearly uncorrelated—as measured by the tra-

E X H I B I T 1–6

Summary Statistics on Currency Returns from Various Studies
Summary of Statistics for Intraday Currency Returns on USD/CHF
Five-Minute Observations during 231 Trading Days in 1983, Bid Prices

	Average Return per Day	Std. Dev. per Day	Skewness	Kurtosis	Autocorrelation	
					Lag 1	Lag 2
Mean	0.02	0.66	−0.19	4.79	−0.13	0.03
Std. dev.	0.99	0.26	0.91	7.40	0.15	0.12
Minimum	−3.64	0.27	−5.16	−0.52	−0.49	−0.29
Maximum	3.69	1.53	3.8	41.69	0.26	0.36

Source: Wasserfallen (1989).

Summary Statistics for Daily Currency Returns, 1974–83

	GBP	CAD	DEM	JPY	CHF
Mean	−0.0184	−0.0089	0.0005	0.0077	0.0171
Median	0.0000	0.0098	0.0000	0.0000	0.0000
Std. dev.	0.5921	0.2234	0.6372	0.6260	0.7889
Skewness	−0.4136	−0.3149	−0.4249	−0.2044	−0.2835
Kurtosis	8.90	8.61	12.79	11.27	10.22
Maximum	3.7496	1.5492	3.6686	3.5703	4.4466
Minimum	−4.6623	−1.8677	−7.0967	−6.2566	−7.0054
Runs test:	1.96	−0.86	2.38	0.64	0.77
$N(0,1)$	(0.0500)	(0.3898)	(0.0173)	(0.5222)	(0.4413)

Source: Hsieh (1989).

ditional Pearson correlation coefficient—yet be nonlinearly dependent for a nonnormal population.

Turning to the issue of distributional form, the histogram of monthly currency returns for the German mark (Exhibit 1–7) shows a broad resemblance to the normal distribution except that there are more outliers, suggesting kurtosis, and peakedness relative to the normal (referred to as a leptokurtic sample). Relative to the normal, a greater number of observations are very near and very far away from the mean, and a fewer number are at intermediate distances from the mean.[6] This is supported by the skewness and kurtosis statistics reported in Exhibits 1–5 and 1–6.

What conclusions can be drawn? While there is ample evidence in the literature in support of the random hypothesis, the new statistical procedures favor the serial dependence hypothesis. On the second issue, empirical evidence seems to overwhelmingly reject the normal distribution for currency returns. However, despite all of the research that has been conducted, no single probability distribution that optimally describes foreign exchange returns has been isolated.

EXHIBIT 1–7

Histogram of Monthly Returns on USD/DEM
January 1986–May 1995

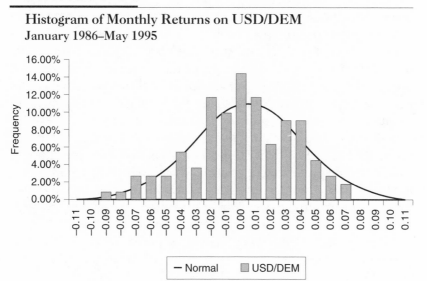

Mathematically speaking, the random model for foreign exchange is familiar to students of empirical finance because it is often used to describe the behavior of stock market prices. But an important difference between currencies and stocks must be mentioned and maybe even stressed: There is no evidence that currencies, unlike stocks and bonds, contain a market-determined risk premium. This is not to say that currencies are not risky. As can be seen in the data displayed in Exhibits 1–3 and 1–4, currency risk can materially affect investment performance. The distinction is that currency risk may not be "economic" risk, at least as it is perceived and priced in the marketplace. One notion is that currencies resemble agricultural and industrial commodities, both of which are known to be volatile in price but thought to have no risk premium. Nevertheless, speaking in an abstract context, the general resemblance of the behavior of exchange rates to that of stock prices, apart from the risk premium issue, is fortunate. It means that many scientific discoveries about the stock market and its derivative markets, such as option pricing theory, can be applied to currency markets with little or no modification.

The minor currencies can be quite a different story. They have been known to exhibit large, discontinuous price movements, particularly in an environment of government-sponsored price fixing. Governments have sometimes gone to extraordinary lengths to fight the market's determination of their currency's value. As a general rule, the very currencies that have received the most extensive support have proven to be the most dangerous for investors. Catastrophic declines in value, sometimes in the course of a single day, have followed the abandonment of stabilization policies that have become too costly to maintain. A recent example is the Mexican peso, which in December 1994 lost over 50 percent of its value in the 72 hours following the government's retreat from an exchange rate stabilization policy. Usually, investors find it impossible to hedge this type of catastrophic risk except at exorbitant prices for forwards, swaps, and options. In extreme situations, no market whatsoever may exist for a currency that exhibits chaotic, discontinuous behavior because no counterparty is willing to take the other side of what could turn out to be a wholly ruinous trade.

THE DEBATE ON FOREIGN EXCHANGE HEDGING

The literature from academicians and practitioners contains no shortage of advice on what should be done about the foreign exchange risk associated with international portfolio management (see Gastineau 1995). Unfortunately, no single, generally accepted view has emerged from the debate.

A large part of what has been written addresses the question of whether or not foreign exchange risk should as a rule be permanently—or "statically"—hedged. There are three prominent opinions.

The first comes from Perold and Schulman (1988), who believe that foreign exchange risk should be hedged all of the time. They reach this conclusion based in part on the proposition that foreign currency hedging has no risk premium:

> When one buys foreign currency, the seller is buying U.S. dollars. To assume one will receive a premium for holding foreign currency is to assume the other side of the transaction will pay a premium for U.S. dollars, that "they need our currency more than we need theirs." Certainly, on occasion one might expect rewards for taking currency risk, but there is little reason to believe that, in the long run, the rewards for bearing foreign currency risk will be one-sided. . . . There are good grounds for believing that, over relatively short periods, the expected return from currency hedging (equivalently, currency exposure) will be non-zero. However, there are not good grounds for believing that these premiums will be consistently positive or consistently negative. (p. 47)

Perold and Schulman present evidence that currency hedging can materially reduce the risk of investing in assets denominated in a foreign currency. They examine the volatility of hedged and unhedged, quarterly, real U.S. dollar rates of return over the decade ending December 1987 for investments made in the stock and bond markets of Japan, the United Kingdom, and Germany. The volatility of hedged returns is significantly and uniformly lower than the volatility of unhedged returns. Given their no risk-premium assertion, Perold and Schulman conclude that currency hedging is a "free lunch."

A second view comes from Black (1989 and 1990), who advises that although some hedging is desirable, investors in international equities should retain some exposure to foreign exchange risk.[7]

Black derives an optimal hedge ratio (meaning the fraction of exchange rate exposure that needs to be hedged)

$$\frac{\mu_m - \sigma_m^2}{\mu_m - \frac{1}{2}\sigma_e^2}$$

where μ_m is the average world market portfolio expected excess return (above the riskless rate) on the world market equity portfolio, σ_m^2 is the average world market portfolio excess return variance, and σ_e^2 is the average exchange rate variance across all pairs of countries. For example, if one were to use $\mu_m = 8\%$, $\sigma_m = 15\%$, and $\sigma_e = 10\%$ (which are plausible given any number of empirical studies on historical rates of return and volatility), the universal hedge ratio would be equal to 77 percent. Black acknowledges that a different set of parameter values can greatly modify the calculated universal hedge ratio.

Black's derivation rests in part on a somewhat obscure mathematical principle called Siegel's paradox (or to a related concept known as Jensen's inequality). The paradox concerns the asymmetrical effect of a movement in exchange rates as considered by consumers whose wealth and income are denominated on opposite sides of an exchange rate. For example, a decline in dollar/mark from 1.5000 to 1.4500 would represent a loss of 3.33 percent in foreign purchasing power for dollar-based consumers but a gain of 3.44 percent in foreign purchasing power for mark-based consumers. Black argues that this seemingly paradoxical asymmetry represents an exploitable profit opportunity if some portion of one's foreign exchange exposure were left unhedged. The optimal hedge ratio is "universal" because, in his words:

> The formula applies to every investor who holds foreign securities. It applies to a U.S. investor holding Japanese assets, a Japanese investor holding British assets, and a British investor holding U.S. assets. (Black 1989, p. 16)

A third opinion comes from Froot (1993), who studies long-term movements of exchange rates. Froot argues that the benefits from currency hedging are short term in nature. Over longer periods, he finds that there is either no benefit or actually a cost to hedging. His argument hinges on his empirical finding that real exchange rates are mean-reverting, a condition that would explain why hedging appears to be so different in the short and long runs. Froot writes:

> I argue . . . that currency hedges have very different properties at long horizons compared with short horizons. . . . The properties of currencies hedges vary with horizon in part because hedge returns at different horizons are driven by very different factors. At relatively short horizons, hedge returns are dominated by changes in real exchange rates, i.e., in the purchasing power of one currency compared with another. However, mean reversion in the real exchange rates implies that these purchasing powers tend toward parity, so that real exchange rates over time remain roughly constant. At long horizons, hedge returns are instead dominated by fluctuations in cross-country differences in unexpected inflation and real interest differentials. The importance of this latter component grows the longer the hedge remains in place. (p. 2)

An entirely different group of opinions is based on the assumed existence of exploitable inefficiencies in foreign exchange. As has already been discussed, Kritzman (1989) argues that currency returns are nonrandom on the grounds of variance ratio tests. He argues that central bank activity in the market induces serial dependence in exchange rates that can be exploited by what he terms convex investment strategies. Convex strategies are basically trend-following investment rules. They buy or add to a position in a currency as its exchange rate increases and sell or reduce a position as its exchange rate declines. In a similar line, Levich and Thomas (1993) propose that nonrandomness in currency futures prices can be exploited with an agglomeration of filter rules and moving-average crossover rules. They write:

> Our analysis of daily currency futures prices over the 1976–90 period shows that exchange rates have not evolved randomly.

Simple trend-following trading rules have historically earned economically and statistically significant profits. . . . To date, most contributors to the currency hedging debate have either implicitly or explicitly assumed that foreign currency positions do not promise abnormal risk-adjusted returns. But if foreign exchange markets offer unusual profit opportunities, the arguments for always hedging are weakened. Our results suggest that selective hedging may produce superior investment performance. (p. 68)

Kritzman (1993) calls attention to another potentially exploitable market anomaly, which has to do with the forward exchange rate. In some circles, classical economic theory is believed to postulate that the forward exchange rate is an unbiased estimator of the future spot exchange rate—the so-called uncovered interest parity theorem. Yet the body of empirical evidence roundly rejects this notion. Kritzman writes:

Since 1973, the beginning of the modern era of floating exchange rates, the forward rate has systematically and significantly overestimated the subsequent change in the spot rate. On balance, hedgers have suffered losses when they sold currency forward contracts at discounts or purchased them at premiums, while they have reaped gains when they sold currency forward contracts at premiums and purchased them at discounts. (p. 96)

Kritzman develops a normative approach for currency hedging that takes advantage of the supposed forward rate bias. Hazuka and Huberts (1994) take it one step further. They recommend an approach that prefers currencies with comparatively high real interest rates. Their empirical work gives evidence of outperformance of their alternative method over simply favoring high nominal interest rate, meaning discount, currencies.

What characterizes the work of Levitch and Thomas, Kritzman, and Hazuka and Huberts is the belief that there is no optimal, static hedging policy. Each advocates implementation of decision rules that are based on market anomalies.

Finally, it should be recognized that none of the above mentioned research stands in the way of active management of currency hedging to express views on the future direction of exchange rates.

DERIVATIVES AND PUBLIC POLICY

A ferocious public debate concerning derivative securities erupted in the course of the preparation of the second edition of this book. At issue is the emergence of some spectacular losses to investors associated with derivative instruments. These losses, which almost always were preceded by years of hefty profits, have fallen upon investors who would not ordinarily have been deemed suited to speculative risk taking. This has led to new demands for regulation of the derivatives segment of the capital market. Beyond the suitability issue, there are two important questions. First, are derivative instruments inherently risky? The answer is no, but that must be qualified by the presumption that the investor has a proper understanding of risk. The second question is, Are derivative instruments inherently profitable? The answer is no: Derivatives are not automatic wealth-producing machines. On the other hand, derivatives are powerful—if not indispensable—tools for risk management, which should become apparent to readers of this book.

NOTES

1. InterSec Research of Stamford Connecticut surveys investment managers. InterSec cautions that these data exclude foreign investment holdings in accounts not designated as international or global strategies.

2. Greenwich Associates conducts surveys of foreign exchange product end users. The 1994 survey included 966 corporations, which was comprised of industrials, commercial enterprises, construction firms, services, and utilities. Total foreign exchange transactions in spot, forward, swaps, currency options, and currency futures were $1,526 billion (United States), $3,886 billion (top-tier continental Europe), £477 billion (United Kingdom), and $466 billion (Japan). Greenwich Associates also surveyed 351 financial institutions in the same four centers. Financial institutions included investment portfolio managers, investment banks, hedge funds, insurance

companies, and other financials. The survey estimates were $7,648 billion (United States), $1,642 billion (continental Europe), £1,568 billion (United Kingdom), and $546 billion (Japan).

3. The following is an example of how triangular arbitrage holds the cross rates in place. Suppose that dollar/yen were quoted at 105.00 – 105.05 and dollar/mark at 1.5825 – 1.5830. To synthesize a long position in mark/yen (i.e., long marks/short yen), a trader could sell one million dollars against marks at 1.5825. At this rate, the trader would be short one million USD against 1,582,500 DEM. Next, the trader could buy one million USD against yen at 105.05. This implies a rounded synthetic exchange rate offer equal to 66.38 for mark/yen. To synthesize a short mark/yen position, the trader could buy one million USD against DEM at 1.5830 and sell the dollars against yen at 105.00 to arrive at a synthetic exchange rate bid equal to 66.33. A direct quotation on the mark/yen cross outside of 66.33 – 66.38 would never trade.

4. The 1995 survey results are preliminary numbers as reported in a press communique from the Bank for International Settlements, dated 24 October 1995, entitled "Central Bank Survey of Foreign Exchange Market Activity in April 1995: Preliminary Global Findings." The 1995 survey separated futures and options trading from foreign exchange turnover, which was not done in previous surveys. Data for options trading were reported in a press communique from the Bank for International Settlements, dated 18 December 1995, entitled "Central Bank Survey of Derivatives Market Activity: Release of Preliminary Global Totals."

5. Strictly speaking, the kurtosis statistic is equal to three for a normal population. However, it is common practice to subtract three from the statistic for a sample to make a comparison to zero. The skewness statistic is zero for a normal population. The standard error of the autocorrelation function is $1/\sqrt{N}$ where N is the sample size,

given the null hypothesis that the population autocorrelation is zero. Q is the adjusted Box–Pierce statistic. Q is a joint test that autocorrelation coefficients 1 to k are zero. $Q(k)$ is given by

$$N(N+2)\sum_{i=1}^{k}\frac{r_i^2}{(N-k)}$$

where r_i is the sample autocorrelation coefficient at lag i. Q is distributed chi-square with k degrees of freedom under the null hypothesis (see Roberts and Ling 1982). The expected number of runs in a sample of N observations where N_1 are positive and N_2 are negative is given by

$$E(\text{Runs}) = \frac{2N_1N_2}{N} + 1$$

and the standard deviation (Roberts and Ling 1982) is given by

$$\sqrt{\frac{2N_1N_2(2N_1N_2 - N)}{N^2(N-1)}}$$

6. For further reading on the controversy about the distributional form of exchange returns, see Westerfield (1977); Rogalski and Vinso (1978); Freidman and Vandersteel (1982); McFarland, Pettit, and Sung (1982); Wasserfallen and Zimmermann (1985); and Wasserfallen (1989).

7. Black makes his argument only for international equity portfolios. His universal hedge ratio is 100 percent for international fixed-income portfolios.

CHAPTER 2

An Overview
of the International
Monetary System

In the period following the end of the second world war, the governments of the major industrialized countries experimented with a variety of exchange rate systems while in search of a workable, stable international monetary system. This chapter outlines this history and describes the foreign exchange regimes that exist today.

FROM BRETTON WOODS TO TODAY

With the end of the second world war in sight, the leaders of the Allied countries met at a resort at Bretton Woods, New Hampshire, in July 1944 to agree on a design for a new international monetary system. The cornerstone of the Bretton Woods agreement was a pledge of cooperation between central banks. The agreement called for the creation of the International Monetary Fund (IMF). The most important outcome of Bretton Woods was a resolution to fix the value of all major currencies to the U.S. dollar within a narrow tolerance band. The U.S. dollar, as a consequence, together with gold, became the primary medium of international exchange. The exact rules were as follows:

1. The central banks of all IMF countries would keep their foreign exchange reserves in U.S. dollars, British pounds, or gold.

2. Each IMF member country would establish its currency's par value against the U.S. dollar. Thereafter, it would be responsible for maintaining its currency against the dollar within a band of plus or minus 1 percent of par value. This would be accomplished with appropriate domestic fiscal and monetary policies, and open market purchase and sales of foreign exchange. The IMF would help countries by extending foreign exchange loans to enable central banks to carry out stabilizing transactions.

3. The United States would maintain the value of the dollar by the purchase and sale of gold at a fixed price of $35 per ounce.

From time to time, adjustments to par value exchange rates, called devaluations and revaluations, were required to keep the Bretton Woods superstructure functioning. Critics began to call it the system of "creeping pegs." In the first 25 years, the largest devaluation occurred in 1949, when the British pound was devalued from $4.03 to $2.80. The British pound was devalued again in 1967 from $2.80 to $2.40. The French franc was devalued by 11 percent in 1969.

The most serious challenge to the Bretton Woods system was the "dollar crisis" of 1971. The dollar had become regarded as a depreciating currency, yet it was the principal monetary reserve for the free world. The United States was running serious balance of payments deficits, and there were well-founded reasons to fear that inflation would erode the dollar's purchasing power. At the extreme, there were doubts as to whether the United States could maintain the convertibility of the dollar into gold at $35. In the face of this acute loss of confidence, President Nixon suspended the dollar's convertibility into gold at the $35 per ounce level in August 1971. Mr. Nixon simultaneously imposed price and wage controls in an attempt to curb inflation. The president also placed a temporary surcharge on goods imported into the United States, presumably to ameliorate the pressure on the dollar. In December 1971, the Smithsonian Agreement, a restructuring of Bretton Woods, was announced with great ceremony. The price of gold was raised to $38 (i.e., the dollar was devalued), and the permitted band of fluctuation around the dollar was widened to 2.25 percent, up or down, for all participating currencies.

In the end, the Smithsonian modifications failed to save the Bretton Woods system. The system of pegged dollar exchange rates collapsed in 1973. Ever since that time, the dollar has mostly been allowed to float, its value being determined by free market forces of supply and demand.

EUROPE'S ATTEMPTS TO STABILIZE EXCHANGE RATES

The treaty of Rome in 1957 called for the creation of the European Economic Community (EEC). This started the process of European economic unification that led to the establishment of the European Monetary System (EMS) in 1979.

European governments exhibit a particularly strong aversion to exchange rate volatility. The reasons for this are not readily apparent to non-European observers. Giavazzi and Giovannini (1989) provide an explanation:

> Analyzing the EMS without considering why Europeans are averse to exchange rate fluctuations would not give a clear picture of the system. The EMS is just one element of a much richer set of agreements among European countries in the trade, industrial and agricultural areas. These agreements rest on exchange rate stability, and thus lend credibility to intra-European exchange rate targets. (p. 1)

Following in the spirit of the Smithsonian Agreement, the EEC suggested in December 1972 that its member countries limit the movement of their bilateral exchange rates to one-half of the new 2.25 percent band. Members of the EEC voluntarily joined (and left and sometimes later rejoined) this system. It became known as the "snake in the tunnel" (or simply the "snake"). Schwartz (1987) relates a brief history of the snake:

> Six countries (France, Germany, Italy, Belgium, Luxembourg, the Netherlands) originally joined the snake, three others joined in May 1972 but left in June (UK, Denmark, Eire). Denmark rejoined in October 1972, Italy left in December 1972, France left in January

> 1974, rejoined in July 1975, and left again in March 1976. Sweden
> and Norway, non-EEC countries, joined in May 1972. Sweden left
> in August 1977 [and] many changes in exchange rates within the
> snake were made. (p. 349)

The experiment with the snake clearly failed, yet it may have
inspired the creation later of the European exchange rate
mechanism.[1]

At the start, the EMS called for the creation of a new currency, the ECU (European currency unit). The ECU was originally
a GDP-weighted average of the EMS currencies. Periodically, its
composition was modified to reflect changes in the relative GDP
of member nations. The composition of the ECU also changed
when a new currency was admitted to the EMS. In November
1993, the composition of the ECU was permanently fixed to the
weights first established in September 1989. Exhibit 2–1 shows the
composition of the ECU upon the admission of Greece in 1984
and Spain and Portugal in 1989.

The theoretical value of the ECU is calculated in the following manner. Each currency is allocated a fixed share in the ECU
equal to a certain number of units of currency (for example,
.6242 German mark, as of September 20, 1989, Exhibit 2–1). To
arrive at the value of the ECU in terms of U.S. dollars, multiply
the fixed amount of each currency by the exchange rate of that
currency for dollars. Exhibit 2–2 shows this calculation to arrive
at the theoretical dollar value of the ECU on June 8, 1995, of U.S.
dollars 1.3202. Note that the German mark is 33.43 percent of the
ECU. This is followed by the French franc at 20.32 percent and
the British pound at 10.59 percent.

The second feature of the EMS that was adopted by many
of its members is the exchange rate mechanism (ERM). Each
ERM currency has an assigned ECU central rate, which is its targeted rate of exchange for the ECU, measured as the number of
units of currency equal to one ECU. The ratio of any two currencies' ECU central rates is defined as their bilateral central rate.
For example, using the ECU central rate for the German mark of
1.91007 and the ECU central rate for the French franc of 6.40608,
one can calculate that the bilateral central rate must be 3.35386
francs for one mark. All bilateral central rates taken together

E X H I B I T 2-1

The Changing Composition of the ECU

| | March 13, 1979 (1) | | Sept 17, 1984 (1) | | Sept 20, 1989 (2) | |
	FX Amt	Percent	FX Amt	Percent	FX Amt	Percent
German mark	0.828	33.0%	0.719	32.0%	0.6242	30.1%
French franc	1.15	19.8%	1.31	19.0%	1.332	19.0%
British pound	0.0885	13.3%	0.0878	15.0%	0.0874	13.0%
Dutch guilder	0.286	10.5%	0.256	10.1%	0.2198	9.4%
Italian lire	109	9.5%	140	10.2%	151.8	10.2%
Belgian franc	3.66	9.3%	3.71	8.2%	3.301	7.6%
Danish kroner	0.217	3.1%	0.219	2.7%	0.1976	2.4%
Irish punt	0.00759	1.1%	0.00871	1.2%	0.008552	1.1%
Luxembourgian franc	0.14	0.4%	0.14	0.3%	0.13	0.3%
Greek drachmas	—	—	1.15	1.3%	1.44	0.8%
Spanish peseta	—	—	—	—	6.885	5.3%
Portuguese escudo	—	—	—	—	1.393	0.8%
		100%		100%		100%

(1) Source: Ungerer (1986).
(2) Source: Goldman Sachs.

29

EXHIBIT 2–2

Calculation of Theoretical Value of the ECU, June 8, 1995

	Amount of Currency	Exchange Rate	Cross Product	Weight in ECU	FX/ECU
Germany	0.6242	1.4145	0.441	33.43%	0.9333
France	1.332	4.9665	0.268	20.32%	0.02651
U.K.	0.08784	1.5910	0.140	10.59%	0.82976
Italy	151.8	1644.35	0.092	6.99%	0.00080
Netherlands	0.2198	1.5821	0.139	10.52%	0.83443
Belgium	3.301	29.0570	0.114	8.61%	0.04543
Spain	6.885	122.45	0.056	4.26%	0.01078
Denmark	0.1976	5.5115	0.036	2.72%	0.23953
Ireland	0.00855	1.6170	0.014	1.05%	0.81642
Portugal	1.393	148.80	0.009	0.71%	0.00887
Greece	1.44	227.57	0.006	0.48%	0.00580
Luxembourg	0.13	29.06	0.004	0.34%	0.04543

Theoretical ECU   1.3202

Actual ECU market rate   1.3072

form the ERM Parity Grid (Exhibits 2–3 and 2–4). The crux of the ERM is the requirement that each member must keep its currency's exchange rate for every other ERM currency within a predetermined band around the bilateral central rates. Before the crisis of August 1993, the band was plus or minus 2.25 percent for all currencies except the Spanish peseta, for which the band was plus or minus 6 percent.

Since its inception, the ERM has had a total of 18 realignments affecting 56 central rates in which the parity grid has been adjusted (Exhibit 2–5). There have also been two spectacular currency crises. The September 1992 ERM crisis forced Great Britain and Italy to withdraw from the ERM.[2] In the second ERM crisis, in August 1993, the EMS was compelled to widen the bands to plus or minus 15 percent (from 2.25 percent), an act that seemingly converted ERM currencies to nearly freely floating exchange rates. Nonetheless, Spain and Portugal were forced to devalue yet again on March 6, 1995. Exhibit 2–3 shows the ERM grid as it stood before the August 1993 crisis with its narrow, 2.25 percent bands. Exhibit 2–4 shows the grid as of March 6, 1995, with widened, 15 percent bands. In addition, the Nordic countries, Sweden, Norway, and Finland, have all experienced separate crises of their own as a consequence of having voluntarily tied their currencies to the ECU.

CENTRAL BANK INTERVENTION AND THE G-7

Ministers of finance and heads of central banks have shown a remarkable and persistent enthusiasm for intervention as a tool for regulating foreign exchange markets ever since the dollar became a floating currency. Some intervention is accomplished by way of timing and wording of policy statements, what is termed in the market as jawboning. Other times, intervention consists of a single central bank directly entering the market to buy or sell foreign exchange. On the grand scale, as many as two dozen central banks have been known to enter the market simultaneously in a coordinated or concerted intervention.

Some of the more historic interventions have been orchestrated by the G-7 (the "Group of Seven" large industrial countries). The G-7 consists of representatives of the United States, Japan, Germany, the United Kingdom, France, Italy, and Canada. In the spirit of cooperation among central banks established by the Bretton Woods Agreement, the G-7 ministers attempt to coordinate international policy to foster stable economic growth and to retard inflation.

The strategy of the G-7 appears to change with economic conditions. In September 1985, the G-5 (an earlier version of the G-7 that did not include Canada and Italy) met at the Plaza Hotel in New York where they planned massive coordinated intervention aimed at lowering the U.S. dollar (see Funabashi 1989). It was widely believed that the dollar had "overshot" above the level that could be justified by economic fundamentals. (Some authors refer to this phenomenon as the "dollar bubble.") The results of the Plaza intervention were dramatic; the dollar fell more than 4 percent against major currencies in the first 24 hours of intervention.

European Monetary System: ERM Parity Grid as of May 13, 1993

		Belgium 100 BEL=	Denmark 100 DKK=	France 100 FRF=	Germany 100 DEM=	Ireland 1 IRP=	Netherlands 100 NLG=	Portugal 100 ESC=	Spain 100 PTE=	ECU 1 ECU=
Belgium	S		553.000	628.970	2109.50	50.8605	1872.15	22.1400	27.6810	
	C		540.723	614.977	2062.55	49.7289	1830.54	20.8512	26.0696	40.2123
	B		528.700	601.295	2016.55	48.6230	1789.85	19.6375	24.5520	
Denmark	S	18.9143		116.320	390.160	9.40600	346.240	4.09450	5.11930	
	C	18.4938		113.732	381.443	9.19676	338.537	3.85618	4.82126	7.43679
	B	18.0831		111.200	373.000	8.99220	331.020	3.63170	6.54070	
France	S	16.6310	89.9250		343.050	8.27030	304.440	3.60010	4.50110	
	C	16.2608	87.9257		335.386	8.08631	297.661	3.39056	4.23911	6.53883
	B	15.8990	85.9700		327.920	7.90640	291.040	3.19330	3.99230	
Germany	S	4.95900	26.8100	30.4950		2.466000	90.7700	1.07330	1.34200	
	C	4.84837	26.2162	29.8164		2.441105	88.7526	1.01094	1.26395	1.94964
	B	4.74000	25.6300	29.1500		2.357000	86.7800	0.95200	1.19000	
Ireland	S	2.05664	11.1208	12.6480	42.4268		37.6478	0.445207	0.556630	
	C	2.01090	10.8734	12.3666	41.4757		36.8105	0.419295	0.524232	0.808628
	B	1.96616	10.6315	12.0915	40.5515		35.9919	0.394892	0.493722	

(continued)

European Monetary System: ERM Parity Grid as of May 13, 1993 (concluded)

		Belgium 100 BEL=	Denmark 100 DKK=	France 100 FRF=	Germany 100 DEM=	Ireland 1 IRP=	Netherlands 100 NLG=	Portugal 100 ESC=	Spain 100 PTE=	ECU 1 ECU=
	S	5.58700	30.2100	34.3600	115.2350	2.77840		1.20950	1.51213	
Netherlands	C	5.46286	29.5389	33.5953	112.6730	2.71662		1.13906	1.42413	2.19672
	B	5.34150	28.8825	32.8475	110.1675	2.65620		1.07280	1.34124	
	S	509.230	2753.50	3131.60	10505.20	253.234	9321.40		132.750	
Portugal	C	479.590	2593.24	2949.37	9891.77	238.495	8779.18		125.027	192.854
	B	451.670	2442.30	2777.70	9319.70	224.615	8267.90		117.750	
	S	407.300	2202.30	2504.80	8403.00	202.544	7455.80	84.9260		
Spain	C	383.589	2074.15	2358.98	7911.72	190.755	7021.83	79.9828		154.25
	B	361.260	1953.40	2221.70	7451.50	179.653	6613.20	75.3300		

S is the exchange rate at which the central bank of the country in the left-hand column will sell the currency identified in the row at the top of the table.

C is the bilateral central rate.

B is the exchange rate at which the central bank of the country in the left-hand column will buy the currency identified in the row at the top of the table.

Source: Swiss Bank Corporation.

EXHIBIT 2-4

European Monetary System: ERM Parity Grid Since March 6, 1995

		Belgium 100 BEL=	Denmark 100 DKK=	France 100 FRF=	Germany 100 DEM=	Ireland 1 IRP=	Netherlands 100 NLG=	Portugal 100 ESC=	Spain 100 PTE=	Austria 100 ATS=	ECU 1 ECU=
Belgium	S		627.880	714.030	2395.20	57.7445	2125.60	23.3645	28.1525	340.420	
	C		540.723	614.977	2062.55	49.7289	1830.54	20.1214	24.2447	293.163	39.3960
	B		465.665	529.680	1776.20	42.8260	1576.45	17.3285	20.8795	252.470	
Denmark	S	21.4747		132.066	442.968	10.67920	393.105	4.32100	5.20640	62.9561	
	C	18.4938		113.732	381.443	9.19676	338.537	3.72119	4.48376	54.2170	7.28580
	B	15.9266		97.943	328.461	7.92014	291.544	3.20460	3.86140	46.6910	
France	S	18.8800	102.1000		389.480	9.38950	345.650	3.79920	4.57780	55.3545	
	C	16.2608	87.9257		335.386	8.08631	297.661	3.27188	3.94237	47.6706	6.40608
	B	14.0050	75.7200		288.810	6.96400	256.350	2.81770	3.39510	41.0533	
Germany	S	5.63000	30.4450	34.6250		2.800000	103.0580	1.13280	1.36500	16.5050	
	C	4.84837	26.2162	29.8164		2.441105	88.7526	0.97556	1.17548	14.2136	1.91007
	B	4.17500	22.5750	25.6750		2.076000	76.4326	0.84010	1.01230	12.2410	
Ireland	S	2.33503	12.6261	14.3599	48.1696		42.7439	0.469841	0.566120	6.84544	
	C	2.01090	10.8734	12.3666	41.4757		36.8105	0.404620	0.487537	5.89521	0.792214
	B	1.73176	9.3640	10.6500	35.7143		31.7007	0.348453	0.419859	5.07688	

(continued)

Europcan Monetary System: ERM Parity Grid Since March 6, 1995 (concluded)

		Belgium 100 BEL=	Denmark 100 DKK=	France 100 FRF=	Germany 100 DEM=	Ireland 1 IRP=	Netherlands 100 NLG=	Portugal 100 ESC=	Spain 100 PTE=	Austria 100 ATS=	ECU 1 ECU=
Netherlands	S	6.34340	34.3002	39.0091	130.8340	3.15450		1.27637	1.53793	18.5963	
	C	5.46286	29.5389	33.5953	112.6730	2.71662		1.09920	1.32445	16.0149	2.15214
	B	4.70454	25.4385	28.9381	97.0325	2.33952		0.94661	1.14060	13.7918	
Portugal	S	577.090	3120.50	3549.00	11903.30	286.983	10564.00		139.920	1691.80	
	C	496.984	2687.31	3056.35	10250.50	247.145	9097.55		120.493	1456.97	195.792
	B	428.000	2314.30	2632.10	8827.70	212.838	7834.70		103.770	1254.70	
Spain	S	478.944	2408.50	2945.40	9878.50	238.175	8767.30	96.3670		1404.10	
	C	412.461	2074.15	2536.54	8507.18	205.113	7550.30	82.9927		1209.18	162.49
	B	355.206	1786.20	2184.40	7326.00	176.641	6502.20	71.4690		1041.30	
Austria	S	39.6089	214.174	243.586	816.927	19.6971	725.065	7.97000	9.6034		
	C	34.1107	184.444	209.773	703.550	16.9629	624.417	6.86356	8.2701		13.4383
	B	29.3757	158.841	180.654	605.877	14.6082	537.740	5.91086	7.1220		

S is the exchange rate at which the central bank of the country in the left-hand column will sell the currency identified in the row at the top of the table.

C is the bilateral central rate.

B is the exchange rate at which the central bank of the country in the left-hand column will buy the currency identified in the row at the top of the table.

Source: European Commission.

The History of the EMS/ERM

	B/LF	DKK	DEM	GRD	ESP	FRF	IEP	ITL	NLG	ATS	PTE	GBP
13-Mar-79	The European Monetary System (EMS) starts with B/LF, DKK, DEM, FRF, EIP, ITL, NLG, and GBP. B/LF, DKK, DEM, FRF, IEP, ITL, NLG, and GBP are components of the ECU basket. B/LF, DKK, DEM, FRF, IEP, ITL, and NLG (but not GBP) participate in the exchange rate mechanism (ERM). They are in the narrow band (2.25% fluctuation) of the ERM, except the ITL in the wide band (6% fluctuation).											
24-Sep-79 Realignment	0	−3.00	+2.00			0	0	0	0			
30-Nov-79 Realignment	0	−5.00	0			0	0	0	0			
23-Mar-81 Realignment	0	0	0			0	0	−6.00	0			
05-Oct-81 Realignment	0	0	+5.50			−3.00	0	−3.00	+5.50			
22-Feb-82 Realignment	−8.50	−3.00	0			0	0	0	0			
14-Jun-82 Realignment	0	0	+4.25			−5.75	0	−2.75	+4.25			
22-Mar-83 Realignment	+1.50	+2.50	+5.50			−2.50	−3.50	−2.50	+3.50			
17-Sep-84	Revision of the ECU composition (drachma enters into the ECU basket without participating in the ERM).											
22-Jul-85 Realignment	+2.00	+2.00	+2.00			+2.00	+2.00	−6.00	+2.00			
07-Apr-86 Realignment	+1.00	+1.00	+3.00			−3.00	0	0	+3.00			
04-Aug-86 Realignment	0	0	0			0	−8.00	0	0			
12-Jan-87 Realignment	+2.00	0	+3.00			0	0	0	+3.00			
19-Jun-89	Though not in the ECU basket yet, peseta joins the EMS by entering into the wide band of the ERM.											
21-Sep-89	Revision of the ECU composition: Peseta and escudo enter into the ECU basket. Escudo does not participate in the ERM.											
08-Jan-90	Italian lira (formerly in the wide band of the ERM) joins the narrow band of the ERM.											

(continued)

The History of the EMS/ERM (concluded)

		B/LF	DKK	DEM	GRD	ESP	FRF	IEP	ITL	NLG	ATS	PTE	GBP
08-Jan-90	Realignment	0	0	0		0	0	0	-3.6774	0			
08-Oct-90	Sterling enters into the wide band of the ERM.												
06-Apr-92	Escudo enters into the wide band of the ERM.												
14-Sep-92	Realignment	+3.50	+3.50	+3.50		+3.50	+3.50	+3.50	-3.50	+3.50		+3.50	+3.50
17-Sep-92	Sterling and lira suspend their participation in the ERM.												
17-Sep-92	Realignment	0	0	0		-5.00	0	0		0		0	
23-Nov-92	Realignment	0	0	0		-6.00	0	0		0		-6.00	
01-Feb-93	Realignment	0	0	0		0	0	-10.00		0		0	
14-May-93	Realignment	0	0	0		-8.00	0	0		0		-6.50	
02-Aug-93	ERM currencies may fluctuate by 15%. Drachma, lira, and sterling still floating.												
01-Nov-93	Composition of ECU basket frozen.												
01-Jan-95	Austrian schilling, Finnish markka, and Swedish krona become members of EMS.												
09-Jan-95	Schilling enters ERM (but it is not part of the ECU basket).												

Currency not in EMS
Currency not in ERM

Source: European Commission.

The next major G-7 milestone came in February 1987, when the ministers met at the Louvre. Their collective judgment was that the dollar had fallen sufficiently from its levels in 1985 to achieve the objectives of the Plaza Accord. Their attention shifted to stabilizing exchange rates, meaning taking steps to limit the size of exchange rate fluctuations, especially between the dollar, yen, and mark. The weapon of choice again was coordinated intervention.[3] By April 1990, the G-7 seemed to have all but abandoned its interest in exchange rates, as evidenced by its reluctance to provide substantial aid for the Japanese to support the then depressed yen. Attention had focused away from exchange rates towards directing macroeconomic policy designed to promote economic growth and contain inflationary pressures. In 1994, interest in exchange rates was rekindled when the United States convinced the G-7, and a good many other central banks, to intervene repeatedly to limit the fall of the dollar.

The history of the G-7's foreign exchange operations calls the effectiveness of central bank intervention into question. The Plaza Accord is widely regarded as the most successful intervention in the postwar period. Critics of intervention hasten to point out that the dollar had already peaked in February of the same year. So it is not clear that the Plaza intervention did anything more than speed the dollar's descent and create substantial market volatility. The Louvre Accord also justifiably can be criticized for having failed in its stated purpose to stabilize the value of the dollar.[4]

ALTERNATIVE EXCHANGE ARRANGEMENTS

The International Monetary Fund (1994) reports that 241 countries have their own currencies. (A partial list is displayed in Exhibit 2–6.) Very few have freely floating exchange rates. Most exchange rates are either fixed absolutely or at least in part, and many of the others are managed through outright intervention or by other less obvious means. The IMF classifies exchange rate regimes into three major categories: currencies that are pegged, currencies with limited flexibility, and currencies with more flexibility.

The purest example of a pegged currency is the Panamanian balboa. (One balboa = one U.S. dollar.) What is unusual about Panama is that the U.S. dollar is legal tender—U.S. dollars freely circulate alongside the balboa—which is tantamount to the balboa being a private label dollar. Argentina, Estonia, and Hong Kong operate currency boards to peg their exchange rates. Currency boards are artifacts of the days of the British Empire when practically every colony pegged its currency to sterling.[5] A currency board operates by holding 100 percent backing for the domestic currency in the form of a foreign reserve currency (which is the U.S. dollar in the case of Hong Kong and Argentina today). The board agrees to stand ready to exchange its domestic currency for the reserve currency at the specified fixed rate. Of course, many countries peg their currencies without the formal discipline of a currency board. Many Caribbean nations and some Middle Eastern countries peg their exchange rate to the U.S. dollar. Some former French colonies in Africa peg their currencies to the French franc, and a few of the newly independent former Soviet states peg to the Russian ruble. Four countries peg to the SDR. Still others peg to a composite basket of external currencies. The Thai baht, for example, is pegged to a basket of U.S. dollars, Japanese yen, and German marks.

Currencies with limited flexibility, the second IMF category, fall into two groups. Four of the Arabian gulf states fix their currencies in a narrow trading range to the U.S. dollar, which derives from the fact that crude oil exports are primarily U.S. dollar deals. The other group seeking limited flexibility is comprised of the EMS/ERM countries, as was previously discussed.

The third IMF category is comprised of currencies with more flexibility, other than independent floating ones. This includes those currencies adjusted to a set of indicators and those that are subject to a managed float. Among the former is the Chilean peso (IMF 1994). The Chilean central bank's exchange rate for the peso is the adjusted value of a basket consisting of the U.S. dollar, German mark, and Japanese yen. The basket is adjusted daily for the difference between the domestic rate of inflation and the rates of inflation in the three external basket currency countries.

E X H I B I T 2-6

Exchange Rate Arrangements

Currency Pegged to

U.S. Dollar	French Franc	Ruble	Another Currency	SDR	Another Composite
Angola	Benin	Armenia	Bhutan	Libya	Algeria
Antigua and Barbuda	Burkina Faso	Azerbaijan	(Indian Rupee)	Myanmar	Austria
Argentina	Cameroon	Belarus	Estonia	Rwanda	Bangladesh
Bahamas	Central African Rep.	Kazakhstan	(Deutsche Mark)	Seychelles	Botswana
Belize	Chad	Turkmenistan	Kiribati		Burundi
Djibouti	Comoros		(Australian Dollar)		Cape Verde
Dominica	Congo		Lesotho		Cyprus
Grenada	Cote d'Ivoire		(South African Rand)		Fiji
Hong Kong	Equatorial Guinea		Namibia		Hungary
Iraq	Gabon		(South African Rand)		Iceland
Liberia	Mali		San Marino		Jordan
Marshall Islands	Niger		(Italian Lire)		Kenya
Oman	Senegal		Swaziland		Kuwait
Panama	Togo		(South African Rand)		Malawi
St. Kitts and Nevis					Malta
St. Lucia					Mauritania
St. Vincent and					Mauritius
the Grenadines					Morocco
Surinam					Nepal
Syria					Papua New Guinea
Yemen					Solomon Islands
					Thailand
					Tonga
					Vanuatu
					Western Samoa
					Zimbabwe

(continued)

Exchange Rate Arrangements (concluded)

Currency with Limited Flexibility		Currency with More Flexibility		
Vis-à-Vis a Single Currency	**Cooperative Exchange Rate Arrangements**	**Adjusted According to a Set of Indicators**	**Other Managed Floating**	**Independent Floating**
Bahrain	Belgium	Chile	Cambodia	Afghanistan	Kyrgytan
Qatar	Denmark	Colombia	China	Albania	Latvia
Saudi Arabia	France	Madagascar	Croatia	Austria	Lithuania
United Arab Emirates	Germany	Nicaragua	Ecuador	Bolivia	Moldova
	Ireland		Egypt	Brazil	Mongolia
	Luxembourg		Greece	Bulgaria	Mozambique
	Netherlands		Guinea	Canada	New Zealand
	Portugal		Guinea-Biseau	Costa Rica	Nigeria
	Spain		Indonesia	Dominican Republic	Norway
			Israel	El Salvador	Paraguay
			Korea	Ethiopia	Peru
			Malaysia	Finland	Philippines
			Maldives	Gambia	Romania
			Mexico	Georgia	Russian Federation
			Pakistan	Ghana	Sierra Leone
			Poland	Great Britain and Northern Ireland	South Africa
			Sao Tome and Principe	Guatemala	Sudan
			Singapore	Guyana	Sweden
			Slovenia	Haiti	Switzerland
			Somalia	Honduras	Tanzania
			Sri Lanka	India	Trinidad and Tobago
			Tunisia	Iran	Uganda
			Turkey	Italy	Ukraine
			Uruguay	Jamaica	United States
			Venezuela	Japan	Zaire
			Viet Nam		Zambia

Source: Deutsche Bundesbank, *Exchange Rate Statistics 1994*, and the International Monetary Fund.

Managed float currencies can also be subject to a complex set of rules. Prior to December 20, 1994, the Mexican peso was contained inside a narrow band. The upper limit expanded by .0004 Mexican pesos per calendar day to allow for an orderly and scheduled devaluation. The Indonesian rupiah functions in a similar way. Bank Indonesia keeps the rupiah within a narrow rupiah band (30 rupiah at present), the width of which is continuously adjusted to allow for a planned rate of devaluation (4 percent annually at present). Some governments take exchange rate management to other dimensions beyond direct intervention. The Singapore dollar is a floating currency, but the government has made it clear that it strongly opposes what it calls the "internationalization" of their currency. The same can be said for the Malaysian ringgit. Malaysia stands out as a country that at times has taken extraordinary measures to discourage speculation in the ringgit, measures that have included restrictions on interest being paid on foreign funds.

WHAT MAKES A CURRENCY SUITABLE FOR INVESTMENT?

The history of foreign exchange is the story of confrontations between traders and government officials. Ministers of finance are especially susceptible to the belief that their currency is mispriced or disadvantaged by the market. Consider a rather blunt opinion given by John Maynard Keynes in the introduction to the French translation of his *Tract on Monetary Reform:*

> Each time the franc loses value, the Minister of Finance is convinced that the fact arises from everything but economic causes. He attributes it to the presence of foreigners in the corridors of the Bourse, to unwholesome and malign forces of speculation. (pp. xvi–xvii)

He might have also written that whenever the franc gains value, the Minister of Finance attributes this completely to economic causes, specifically his own masterful handling of the French economy. Governments have sometimes embarked on extraordinary, and not always successful, programs to regulate exchange rates (Funabashi 1989). Among the most memorable was the defense of the British pound in September 1992 when the British government absorbed over 15 billion pounds against marks in a single day. The exact size of the loss to the British treasury has never been released but it is estimated to be between three and five billion pounds. Episodes like this bring into question whether intervention policies are ever to be recommended.

One standard argument for interventionist policy is that it is needed to preserve the value of the nation's currency in order to create a hospitable environment for foreign investors. In reality, a depreciating currency is not an insurmountable problem as long as there is a well-functioning foreign exchange market. Sophisticated investors will be able to hedge by transferring risk to specialized economic agents. The problem is that intervention can change the nature of the market itself in subtle ways that diminish the efficiency of the price formation process. For example, the focus of market participants can switch away from assessing the impact of natural economic forces to watching for signs of impending government action. In a market that has become nothing more than a guessing game about the next round of policy, the cost of hedging foreign exchange risk is likely to be erratic and arbitrarily exorbitant. The worst environment is where there is a foreign exchange stabilization program that is in doubt of survival. This is the perfect breeding ground for a large, discontinuous move in exchange rates, as was the case with the Mexican peso in December 1994. The cure can be far worse than the disease; the lesson that always repeats itself is that freely floating exchange rates are the best environment for attracting international investors.

NOTES

1. See Milton Friedman, "Deja Vu in Currency Markets," *The Wall Street Journal*, September 22, 1992.

2. See International Monetary Fund, *International Capital Markets*, Part I, *Exchange Rate Management and International Capital Flows*, April 1993.

3. See Martin Feldstein, "Time to Bid Farewell to the Louvre Accord," *Financial Times*, March 29, 1990.

4. The most complete study of central bank intervention is Dominguez and Frankel (1993), but also see Goodhart and Hesse (1993).

5. See David Hale, "How to End Mexico's Meltdown," *The Wall Street Journal*, January 19, 1995.

CHAPTER 3

Mechanics of Foreign Exchange

Having some knowledge of the mechanics of trading foreign exchange in its various forms is essential for all practitioners in today's world of international finance. This chapter discusses some of the practical aspects of trading spot and forward foreign exchange, currency futures, and currency options.

THE FOREIGN EXCHANGE MARKET
Interbank Dealing Activities

Foreign exchange is traded by a wide international network of dealers, most of whom are commercial banks and investment banking firms.

As was discussed in Chapter 1, the trading volume is enormous—it was estimated at well over one billion dollars per day in 1995. A simple confirmation that the size must be large comes from the fact that in this busy market quotations are made in pieces of one million units of currency. For example, when a trader says "10 dollars," it is understood to mean 10 million dollars. Likewise, "50 marks" means 50 million marks. Some amounts are quoted in units of billions, which are called yards; "one yard of yen" means one billion yen.

London, New York, and Tokyo are the three largest centers for foreign exchange, by respective volume of trading. But dealing institutions are located in many other cities throughout Asia, Europe, and the United States. The center of trading rotates around the globe throughout the day. New Zealand and Australia open the day in what is known as the Austral–Asian trading time zone. The official start of the foreign exchange day is 6 A.M. Sydney time. Japan, Hong Kong, and Singapore join in a few hours later. Next, the center moves to the European trading time zone. Trading takes place mainly in London, but Zurich, Frankfurt, and Paris are also important, along with many other European cities. In the American trading time zone, New York dominates, but Chicago, Los Angeles, Toronto, and Montreal are also sizable participants. Trading for the day closes at 5 P.M. New York time.

Foreign exchange is a dealer's market. By definition, a dealer is a principal party who "makes a market"—that is, provides two-way quotes, both bid and offer, on foreign exchange in meaningful size (which is usually a minimum of $10 million worth of currency). As a principal, the dealer buys and sells for his own account (called his book) by taking the other side of trades. When a counterparty buys, the dealer sells, and when a counterparty sells, the dealer buys. Profits arise from situations wherein the dealer can capture a small price advantage from the bid–offer spread or when the dealer's book is correctly positioned to benefit from directional moves in exchange rates. Dealing also means facing the risk of getting caught with a long position in a falling market or with a short position in a rising market. This is why being a dealer presumes a willingness to assume considerable financial risk and requires the commitment of large amounts of reserve capital to cover potential short-term losses. Consequently, not all banks are in a position to deal in foreign exchange. Still, many banks do have active roles in the market, not as market makers but as agents who arrange foreign exchange transactions for their customers. Putting none of their own capital at risk, they match each customer transaction back-to-back with a trade in the interbank market using exchange rates obtained from the market makers.

Foreign exchange dealers set out to accomplish two basic functions. The first combines market making and customer order facilitation. Market making is primarily an interbank activity that is dominated by the money-center institutions. The customer side of the business may include investment managers, corporate treasurers, financial institutions, and private individuals. Customers call into the dealing room for quotes and to transact in spot and forward foreign exchange and currency derivatives. The largest volume of trading is done for spot settlement (also called the cash market). A spot transaction normally requires settlement two bank business days later. Forward transactions are the same in structure as spot transactions except that settlement occurs at some time in the future beyond two bank business days. Currency derivatives include futures, options, futures options, and a whole host of new exotic instruments and structured products. Practically every foreign exchange dealer is a member of or has access to the Chicago Mercantile Exchange's International Monetary Market (for currency futures and futures options) and the Philadelphia Stock Exchange (for currency options) and therefore can execute exchange-listed currency derivatives contracts for customers and for their own trading. The largest portion of trading in currency derivatives is done over-the-counter by money center banks that make markets in currency options in tandem with their dealing in spot and forward foreign exchange.

The second function of the dealing room is proprietary or strategic trading. Here, the bank puts its own capital at risk, sometimes in size and for prolonged periods of time. Some proprietary trading is nothing more than riskless or nearly riskless arbitrage. This is true for cash-futures arbitrage, which attempts to exploit temporary mispricing opportunities between the interbank cash market and listed currency derivatives. Genuine strategic trading involves taking aggressive positions in spot, futures, and options to express directional views on the future exchange rate movements. Other, more intricate strategies involve views on the volatility of exchange rates and the term structure of interest rate spreads between currencies. In all of these endeavors, risk analysis and loss control are essential for success, if not survival. To this end, institutions with serious appetites for proprietary trading have invested serious amounts of resources in risk-analysis systems and software.

The Foreign Exchange Dealing Room

A foreign exchange dealing (or trading) room can be a formidable place. The level of noise can be deafening at times, especially when traders shout across the room for prices as some major news event hits the market. Space is usually cramped. The room is jam-packed with quotation equipment, telephones, fax machines, computers, and telex machines. The whole apparatus is designed for the one purpose of being able to deal in large quantities of foreign exchange quickly and efficiently. Good communications are of key importance, and the principal modes are the telephone and privately owned computer networks. Most interbank dealing is done over computer networks, of which the Reuters Dealing 2000 and the Electronic Broking Service are examples. Otherwise, client business is usually done over the phone; calls are usually tape-recorded for security reasons and to help settle the odd disputed trade.

Not to be understated is the role of the interbank foreign exchange brokers. A dozen or more of these institutions serve the dealing community by matching dealers seeking to sell with dealers seeking to buy. Brokers themselves do not take positions. Their sole function is to arrange trades, and they are paid commissions for doing so as a direct function of volume. Over the past decade, the number of major dealers in foreign exchange has declined because of bank mergers. This fact, combined with a tremendous increase in dealing volume, has elevated the status of the brokers and has given added importance to the liquidity they provide.

Most dealing rooms are organized in basically the same way, making for a definable taxonomy of trader functions. Sales traders are the point of contact between the dealing room and clients. Each client is assigned a sales trader or team of sales traders who are responsible for the relationship. Sales traders give information and quotations to clients and are responsible for the proper execution of their orders in spot or forward foreign exchange, futures, or options. The traders who actually make markets in exchange rates are called spot dealers inside the trading room. They tend to specialize in one exchange rate by itself, such as dollar/mark, or in exchange rates for a group of related currencies, such as Australian dollars and New Zealand dollars.

Spot dealers are responsible for making a market in their currency throughout their trading time zone. But they are not overnight positions takers as a rule (i.e., they "go home flat on the day"). Forward dealers make markets in forward points that are used in forward outright and swap trading. Their activities combine foreign exchange with interest rate and yield curve trading. Derivatives traders work the listed currency futures, currency options, and futures options markets side by side with the cash market. Listed currency derivatives comprise a small but nonetheless significant sector of the overall foreign exchange market. Over-the-counter currency option dealers make markets in puts and calls as well as in the newer exotic currency options. Successful option dealers today employ highly analytical approaches to managing the risk of their dealing books. Finally, the proprietary trader's job is to employ the dealing firm's capital to take risk positions in spot, forward, futures, and options, as was described above. Further specialization of trader functions can be expected in the future if the market continues to expand and as new tradable instruments are created.

Currency Basics

There is a simple convention in quoting foreign exchange that prevents much confusion. It is that the first currency mentioned in a currency pair, such as dollar/mark, is the one that is going to be bought or sold.[1] To sell dollar/mark is to sell dollars and buy marks. To buy mark/yen is to buy marks and sell yen.

Some currencies have nicknames. Dollar/mark, the most traded exchange rate, is simply called the dollar. The British pound is called sterling or quid or cable (presumably from the days when overseas trading was done by cablegram). To avoid mixing up the different kinds of francs, the French franc is called French or Paris, the Swiss franc is called Swiss, and the Belgian franc is called Belg. Canada refers to the Canadian dollar but against the dollar is sometimes called funds (an artifact of its special one-day settlement convention). The Spanish peseta is Spain. The Danish krone is Copy, and the Swedish krone, Stocky, both in reference to capital cities.

Most of the dollar exchange rates are quoted European or *indirect*, meaning the number of units of currency equal to one dollar. Examples are dollar/mark, dollar/yen, and dollar/Swiss. Only the British pound, Irish punt, Australian dollar, New Zealand dollar, and the ECU are quoted American or *direct*, meaning the number of dollars per unit of currency.

Cross rates are exchange rates that do not involve the U.S. dollar. As markets have become more international, cross-rate trading has greatly expanded. This is especially pronounced with the European currencies, which by virtue of the EMS now trade primarily against the mark rather than against the dollar. The most actively traded crosses are mark/yen, sterling/mark, and mark/Swiss. As a general rule, the mark crosses are quoted in terms of the number of units of currency equal to one mark. Sterling/mark, however, is quoted as the number of marks equal to one pound.

Spot and Forward Contracts

A spot exchange contract is an agreement to exchange sums of currencies on a value day two bank business days later. There is an exception to this rule. The Canadian dollar settles in one bank business day when traded against the U.S. dollar.

Every spot foreign exchange deal involves two currencies and therefore initiates settlement transactions across borders. On value day, settlement involves the use of banks in the respective countries of domicile of each currency. (Such accounts are called nostro accounts.) Value dates cannot be bank holidays in either country. For example, Boxing Day (the day after Christmas) is not a valid value date for sterling because it is a bank holiday in the United Kingdom. But December 26 is a valid value date for other currencies; dollar/yen can be dealt for value December 26 because Boxing Day is not observed in either the United States or Japan.

A forward exchange contract is an agreement to exchange sums of currencies at a time in the future more distant than the spot value date. Forward contracts can settle on any future date that is a valid spot value date.

Spot and Forward Quotations

Strictly speaking, an actual foreign exchange quotation is a private conversation between a dealer and a counterparty. What appears on quotation screens are public indications of foreign exchange spot levels supplied by dealers to a handful of electronic systems, such as Telerate, Reuters, Knight-Ridder, Bloomberg, and others. In normal market conditions, screen prices are reasonably similar to actual dealing prices. But experienced traders know that screen prices can lag behind current conditions in fast markets.

In the case of Reuters, each contributor has one or more "pages" on the system, each identified by a four-digit alphanumeric code. These are used to broadcast the dealer's indications of exchange rates to all other subscribers. Reuters also collects and formats the most recent indications to make composite pages. The most widely known is the WRLD page (Exhibit 3–1). (The counterpart to WRLD in Europe is FXFX.) To preserve the integrity of the page, Reuters is careful to keep WRLD in the hands of dealers who show timely indications of exchange rates. The column headings of this important page stand for currency (CCY), contributor page (PAGE), dealer or SWIFT address code (DLNG), spot exchange rate indication (SPOT RATE), location of the dealer (LOC), the previous quotation displayed (PREV), and the high and low for the trading area (US HI & LO). The left-hand column gives the time of quotation submission to the system. Currency codes are as follows:

DEM	German mark
JPY	Japanese yen
CHF	Swiss franc
GBP	British pound
CAD	Canadian dollar
AUD	Australian dollar
FRF	French franc

The spot indication displayed in Exhibit 3–1 for dollar/yen of 84.85/95 is a two-way price. The dealer is willing to buy

E X H I B I T 3–1

Spot Exchange Rate Indications
Reuters Composite Page WRLD

	CCY	PAGE	DLNG	SPOT RATE	LOC	PREV	US HI &	LO
0825	DEM	GIBN	GIBN*D	1.4110/15	NYC	00/10	1.4117	1.4075
0826	JPY	MGTX	MGTN*J	84.85/95	NYC	87/90	84.95	84.65
0826	CHF	DNOO	DNOO*C	1.1680/85	OSL	80/90	1.1685	1.1555
0826	GBP	MGTX	MGTN*G	1.5975/85	NYC	68/78	1.6005	1.5975
0826	CAD	HTSA	HTSC*R	1.3748/53	CHI	49/54	1.3775	1.3742
0826	AUD	ANZX	ANZL*T	.7260/65	LON	62/67	0.7270	0.7240
0826	FRF	SOGE	SOGP*F	4.9490/05	PAR	80/10	4.9495	4.9415

dollars at 84.85 and sell dollars at 84.95. Among traders, this quotation would be abbreviated as eighty five–ninety five because the "big figure," 84, is common knowledge. The term *pips* or *points* refers to the last decimal place in the quotation. (In this example, the dealer is offering to buy dollars for 85 pips and to sell dollars for 95 pips.) To help sort out the bid and offer side of the quotation remember that the dealer always quotes to his or her advantage.

There are two types of cross-rate quotations on Reuters. The first is a bona fide cross rate, meaning a cross that is really traded on its own. Mark/yen, sterling/mark, mark/Swiss, mark/Paris, and mark/Spain are all examples. Exhibit 3–2 shows Reuters page WXWY where these and other mark crosses can be found. Some other crosses do not trade on their own, at least directly. Reuters handles this by supplying calculated cross rates, in other words, cross rates that are inferred from other exchange rates (for example, page WXWX, as displayed in Exhibit 3–3).

Forward exchange rates are more difficult to decode. They are constructed from two components. The first is the spot rate, such as 84.85/95 in the dollar/yen example. The second component is called the forward points (or, sometimes, swap rate). Reuters maintains composite pages for forward points on several dozen currencies. (There is a helpful index on Reuters page

E X H I B I T   3–2

German Mark Cross Exchange Rates
Reuters Composite Page WXWY

CCY	TIME	DEAL	CONTRIBUTOR	LOC	
JPY	1227	TRFX	TRANSFOREX	NYC	60.15/18
GBP	1226	AIBI	ALLIED IRISH	DUB	2.2540/50
CHF	1226	SBCB	SWISS BK	BAS	.8277/80
FRF	1226	PYNY	PREBON	NYC	3.5080/88
NLG	1226	ABNR	ABN AMRO	ROT	1.119275/350
ITL	1226	ROMR	BANCA ROMA	ROM	1168.25/1169.25
ECU	1226	INDP	INDOSUEZ	PAR	1.8505/10

E X H I B I T   3–3

Calculated Cross Exchange Rates
Reuters Composite Page WXWX

	DEM	GBP	JPY	CHF	FRF
DEM	*	.4436/40	60.16/19	.8281/84	3.5082/87
GBP	2.2529/39	*	135.68/80	1.8651/78	7.9010/07
JPY	1.6609/31	.7363/72	*	1.3751/71	5.8271/40
CHF	120.66/80	.5354/62	72.65/70	*	4.2327/89
FRF	.2850/52	.1263/64	17.13/18	.2359/62	*

Reproduced by permission from Reuters Information Services, Inc.

FWDS.) Exhibit 3–4 shows the composite page FWDU for the Japanese yen. The left-hand column gives the time of quotation. The next column gives standard forward value dates. (M stands for months.) The entries O/N, T/N, and S/W stand for over/night, tom/next, and spot/week, which are specialized forward transactions. Although it is common practice to indicate quotations on 1-, 2-, 3-, 6-, 9-, and 12-month forwards, dealers will quote forward points for any valid value date. Some dealers selectively quote forward points for one, two, three, and more years. Forward points are added to or subtracted from the spot rate to arrive at the forward outright, a term meaning the forward exchange rate.

To continue with the example of the Japanese yen, two-month forward points for yen are quoted as –71/–70 in Exhibit 3–4. The convention is to subtract forward points from the spot level when they are quoted with the larger number first to arrive at the outright (this is confirmed by the minus signs in this quote, as occurs here). Conversely, when points are quoted with the smaller number first and the larger number second, points are added to the spot rate to obtain the outright. Why is it that points sometimes are added and sometimes subtracted? The short answer concerns the interest rate spread between the dollar and the foreign currency. The long answer will come in the next chapter (the interest parity theorem).

EXHIBIT 3-4

Japanese Yen Forwards
Reuters Composite Page FWDU

0634	O/N	TKAI	−1.2/−1.1
0635	T/N	TKAI	−3.4/−3.3
1055	S/W	SNWA	−8/−7.9
1143	1 M	RBCC	−33.8/−33.5
1143	2 M	RBCC	−71/−70
1230	3 M	SUMQ	−104/−99
1229	6 M	SUMQ	−205/−194
1223	9 M	UBZF	−293/−288
1229	12 M	SUMQ	−390/−375

Reproduced by permission from Reuters Information Services, Inc.

The forward outright bid–offer in the example of the two-month forward dollar/yen would be:

Spot bid/offer	84.85 / 84.95
2M forward points	−71 / −70
Outright	84.14 / 84.25

Note that the forward points are right-justified against the spot exchange rate to determine the position of the decimal point.

An Example of a Basic Spot Trade

Say that a dollar-based portfolio manager needs to buy Japanese yen in order to buy shares in a Japanese bank. Her dealer quotes a two-way price, meaning a bid and offer. A conversation leading to a trade (sometimes called a deal) might go something like this:

Portfolio manager customer: Dollar/yen on 10 dollars, please.

Dealer: 85–95.

Portfolio manager customer: Yours at 85.

Dealer: Thanks, I buy 10 dollars at 84.85.

In the first line of this conversation, the portfolio manager discloses that the size of the deal is $10 million against yen but does not reveal whether she wants to buy or to sell. The dealer responds with a price of "85–95." The "handle" or "figure," equal to 84 in this case, is known from quotation screens. The dealer is making the customer a price on $10 million, where she can buy dollars at the rate of 84.95 yen per dollar or sell dollars at the rate of 84.85 yen per dollar. In the next line, the portfolio manager sells $10 million. The expression "yours" means that she is selling the dollars to the dealer. If she had said "mine at 95," it would have meant that she was buying $10 at the rate of 84.95 yen per dollar.

In strict observance, dealing room quotes are good for only three seconds. Also, the dealer has the right to say "change" and then announce a new set of prices at any time before the customer responds. On some large orders, the customer may be asked whether it is her "full amount." For example, if the customer asks for dollar/mark on five hundred dollars, full amount means that she is not simultaneously asking another bank for a price quote on additional dollars.[2] The dealer may be willing to make a tighter spread on a full amount order because he is apt to have no competition in laying off the position.

A sample trade ticket written from the customer's perspective is shown in Exhibit 3–5. Since spot transactions settle in two bank business days after the trade date, we have denoted settlement day as "day 3." On that day, the portfolio manager must wire the dealing bank $10 million and will receive ¥848,500,000 in an account in a bank in Japan, since

$$\$10,000,000 \times 84.85 = ¥848,500,000$$

Shifting the circumstances of the example, suppose the sale of $10 million against yen were done by a trader at a leveraged currency hedge fund as a directional bet that the dollar would weaken. Also suppose the dollar trades down to 84.00/10 later in the same day and that the hedge fund wants to close the position to take profits. The closing trade could be done either in terms of dollars (i.e., buy dollars against yen) or in terms of yen (sell yen against dollars). Assume that the closing trade sells

EXHIBIT 3-5

Spot Currency Transaction from Customer's Perspective

Buy	Sell	Trade date	Value date
848,500,000 JPY	10,000,000 USD	Day 1	Day 3

Description of trade			
Buy 848,500,000 JPY against 10,000,000 USD Spot			

Spot	Forward points	Commission	Outright
84.85			

Settlement instructions			
Pay 10,000,000 USD to SBC NY on Day 3			
Receive 848,500,000 JPY in Account at SBC Tokyo on Day 3			

Counterparty	Dealer code	Trader	
Swiss Bank New York	SBCN	G-Man	

57

¥848,500,000 against $10,089,179.55 at the rate of 84.10. The profit[3] would be the residual sum of dollars netted out from the opening and closing spot trades.

		Dollars	Yen
Opening trade	84.85	($10,000,000.00)	848,500,000
Closing trade	84.10	$10,089,179.55	(848,500,000)
		$89,179.55	- 0 -

But if the closing transaction had been to buy 10 million dollars against yen, the profit would be a residual sum of 7.5 million yen.

		Dollars	Yen
Opening trade	84.85	($10,000,000)	848,500,000
Closing trade	84.10	$10,000,000	(841,000,000)
		- 0 -	7,500,000

The Taxonomy of Spot Orders

Foreign exchange dealers accept various types of orders, in much the same way as is done in equity markets. The most common case is a customer who asks for a bid–ask quotation in a reasonable size. This was the case described above in the dollar/yen spot trade on 10 dollars. Larger orders are often given to a dealer on an "at-best" basis. This instructs the dealer to buy or sell a large amount on a best efforts basis. Sometimes this is qualified with an upper limit to pay or a lower limit to sell. For example, if dollar/mark is quoted 1.4110/15, an at-best market order to buy five hundred dollars might be qualified with "don't pay more than 1.4150."

Limit orders are orders that are not immediately executable at current market levels. At our quote of 1.4110/15, a limit order might be entered as "buy 50 dollars at 1.4100 the figure." Limit orders can be filled in whole or in part. For example, if the rate were briefly offered at 1.4100, the dealer might be able to buy 10 dollars out of the total order of 50 before a market rally. Some clients give dealers limited discretionary flexibility. "I am a buyer of 50 dollars at 1.4100 with 5 pips discretion" translates into "Buy up to 50 dollars around 1.4100 but do not pay above 1.4105 on average." A special case of a limit order is a "take-profit order." The protocol for execution of a take-profit order is no different from any other limit order except that the client reveals that the order has been placed to exit from a position.

Spot dealers accept stop orders.[4] They function in a similar way to stop orders in listed equity markets. Stop orders are extensively employed in foreign exchange trading to control risk. For example, say the customer sells dollars against marks at 1.4110 to establish a new short U.S. dollar position. The customer is hoping that dollar/mark will fall; but if he is wrong, and the dollar rises against the mark, he will suffer a loss. For protection, he might tell the dealer to "Stop me out at 50." This means that if the dollar ever trades at 1.4150, the dealer should liquidate the position by buying 10 dollars. If 1.4150 does in fact trade, the customer's liquidation order turns into a market order to buy dollars. Because stop-loss orders are handled on a best efforts basis, there is no guarantee that the order can be filled at 1.4150. Stop orders often accumulate above and below what traders regard to be key spot levels. When such a level is broken, several dealers may have to execute stops simultaneously, and there might be a scramble to buy or sell with a number of dealers all on the same side of the market. The next available spot price could be substantially away from the triggered stop level. Even so, stop-loss orders are essential in foreign exchange because trading is conducted virtually 24 hours a day. (The market could move while the trader is asleep.) Another way that traders manage risk is to leave a "call level." If the level trades, the dealer will call the customer for a decision. Stop orders can also be used to enter into new positions. An example would be the case of a technical trader who wants to buy dollars but considers the present market levels not to be decisive. On the breech of a higher level, say at 1.4150, the trader might consider that the trend is firmly in place. This could be expressed with an order to "Buy 10 dollars at 1.4160, stop entry."

Examples of Forward Trades

Corporate treasurers use forward trades as anticipatory hedges for future foreign currency cash flows to avoid unwanted exposure to foreign exchange risk. The forward market affords them an opportunity to commit to a prearranged conversion rate. International equity and fixed income portfolio managers use forwards as part of their currency-hedging strategies. Take the example of a manager who is long one billion yen worth of Japanese equities and who is concerned that the value of the yen might deteriorate over the next two months. A direct step would be to sell one billion yen forward for two months against dollars. This hedging transaction is called an opening transaction. At a two-month outright equal to 84.25, the trade would consist of a commitment to deliver one billion yen in two months and receive dollars in the amount equal to $11,869,436.20 since

$$\frac{¥1\ \text{billion}}{84.25} = \$11,869,436.20$$

A sample trade ticket for this transaction is shown in Exhibit 3–6. The comment "No cash moves until day 60" is meant to serve as a reminder that a forward transaction generates no cash flow until value date.

The portfolio manager must make some decisions once the forward hedge is in place. Since portfolio hedgers rarely enter into forward contracts intending to make delivery of currencies, the hedge must be closed or rolled prior to settlement. A forward hedge can be closed anytime before forward value date by means of a closing transaction. This is accomplished by reversing the original hedge with a second transaction that has the same original value date as the opening transaction does. In the example, the hedge might be closed one month later, day 30, by buying one billion yen for settlement on day 60. The new forward rate would be a one-month rate because only one month would now remain until day 60. Suppose that the spot rate now is 84.00/10 and that the forward points are –26/–25. The outright for value in 30 days would be 83.74/85. The closing transaction would be a purchase of one billion yen against

EXHIBIT 3-6

Forward Currency Transaction: Opening Trade from Customer's Perspective

Buy	Sell	Trade date	Value date
11,869,436.20 USD	1 yard JPY	Day 1	Day 60

Description of trade

Sell 1 yard JPY against USD for value in 60 Days

Spot	Forward points	Commission	Outright
84.95	−0.70	0	84.25

Settlement instructions

No Cash Moves Until Day 60
Pay 1 yard JPY to SBC Tokyo on Day 60
Receive 11,869,436.20 USD in Account at SBC NY on Day 60

Counterparty	Dealer code	Trader
Swiss Bank New York	SBCN	D-Squared

$11,941,724.39 at a rate of 83.74. If the opening and closing trades were done with two different banks, they would have to be settled in the usual way: To settle the opening trade, the portfolio manager delivers one billion yen to the first bank and receives dollars on day 60; to settle the second trade, the portfolio manager receives one billion yen from the second bank and delivers dollars on day 60. However, the portfolio manager might be permitted to take net settlement in cases where both the opening and closing transactions have been done with the same bank. In the example, the net loss on the hedge is $72,288.19.

		Dollars	Yen
Opening trade	84.25	$11,869,436.20	(1,000,000,000)
Closing trade	83.74	($11,941,724.39)	1,000,000,000
		($72,288.19)	- 0 -

Under net settlement, this amount would have to be wired directly to the portfolio manager's dealer counterparty on day 60 to complete settlement of both the opening and closing trades (see Exhibit 3–7).

On the other hand, the portfolio manager might wish to keep the yen hedge in place indefinitely. In a technique called rolling forwards, the manager would do a spot transaction on day 58 to take care of the original forward transaction that settles on day 60 plus simultaneously reestablish the hedge with a new two-month forward trade. Gains or losses are settled each time the hedge is rolled. Rolling the hedge by opening and closing forward contracts is popular in the United States and Europe but much less so in Japan.

In Japan, another settlement procedure called historical rate rollover is popular. An argument often presented is that historical rate rollover is better suited to Japanese accounting practices. Cash gains and losses on forward transactions are delayed until some future date. Each time there is a forward roll, the market rate is adjusted to cover any profits or losses along with any financing costs. Suppose the forward transaction to sell one billion yen on day 1 for value on day 60 were going to be settled and reestablished for two months using historical rate rollover.

EXHIBIT 3-7

Forward Currency Transaction: Closing Trade from Customer's Perspective

Buy	Sell	Trade date	Value date
1 yard JPY	11,941,724.39 USD	Day 30	Day 60

Description of trade

Buy 1 yard JPY against USD to close previous forward trade. Value Day 60

Spot	Forward points	Commission	Outright
84.00	−0.26	0	83.74

Settlement instructions

Net Settlement on Day 60

Pay 72,288.19 USD to SBC NY

Counterparty	Dealer code	Trader
Swiss Bank New York	SBCN	T-Bone

Assume that the new spot rate and two-month forward outright are 84.00/10 and 83.30/39 on day 58. Closing the forward would generate a loss of $35,325.70. Using an interest rate of 5 percent, the future value at the next two-month value date of this sum is $35,621.31. Let the adjusted outright be denoted as x. The goal is to find x so that no matter what the spot rate at settlement turns out to be, there will a loss of $35,621.31 that would not be in existence had the new forward been struck at the outright rate of 83.39. Algebraically

$$\text{¥1 billion} \left[\frac{1}{x} - \frac{1}{83.39} \right] = -\$35,621.31$$

which solves for 83.6384. This is the adjusted forward rate for the new forward hedge. When the new settlement day, day 120, arrives, the contract could be extended again using another historical rate rollover or simply closed. It should be noted that banks in the United States and Europe frown upon the use of historical rate rollover on the grounds that it leads to deferrals of losses, which may in an extreme case jeopardize the creditworthiness of the counterparty.[5]

Tom/Next and Spot/Next Swaps

Spot currency deals ordinarily settle in two bank business days, but the value date can be extended one extra day by executing either a tom/next or spot/next transaction, depending on when the roll occurs. Suppose that on day 1, a trader sold 10 million U.S. dollars against yen at spot at the rate of 84.85. He would have to deliver $10 million and receive ¥848,500,000 on day 3. (For simplicity, we will assume that there are no holidays during this week.) Before the close of trading on day 1, a spot/next transaction would extend the value date to day 4. Spot/next gets its name from the fact that it extends settlement from the current spot value date (day 3) to the "next" value date (day 4). The spot/next swap has two parts. The first takes care of the original spot trade by doing a second spot trade to deliver ¥848,500,000 against dollars on day 3. The second part is a forward outright to sell dollars against yen for delivery on day 4. The same thing could be done on day 2 with a tom/next swap. The only difference between this and spot/next is that tom/next, which is short for "tomorrow/next," extends the spot delivery that will occur on the next day, meaning day 3. Tom/next and spot/next are quoted the same way as normal forwards. Points are either added or subtracted from the spot level (usually from the midpoint of the bid and offer). Exhibit 3–4 shows that the tom/next points for yen were quoted at –3.4/–3.3. The decimal point is used to position the points one position to the right of the rightmost decimal digit in the spot price quote. The exhibit also shows points for a one-week roll (i.e., "spot/week ").

Credit Considerations

Almost every form of foreign exchange trading constitutes a promise made on one date, the trade date, to exchange sums of currencies at a later date, the value date. In between these two dates, exchange rates are bound to change. For this reason, prudent dealers carefully set credit limits for their potential exposure to every counterparty. The industry practice is to review these limits continuously; they are subject to revision at any time without notice. Some banks require their counterparty customers to conclude margining agreements. These call for the pledge of collateral to cover any accrued losses that exceed some threshold level. For the most part, the risk of counterparty nonperformance is limited to the potential movement in exchange rates—this covers most of the cases. Much more dangerous is the risk that also exists for one-sided delivery. This is a rare but not unknown occurrence that usually surrounds a financial insolvency.

CURRENCY FUTURES CONTRACTS

A currency futures contract differs from a forward contract in that initial margin is required as a good-faith deposit. More importantly, daily variation margin must be satisfied. Futures contracts on currencies are listed on the Chicago Mercantile Exchange's International Monetary Market (IMM), the Philadelphia Board of Trade (PBOT), the Singapore International Monetary Exchange

EXHIBIT 3-8

Listed Currency Futures Contracts

	Chicago Mercantile Exchange (IMM)			Philadelphia Board of Trade		
Currency	Size	Minimum Fluctuation	Minimum Price Change	Size	Minimum Fluctuation	Minimum Price Change
Australian dollar	100,000	0.0001	$10.00	100,000	0.0001	$10.00
British pound*	62,500	0.0002	$12.50	62,500	0.0001	$ 6.25
Canadian dollar	100,000	0.0001	$10.00	100,000	0.0001	$10.00
ECU	NA	NA	NA	125,000	0.0001	$12.50
French franc	500,000	0.00002	$10.00	500,000	0.00002	$10.00
German mark*	125,000	0.0001	$12.50	125,000	0.0001	$12.50
Japanese yen*	12,500,000	0.000001	$12.50	12,500,000	0.000001	$12.50
Swiss franc	125,000	0.0001	$12.50	125,000	0.0001	$12.50
Mexican peso	500,000	0.000025	$12.50	NA	NA	NA
Brazilian real	100,000	.0001	$10.00	NA	NA	NA

Additional Specifications

Chicago Mercantile Exchange (IMM)

Months	1, 3, 4, 6, 7, 9, 12 plus spot month
Last trading day	Second business day before third Wednesday
First delivery day	Third Wednesday

Philadelphia Board of Trade

Months	3, 6, 9, 12, and two additional near months
Last trading day	Friday before third Wednesday
First delivery day	Third Wednesday

*Denotes simultaneous SIMEX listing.

(SIMEX), the MidAmerica Commodities Exchange, FINEX, and the Bolsa de Mercadorias & Futuros (Brazil).[6] Exhibit 3–8 summarizes the contract specifications for the IMM and PBOT. Currency futures contracts are quoted as the dollar value of one unit of foreign currency, except the yen, which is quoted as the dollar value of one hundred yen. Futures markets are open outcry markets. Trading is done in trading pits on the exchange floors.

The other side of every IMM futures contract is the Chicago Mercantile Exchange Clearinghouse, which acts as a guarantor of the contract. The Intermarket Clearing Corporation, a subsidiary of the Options Clearing Corporation, issues and guarantees PBOT futures. IMM futures contracts on the German mark, Japanese yen, and British pound are eligible for the Mutual Offset System facility with SIMEX. This means that IMM member firms can execute trades on SIMEX and have them transferred back to the IMM as new or liquidating trades. Similarly, SIMEX members can execute trades on the IMM and have them transferred back to SIMEX.

The clearinghouses of the futures exchanges set initial margin requirements. The amount of initial margin may vary by currency and market conditions. The IMM has two levels of initial margin, one for speculators and another for hedgers. The initial margin for speculators is larger than the one for hedgers. Each day, during the last moments before the close of trading, an exchange employee enters the trading pit to determine the settlement price for each contract. Theoretically, the settlement price is the last legitimate price at which a contract traded, but in active trading it can be the average of the highest and lowest trades done at close. The settlement price determines the variation margin for the day.

Long positions receive positive variation margin and pay negative variation margin. Short positions pay positive variation and receive negative variation margin. Variation margin is given by

$$\text{Price change measured in points} \\ \times \\ \text{Dollar value of one point} \\ \times \\ \text{Number of contracts}$$

Variation margin on a new position is calculated on the difference between the traded price and the day's settlement price. After the first day, variation margin is based on successive changes in settlement price. When the position is closed, variation margin is calculated on the difference between the exit price and the previous day's settlement price. For example, the variation margin for transactions in the German mark futures (one point equals $12.50) would be as follows:

> Day 1   Buy one contract at .5800
> Settlement price = .5790
> Net change = –10 points
> Variation margin = –$125

> Day 2   Carry long position
> Settlement price = .5850
> Net change = +60 points
> Variation margin = +$750

> Day 3   Sell contract at .5870
> Net change = .20 points
> Variation margin = +$250

The difference between the futures price and the spot exchange rate is called the futures basis. This quantity is a gauge of how fairly priced the futures are compared to spot. (There is a model for the fair value of the futures basis in Chapter 4.) Theoretically speaking, futures on currencies that have higher interest rates than the dollar will have negative bases. Futures on currencies with lower interest rates than the dollar will have positive bases.

Currency futures are listed for expiration in the March-June-September-December cycle, but contracts with other settlement months are sometimes listed. The difference between the futures price of the front contract and the next one on the delivery calendar is called the calendar basis. If the foreign currency interest rate is greater than the dollar interest rate, next contracts will be cheaper than the front contract. If the foreign currency interest rate is below the dollar interest rate, the front contract will be cheaper than the next contract.

Exchange for Physical Transactions

Futures and spot foreign exchange are linked though a specialized trading market in exchange for physical (EFP) transactions. In an EFP trade, a long or short position in a currency futures contract is exchanged for an equivalent face position in spot foreign exchange. This is referred to as an ex-pit transaction because it is executed at an off-market price. The price is a two-way quotation for either buying futures/selling spot or selling futures/buying spot. In normal markets, the EFP market closely follows the level of the swap points in the forward market that are quoted for value on futures expiration date.

One important function of the EFP market is to allow currency futures traders to unwind executed cash stop-loss orders that were triggered outside of floor trading hours. For example, suppose a trader is long yen by virtue of owning IMM yen currency futures contracts. During exchange hours, the trader can protect against a drop in the price of the yen by placing a futures stop-loss order. But after hours, the trader must use the cash market for stop-loss protection. A stop-loss order to buy dollars/sell yen can be given to a foreign exchange dealing bank. If the cash market stop order is executed, the trader will have a flat position only in theory; there will actually be two symmetrically opposite positions: one long futures (i.e., short dollars/long yen) and the other in cash (long dollars/short yen). The purpose of an EFP trade is to swap the futures and cash positions to flatten both positions.

OPTIONS ON CURRENCIES
AND CURRENCY FUTURES OPTIONS

Introduction to Options

The market for foreign exchange options is the second largest option market. Only the option market for fixed-income securities is thought to be larger. The largest portion of the currency option market is the interbank market, which is also called the over-the-counter (OTC) market. But there are also listed, meaning exchange-traded, currency options. The Philadelphia Stock Exchange lists options on actual foreign currency, and the

Chicago Mercantile Exchange's International Monetary Market lists options on currency futures (i.e., futures options).

Currency options can be either calls or puts. A currency call is the right but not the obligation to buy a sum of foreign currency at a fixed exchange rate, called the strike, on or before the option's expiration date. A put is an option to sell a sum of foreign exchange. Suppose a dollar/mark call is struck at 1.4100 on a face amount of 10 million dollars. This option grants the right but not the obligation to receive 10 million dollars against delivering 14.1 million marks. It is a call on dollars, but it is also a put on marks. To minimize the chance of what could be a costly misunderstanding, it is good practice to mention both currencies, tagging each with a call or a put identifier. The unambiguous name for the option is "dollar call/mark put." Currency options have the usual variety of exercise conventions. European style exercise options can be exercised only on the exercise date, but American style options can be exercised at any time before or on the expiration date.

The Interbank Over-the-Counter
Currency Option Market

The interbank currency option market trades 24 hours per day, right alongside spot and forward foreign exchange. All of the top-tier foreign exchange dealers make markets in currency options. Options are dealt on practically every exchange rate, but the bulk of trading is done in options on the major currencies. European exercise is more popular than American exercise. There is also a brisk and rapidly growing interest in exotic currency options, meaning options with nonstandard features, such as knock-outs, average rate options, basket options, and compound options.

Currency options are identified by five parameters: expiration, exchange rate, option type, strike, and face amount. A complete identification of the option in the example would be "European, three-month, dollar call/mark put, 1.4100 strike on 10 dollars." Unless otherwise specified, expiration is assumed to be European style at 10 A.M. New York time. Traders use one additional parameter, the delta, to fully identify options. As is discussed in Chapter 6, delta is the first derivative of the option price with respect to the exchange rate. The greater the delta, the more the option's value will change when the exchange rate moves. Delta is scaled between zero and 100. There are some general rules of first approximation about deltas that are part of most traders' common understanding of options. The delta of an option struck at the forward exchange rate (called "at-the-money-forward") is 50.[7] This means that if the spot exchange rate changes by 10 pips, say, the value of the call would increase by about 5 pips. The delta of an in-the-money-forward option is between 50 and 100; and the delta of an option out-of-the-money-forward is between 50 and zero. For the option that has been serving as the example, the trader might have inquired for a "European, three-month, 50 delta dollar call/mark put."

Options in the interbank market are quoted in terms of implied volatility. The concept of implied volatility, like that of delta, goes back to option math. Implied volatility is a parameter in currency option models that is measured in standard deviations. As a rough measure, implied volatilities for options on major currencies range between 3 percent and 20 percent, but they can be much higher in times of crisis. Puts and calls are worth more at higher levels of implied volatility. A sample conversation between a client and dealer is

> *Client:* Three-month, 50 delta dollar call/mark put on 10 dollars, please.
>
> *Dealer:* 14.00 – 14.50 percent.
>
> *Client:* Mine at 14.50 percent.
>
> *Dealer:* I sell a European, three-month, 50 delta dollar call/mark put at 14.50.

"14.00–14.50 percent" is the dealer's bid–offer quote. Because option value is a positive function of implied volatility, the smaller number, 14.00 percent, is known to be the dealer's bid (where he would buy the option) and the larger number, 14.50 percent, is the dealer's offer (where he would sell the option). In this conversation, the client buys the dollar call/mark put by saying "mine" at the dealer's offer of 14.50 percent. Once the implied volatility is known, the exact price of the option can be calculated given the level of the spot exchange rate and forward points. This calculation requires the help of an option pricing model. The option price, called the premium, can be quoted in at least five ways: total dollars, total marks, the percentage of face value, the number of dollar pips per mark, or the number of mark pips per dollar.

OTC option exercise for European options is marked at a date and time. (Popular "cuts" are 10 A.M. New York and 3 P.M. Tokyo.) Option exercise is the same in format as a spot exchange deal. In the example, assume that the spot dollar/mark exchange rate has moved up to 1.4500. In the process of exercise, the holder of the dollar call/mark put buys 10 dollars and sells marks at a strike exchange rate of 1.4100 for settlement in two bank business days. The option holder might want to continue with the long dollar/short mark spot position or immediately sell the dollars to take the profit. If the position can be liquidated at the spot rate of 1.4500, the profit gross of the expense of having bought the option would be equal to

$$\$10,000,000 \times \frac{(1.4500 - 1.4100)}{1.4500} = \$275,862.07$$

The Listed Market for Currency Options[8]

The Philadelphia Stock Exchange (the Philly) lists options on foreign currencies, which are both European and American in exercise convention. As in the case of OTC currency options, the Philly options deliver actual foreign currency upon exercise.[9] Philly options clear through and are guaranteed by the Options Clearing Corporation. The exchange sets standardized contract sizes, fixes expiration dates, and establishes strikes (Exhibit 3–9). Philly options are quoted in U.S. cents per unit of foreign exchange. There are two exceptions: the Japanese yen contract, which is quoted in hundredths of one cent per yen, and the French franc contract, which is quoted in tenths of one cent per franc. The value of a Philly option can be found by multiplying

Listed Currency Options and Futures Options

Currency	Chicago Mercantile Exchange (IMM) Options on Futures			Philadelphia Stock Exchange Options on Foreign Exchange		
	Size	Minimum Fluctuation	Minimum Price Change	Size	Minimum Fluctuation	Minimum Price Change
Australian dollar	1 futures contract	0.0001	$10.00	50,000	0.01	$5.00
British pound	1 futures contract	0.0002	$12.50	31,250	0.01	$3.125
Canadian dollar	1 futures contract	0.0001	$10.00	50,000	0.01	$5.00
ECU	NA	NA	NA	62,500	0.01	$6.25
French franc	1 futures contract	0.00002	$10.00	250,000	0.02	$5.00
German mark	1 futures contract	0.0001	$12.50	62,500	0.01	$6.25
Japanese yen	1 futures contract	0.000001	$12.50	6,250,000	0.01	$6.25
Swiss franc	1 futures contract	0.0001	$12.50	62,500	0.01	$6.25
Mexican peso	1 futures contract	0.000025	$12.50	NA	NA	NA

Additional Specifications

	Chicago Mercantile Exchange (IMM)	Philadelphia Stock Exchange
Months	3, 6, 7, 9, 12 plus two serial months and four weekly expirations	3, 6, 9, 12, and two additional near months
Last trading day	Second Friday before third Wednesday*	Friday before third Wednesday
First delivery day	Exercise into currency futures contract	Third Wednesday
Exercise	American	American and European

*Weeklies expire on all other Fridays in contract month.

73

the contract face amount by the quoted option price. To take the example, the dollar value of a German mark call quoted at 0.66 is $412.50, since

$$62,500 \text{ DEM} \times .66 \times .01 = \$412.50$$

The Philly sets margin rules for currency options. The most recent set, promulgated in the summer of 1990, is described in Appendix B to this chapter.

The International Monetary Market (IMM) of the Chicago Mercantile Exchange lists American style options on its currency futures (Exhibit 3–9). IMM currency futures options are guaranteed by the Chicago Mercantile Exchange Clearinghouse; it is the counterparty to every transaction. The IMM options match the specifications of the futures contracts with respect to quotation convention and size. The IMM futures options deliver currency futures in the March-June-September-December cycle. For example, the October option would exercise into the December futures contract. Upon exercise, the buyer of a long call or short put is credited with a long position in a currency futures contract. Likewise, the writer of a call or buyer of a put is debited with a futures contract at exercise. At exercise, there is a mark-to-market equal to the spread between the strike and the settlement price.

IMM currency futures options work the same as the Philly currency options in terms of quotation: The rule is to multiply the quoted price by the contract size. For example, a German mark call quoted at .55 would be worth $687.50, since

$$125,000 \text{ DEM} \times .55 \times .01 = \$687.50$$

The Chicago Mercantile Clearinghouse operates a complex risk management program to determine option margin requirements. It is called standard portfolio analysis of risk (SPAN). SPAN generates daily margin requirements based on portfolio risk analysis and scenario models of changing market conditions. The CME provides clearing firms with SPAN arrays daily for the calculation of minimum margin requirements.

NOTES

1. Appendix A describes the hierarchy of major exchange rates.

2. The reason customers are asked to disclose whether a trade is in the full amount is as follows. The dealer always tries to guard against taking a position that is opposite to the very near-term direction of the market. The hazard is that the dealer might not know the full size of a customer order that is large enough to move the market. Say the customer intends to sell 500 million dollars against the Japanese yen but only discloses 100 million to a particular dealer. The dealer makes 84.85/95 and is "given at 85" on 100 million dollars. Thereupon the dealer would normally flatten the new position by selling 100 million dollars in the interbank market. Unfortunately for him, the customer is now trying to do the rest of his order elsewhere, selling the balance of 400 million dollars. Now the market might be 84.10 bid; in the colorful language of the market, the dealer has been "stuffed." This kind of customer is found out quickly in the small world of interbank dealing.

3. A quick way to compute the profit or loss on the spot trade is given by

$$P\&L = \left(\frac{\text{Spot at open} - \text{Spot at close}}{\text{Spot at close}} \right) \times \text{Face amount}$$

In the example, this would be

$$\$10,000,000 \times \left(\frac{84.85 - 84.10}{84.10} \right) = \$89,179.55$$

4. The Association Cambiste Internationale's Code of Conduct (Paris 1991) is the source of a lot of convention on spot dealing. On stop-loss orders, the Code specifies

Any dealer who has received a stop-loss order works to execute it at the designated rate on a best efforts basis. However, an order-receiving bank does not guarantee to execute it at the rate. (p. 8)

5. Historical rate rollover is a controversial topic. The Association Cambiste Internationale's Code of Conduct (Paris 1991) warns against dealing at noncurrent rates, an essential part of any historical rate rollover:

   Deals at non-market rates should generally be avoided, as such practices may result in concealment of a profit or loss; in the perpetration of a fraud; or in the giving of an unauthorized extension of credit. (p. 7)

   Also, the annual report for 1991 of the Foreign Exchange Committee cautions against historical rate rollover except in cases where "(a) customers have a legitimate commercial justification for extending the contract, and (b) senior management of both the customer institution and the dealer institution are fully aware of the transaction and the exposures involved" (pp. 23–24).

6. The Bolsa de Mercadorias & Futuros (Brazil) lists futures and put and call options on the exchange rate of Brazilian reals per U.S. dollar. FINEX lists futures on the following cross rates: sterling/mark, mark/yen, mark/swiss, mark/french, mark/lira, and mark/swedish.

7. Some traders use the spot exchange rate rather than the forward exchange rate as the measure of whether a currency option is at-, in-, or out-of-the-money. The rationale for using the forward exchange rate for European style exercise is that the option can be thought of as a conditional forward transaction.

8. The MATIF (Paris) lists options on dollar/mark, dollar/lira, and sterling/mark.

9. In the case of both Philly and IMM options, exercise is randomly assigned by the clearinghouse to the accounts of clearing brokers. The brokers in turn must decide which of their clients will receive exercise notices.

APPENDIX A

The Hierarchy of Exchange Rates

As described in the chapter, the first currency in an exchange rate pair is the direct object of the trade. To buy 10 mark/Swiss is to buy 10 million marks against the Swiss. Exhibit 3–10 displays as much of an international convention for the hierarchy of currencies as exists. The rule is that the higher currency on the grid is the one that deals. For example, marks deal against yen, but sterling deals against marks. This is accurate in the professional market. There are also local markets with different conventions. In a local market, if the local currency is direct, traders might quote a cross with their own currency first. For example, in Australia, a quote might be given as AUD/ECU. If the local currency is an indirect currency, traders might quote a cross with their own currency second. Examples are JPY/CHF in Switzerland and CHF/DEM for Germany.

EXHIBIT 3–10

Dealing Hierarchy of Major Exchange Rates

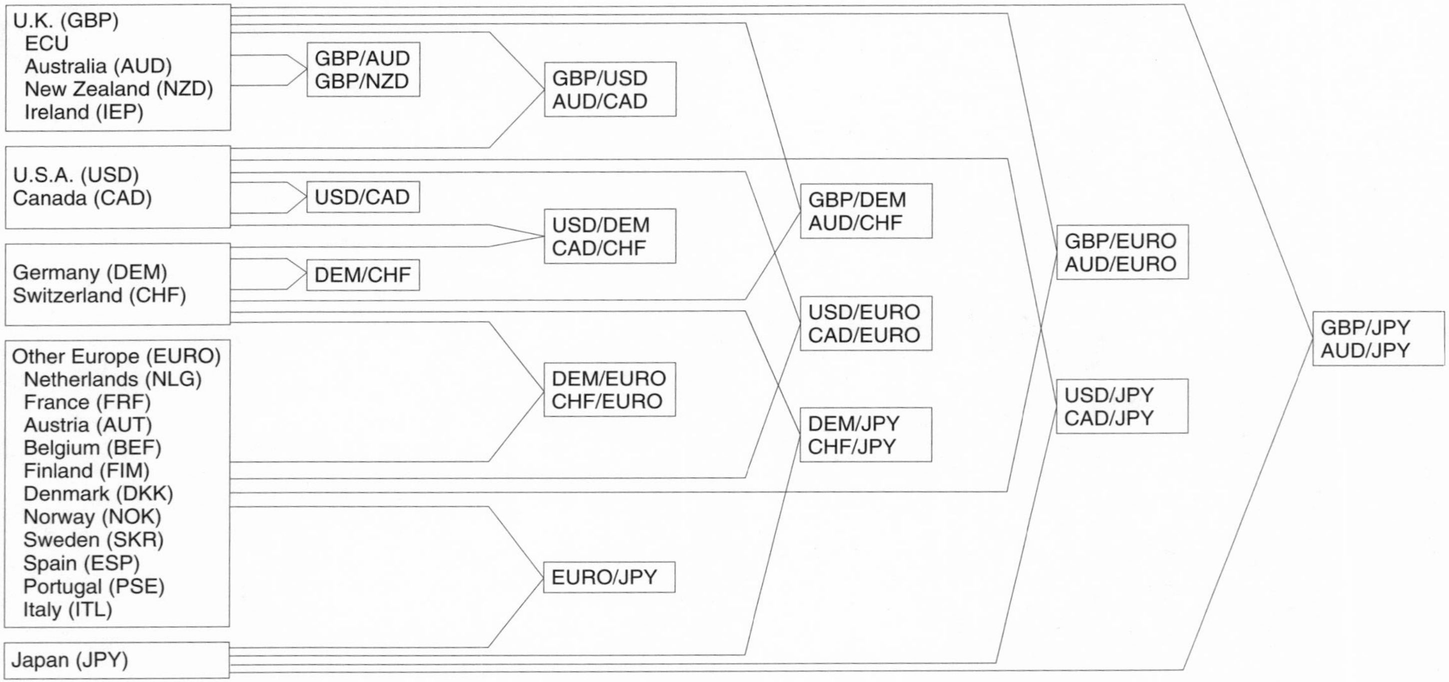

Philadelphia Stock Exchange Margin Rules for Currency Options

Margin Rules for the Philadelphia Stock Exchange on currency options (as per rule 722, Summer 1990):

1. **Long calls and long puts:** Margin is 100 percent of the option's premium.

2. **Uncovered short call or short put:** Margin is 100 percent of premium plus 4 percent of the contract less the out-of-the-money amount, with a minimum of premium plus $\frac{3}{4}$ percent of contract spot amount.

3. **Call spread or put spread** (consisting of a long and short position in calls or puts of the same currency with the same expiration date): 100 percent of the premium on long option plus the lesser of the margin on an uncovered short option or the absolute value of the difference in the strike prices.

4. **Short straddle** (consisting of a short put and a short call with the same strike price and same expiration date): Pay the greater of the margin on the put or the call plus the premium on the other position.

5. **Short currency with a long or short position in an option:** Hedge is not recognized. Pay margin on option as though short currency position did not exist.

6. **Long spot currency and long put:** 100 percent of premium on put.

7. **Long spot currency and short call:** No margin required, but futures contracts are not accepted.

CHAPTER 4

The Interest Parity Theorem and the Valuation of Forward Currency Contracts, Futures, and Swaps

The interest parity theorem is the fundamental law of international finance that links exchange rates and interest rates.[1] The interest parity theorem has broad implications for understanding the pricing of currency forward contracts, futures contracts, currency options, and swaps.[2]

THE INTEREST PARITY THEOREM

The Basic Idea

It is readily observable that interest rates vary widely across countries. This is somewhat of a puzzle. How can the Italian lira interest rate be 10.7 percent, for example, when the U.S. dollar rate is 6.00 percent? What would prevent capital from flowing from the United States to Italy, thereby causing the lira interest rate to fall and the dollar interest rate to rise, until the entire interest rate differential has disappeared? Of course, no such thing occurs. The reason this analysis is wrong is that it does not consider exchange rate risk. An attempt to extract the Italian lira interest rate advantage would require that a dollar-based investor take exposure to the lira. Exchange rate risk—the risk that the lira would depreciate against the dollar—is unavoidable in the transaction. It acts as a barrier of sorts. Exchange rate risk is what permits differentials in interest rates to persist.

Although no riskless arbitrage mechanism exists to bring interest rates around the world to one single level, there is a linkage between interest rates and foreign exchange. This relationship is called the interest parity theorem. Driving the interest parity theorem is the basic principle that well-functioning financial markets generate asset prices and exchange rates that preclude opportunities for riskless profit taking. In the example of the Italian lira, the potential arbitrage is that a dollar-based investor could use the forward market to hedge the exchange rate risk associated with a lira bond yet retain some or all of the interest differential. The no-arbitrage rule here is enforced by the forward exchange rate, which is in effect the spoiler. It trades away from the spot by just enough to exactly capture the spread in interest rates between the domestic and foreign currencies (Exhibit 4–1).

Formal Statement of Interest Parity Theorem

As was previously stated, the foreign exchange market uses two conventions to quote spot and forward rates. This makes it necessary for the theorem to be stated in two ways. The American quotation convention states the exchange rate in terms of the number of U.S. dollars that equate to one unit of currency (1.5900 USD equal one pound). The other convention, European style, quotes the exchange rate in terms of the number of units of currency that equal one U.S. dollar (85.00 yen equal one dollar).

Interest Parity: American Convention

The forward exchange rate, F, is related to the spot rate, S, and to the continuously compounded riskless interest rates on the domestic and foreign currencies, denoted as R_d and R_f, respectively, according to the following equation known as the interest parity theorem:

$$F = Se^{(R_d - R_f)\tau}$$

where e is the base of the natural logarithm. This formulation uses continuously compounded interest.[3] τ is time in years or

EXHIBIT 4-1

A Numerical Example of the Interest Parity Theorem
USD (U.S. dollars) versus DEM (German marks)

Suppose you had 1,000,000 USD to invest for 60 days.
Given the following market conditions,

Spot USD/DEM	1.3950
USD interest rate (60 days)	6.00%
DEM interest rate (60 days)	4.50%

and assuming annual compounding, what 60-day forward exchange rate would have to prevail?

The forward rate that precludes arbitrage makes traders indifferent between:

1. Keeping the funds in USD.

   Invest for 60 days in USD to get $1,010,000.

2. Converting to DEM, investing for 60 days, and buying USD forward.

   a. Convert $1,000,000 to 1,395,000 DEM at the spot rate.
   b. Invest DEM for 60 days to get 1,405,462 DEM.
   c. Buy USD forward to settle in 60 days vs. 1,405,462 DEM.

The only forward price that precludes arbitrage is found by dividing 1,405,462 by 1,010,000 to get 1.3915.

fractions thereof, and the two interest rates R_d and R_f are annualized according to convention.

For example, if the pound sterling were at 1.5975 spot and the six-month interest rates were 7.10 percent and 5.90 percent for sterling and dollars, respectively, the forward exchange rate for six months, using the continuously compounded interest formulation, would be 1.5879 (corresponding to −96 forward points).

The equation also can be written in terms of simple interest:

$$F = S\frac{(1+r_d)^{\tau}}{(1+r_f)^{\tau}}$$

where r_d and r_f are the domestic and foreign annually compounded interest rates.

Interest Parity: European Convention

Denoting the forward and spot exchange rates quoted in European convention as F' and S', the continuously compounded and annually compounded interest formulations become

$$F' = S'e^{(R_f - R_d)\tau}$$

$$F' = S'\frac{(1+r_f)^\tau}{(1+r_d)^\tau}$$

Premium and Discount Currencies

A foreign currency is said to be a premium currency if its interest rate is lower than the domestic currency. A foreign currency that has a higher interest rate than the domestic currency is called a discount currency.

A foreign currency can switch in either direction between being a premium currency and a discount currency if the sign of the interest rate spread changes. It can be a premium currency at some term structure maturities and simultaneously be a discount currency at other maturities.

The interest parity equation reveals a few simple rules about the relationship between forward and spot exchange rates. The forward rate on a premium currency must exceed the spot rate quoted American convention. The forward rate on a discount currency must be lower than the spot rate quoted American. The reverse is true for currencies quoted European: The forward rate on a premium currency must be less than the spot rate; the forward rate on a discount currency must exceed the spot rate.

As discussed in Chapter 3, the difference between the forward and the spot exchange rates is called the forward points. Forward points can be expressed as follows, using the interest parity theorem.

Forward Points (American Convention)

$$S\left(e^{(R_d - R_f)\tau} - 1\right)$$

Forward Points (European Convention)

$$S'\left(e^{(R_f - R_d)\tau} - 1\right)$$

Uncovered Interest Parity

One question that has long held the attention of economists is whether a more generalized form of interest parity holds. To be precise, what has been discussed is called "covered" interest rate parity. The term covered refers to the use of the forward market to hedge, or cover, currency risk. As was demonstrated, arbitrage forces the forward rate to be priced so as to capture the interest rate spread, much the same as the cost of carry is reflected in the pricing of commodity futures and financial derivative instruments. A more generalized form of the theorem, called "uncovered" interest parity, proposes that the forward exchange rate is an unbiased forecast of the future spot exchange rate. An alternative statement is that in a risk-neutral, perfect capital markets setting, the difference between forward and spot exchange rates is equal to the expected future appreciation or depreciation in the exchange rates. A great deal of empirical research has been devoted to testing uncovered interest parity. The results uniformly reject the hypothesis.[4] There are three, non–mutually exclusive explanations for this puzzle. One is that there is a logical flaw in the uncovered interest parity theorem. The second explanation is that there is a risk premium built into the forward exchange rate. But to account for the empirical findings, this risk premium would have to be large and would have to fluctuate somewhat wildly. The third possible explanation is that the forward rate is indeed a predictor of the future spot but that it is a poor predictor. The problem here is that the imputed prediction errors are large and they occur with such predictability that any notion of efficiency with respect to the foreign exchange market must be questioned. Clearly, neither the empirical findings nor any of these three explanations are palatable, which leaves the concept of uncovered interest parity very much in question.

THE VALUATION OF FORWARD CONTRACTS

The Closing Transaction as the Basis of Valuation

A forward contract consists of a promise to exchange one currency for another on a value day in the future. Most forward contracts start out with zero present value by design. Later, as exchange rates and interest rates change and as time to expiration lapses, the contract can take on positive or negative value. As was demonstrated in Chapter 3, a forward contract can be effectively closed at any time before settlement by entering into a second transaction to reverse the purchase or sale of the two currencies. The net profit or loss can be settled in either of the two currencies. The value of the forward contract before settlement must equal the net present value of the gain or loss that would be realized for certain if the forward contract were closed.

Suppose an investor wished to buy 1,000,000 sterling forward against the U.S. dollar for value in one year. Also suppose the initial spot exchange rate was equal to 1.5975 per pound, that the one-year interest rate in dollars was 5.70 percent, and that the interest rate in pounds was 7.50 percent. The one-year forward outright, F, that is consistent with interest parity is

$$F = 1.5975e^{(.057 - .0750)} = 1.5690$$

The forward contract would consist of an agreement to receive £1,000,000 and deliver $1,569,002 USD in one year's time. Now suppose the spot exchange rate was to fall to 1.5700 instantaneously. What would the forward contract now be worth? To unwind the contract and settle in dollars (Exhibit 4–2A), a second transaction, called the closing transaction, could be done. It would sell £1,000,000 for value in one year's time. The number of dollars that would have to be received at settlement with respect to this transaction would depend on the new forward exchange rate, which can be calculated to four decimal digits as

$$F = 1.5700e^{(.057 - .0750)} = 1.5420$$

assuming no change in the interest rates. The closing transaction would call for the investor to deliver £1,000,000 and receive $1,541,993 (the forward outright is not rounded). On a net basis, the pound amounts are equal, and on settlement day a net sum of $27,009 would be deliverable from the counterparty. This sum would have a present value of $25,513 based on the 5.70 percent dollar interest rate. Accordingly, the forward contract would have a value equal to negative $25,513.

E X H I B I T   4–2

Valuation of a Forward Contract
Instantaneous Change in Value—One-Year Forward Contracts

A. American Convention—Settle in Domestic Currency (Forward Purchase of 1,000,000 British Pounds)

Opening Parameters		Closing Parameters	
Spot	1.5975	Spot	1.5700
Forward	1.5690	Forward	1.5420
R_f (GBP)	7.50%	R_f (GBP)	7.50%
R_d (USD)	5.70%	R_d (USD)	5.70%

Opening Transaction		Closing Transaction	
Pay	($1,569,002) USD	Pay	(1,000,000) GBP
Receive	1,000,000 GBP	Receive	$1,541,993 USD
		Net on Settlement—USD	($27,009) USD
		NPV of Forward—USD	($25,513) USD
		NPV of Forward—GBP	(16,250) GBP

B. American Convention—Settle in Foreign Currency (Forward Purchase of 1,000,000 British Pounds)

Opening Parameters		Closing Parameters	
Spot	1.5975	Spot	1.5700
Forward	1.5690	Forward	1.5420
R_f (GBP)	7.50%	R_f (GBP)	7.50%
R_d (USD)	5.70%	R_d (USD)	5.70%

Opening Transaction		Closing Transaction	
Pay	($1,569,002) USD	Pay	(1,017,516) GBP
Receive	1,000,000 GBP	Receive	$1,569,002 USD
		Net on Settlement—GBP	(17,516) GBP
		NPV of Forward—GBP	(16,250) GBP
		NPV of Forward—USD	($25,513) USD

(continued)

Valuation of a Forward Contract (concluded)

C. European Convention—Settle in Domestic Currency (Forward Purchase of 10,000,000 Yen)

Opening Parameters		Closing Parameters	
Spot	84.90	Spot	87.00
Forward	81.08	Forward	83.09
R_f(JPY)	1.10%	R_f(JPY)	1.10%
R_d(USD)	5.70%	R_d(USD)	5.70%

Opening Transaction		Closing Transaction	
Pay	($123,330) USD	Pay	(10,000,000) JPY
Receive	10,000,000 JPY	Receive	$120,353 USD
		Net on Settlement—USD	($2,977)
		NPV of Forward—USD	($2,812) USD
		NPV of Forward—JPY	(244,644) JPY

D. European Convention—Settle in Foreign Currency (Forward Purchase of 10,000,000 Yen)

Opening Parameters		Closing Parameters	
Spot	84.90	Spot	87.00
Forward	81.08	Forward	83.09
R_f(JPY)	1.10%	R_f(JPY)	1.10%
R_d(USD)	5.70%	R_d(USD)	5.70%

Opening Transaction		Closing Transaction	
Pay	($123,330) USD	Receive	(10,247,350) JPY
Receive	10,000,000 JPY	Pay	$123,330 USD
		Net on Settlement—JPY	(247,350) JPY
		NPV of Forward—JPY	(244,644) JPY
		NPV of Forward—USD	($2,812) USD

Alternatively, the closing transaction could be done to settle in pounds (Exhibit 4–2B). The closing transaction would call for $1,569,002 to be received at settlement in exchange for £1,017,516. The amount due at settlement would equal £17,516, which has a present value of negative £16,250, using the interest rate 7.50 percent. Converted to dollars at the new spot rate of 1.5700, the loss would equal \$25,513, which is the same value obtained above where the transaction is settled in dollars.

The closing procedures for a forward contract to buy a European quoted currency, namely the yen, are shown in Exhibit 4–2C and D.

The paradigms outlined in Exhibit 4–2 lead directly to models of forward contract valuation. The mathematics of valuation are most easily understood when the currency is quoted American and when the closing transaction is settled in the domestic currency.

A Model of Forward Contract Valuation[5]

Suppose that a forward contract was opened at time zero at the prevailing forward exchange rate, F_0, for value at time T. The contract will receive one unit of foreign exchange and deliver F_0 dollars. The interest parity level for F_0 is

$$F_0 = S_0 e^{(R_d - R_f)T}$$

The rate F_0 is fixed and does not vary during the contract.

What would the forward contract be worth at some future date, say time t, when $[T - t]$ years remain to settlement? The answer is that the forward contract is worth the net present value of what would be gained or lost to close it out at market prices. Closing the position would consist of selling one unit of foreign currency for settlement at the same day T at the new forward rate that prevails at time t. The present value of the position on day t consists of

U.S. dollars	$-F_0 e^{-R_d(T-t)}$
Foreign currency	$+e^{-R_f(T-t)}$

The first term is the present value of the sum of domestic currency that will be delivered at settlement. The second term is the present value of the unit of foreign currency that is to be received at settlement. To close, one unit of foreign currency must be sold forward at the new forward rate, F_t, to settle at time T. The present value of the closing transaction is

U.S. dollars $\qquad F_t e^{-R_d(T-t)}$

Foreign currency $\qquad -e^{-R_f(T-t)}$

The net is the value of the forward, designated as V_t

$$V_t = F_t e^{-R_d(T-t)} - F_0 e^{-R_d(T-t)}$$

Substituting for F_t in terms of S_t

$$V_t = S_t e^{-R_f(T-t)} - F_0 e^{-R_d(T-t)}$$

The equation can be validated using the paradigm of Exhibit 4–2A; the value of the forward contract to buy pounds would be

$$1 \text{ million GBP} \times [1.5700 e^{-.075} - 1.5690 e^{-.057}] = -\$25{,}511$$

This is slightly different from the result in the exhibit because F_0 is rounded.

The equation shows that the value of the forward contract is positively related to the spot exchange rate. Its sensitivity to changes in the spot rate, called delta (δ), can be found as

$$\delta_{\text{forward contract}} = \frac{\partial V_t}{\partial S_t} = e^{-R_f(T-t)} \le 1$$

Since $(T - t)$ is positive, δ has to be less than one (except if R_f is a negative number). This means that a one-unit change in the spot exchange rate will cause the value of a forward contract to change by less than one unit. Note that δ does not depend on the domestic interest rate because the process of taking present values removes the domestic interest rate. The greater the interest rate on the foreign currency, the smaller the delta of the forward contract for the unit change in spot

$$\frac{\partial}{\partial R_f}\frac{\partial V_t}{\partial S_t} = -(T-t)e^{-R_f(T-t)} < 0$$

As the time remaining to the value date elapses, the delta of the forward contract grows larger, all other things equal, because

$$-\frac{\partial}{\partial(T-t)}\frac{\partial V_t}{\partial S_t} = R_f e^{-R_f(T-t)} > 0$$

Note that $-(T-t)$ is, in effect, the "shrinkage" in the time to settlement as the contract ages. Exhibits 4–3 and 4–4 contain numerical examples of forward contract deltas and their sensitivities to foreign interest rates and time to settlement.

To complete the model, the sensitivities of the value of the forward contract to movements in interest rates and to the passage of time need to be presented. Forward contracts are inversely related to the foreign interest rate and positively related to the domestic rate

$$\frac{\partial V_t}{\partial R_f} = -(T-t)S_t e^{-R_f(T-t)} < 0$$

$$\frac{\partial V_t}{\partial R_d} = (T-t)F_0 e^{-R_d(T-t)} > 0$$

The relationship between the value of the forward contract and time is ambiguous in sign.

$$-\frac{\partial V_t}{\partial(T-t)} = R_f S_t e^{-R_f(T-t)} - R_d F_0 e^{-R_d(T-t)}$$

THE VALUATION OF CURRENCY FUTURES CONTRACTS

Futures Contracts Compared to Forward Contracts

Currency futures contracts resemble forward contracts apart from issues relating to margining and standardization of contract size

EXHIBIT 4-3

The Delta of a Forward Contract
The Impact of a Higher Foreign Interest Rate
Forward Purchase of 1,000,000 British Pounds

		Opening Transaction	
		R_f = 7.50%	R_f = 8.50%
Spot		1.5975	1.5975
Days to settlement		365	365
R_f (GBP)		7.50%	8.50%
R_d (USD)		5.70%	5.70%
Implied forward		1.5690	1.5534
On settlement day			
Pay	USD	($1,569,002)	($1,553,390)
Receive	GBP	1,000,000	1,000,000
		Closing Transaction	
Spot		1.5875	1.5875
Days to settlement		365	365
R_f (GBP)		7.50%	8.50%
R_d (USD)		5.70%	5.70%
Implied forward		1.5592	1.5437
On settlement day			
Receive	USD	$1,559,181	$1,543,667
Pay	GBP	(1,000,000)	(1,000,000)

Gain or Loss on Forward Contract:
Present Values of Settlement Cash Flow

	Amount	PV	Amount	PV
Opening trade	($1,569,002)	($1,482,070)	($1,553,390)	($1,467,323)
Closing trade	$1,559,181	$1,472,793	$1,543,667	$1,458,138
Value of forward contract		($9,277)		($9,185)

Delta of Forward Contract

Change in spot value of pounds		
Original spot value	$1,597,500	$1,597,500
New spot value	$1,587,500	$1,587,500
Change in spot value	($10,000)	($10,000)
Delta of forward contract	**0.928**	**0.919**

For currencies quoted American style, the delta of a forward contract is always less than one. Also, the greater the foreign currency interest rate, the smaller the delta of the forward contract.

EXHIBIT 4-4

Delta of a Forward Contract
The Impact of Time to Expiration
Forward Purchase of 1,000,000 British Pounds

		Opening Transaction	
		Two Months	One Month
Spot		1.5975	1.5975
Days to settlement		60	30
R_f (GBP)		7.50%	7.50%
R_d (USD)		5.70%	5.70%
Implied forward		1.5928	1.5951
On settlement day			
Pay	USD	($1,592,780)	($1,595,138)
Receive	GBP	1,000,000	1,000,000
		Closing Transaction	
Spot		1.5875	1.5875
Days to settlement		60	30
R_f (GBP)		7.50%	7.50%
R_d (USD)		5.70%	5.70%
Implied forward		1.5828	1.5852
On settlement day			
Receive		$1,582,810	$1,585,153
Pay		(1,000,000)	(1,000,000)

Gain or Loss on Forward Contract:
Present Values of Settlement Cash Flow

	Amount	PV	Amount	PV
Opening trade	($1,592,780)	($1,577,926)	($1,595,138)	($1,587,683)
Closing trade	$1,582,810	$1,568,048	$1,585,153	$1,577,744
Value of forward contract		($9,877)		($9,939)

Delta of Forward Contract

Change in spot value of pounds		
Original spot value	$1,597,500	$1,597,500
New spot value	$1,587,500	$1,587,500
Change in spot value	($10,000)	($10,000)
Delta of forward contract	**0.988**	**0.994**

For currencies quoted American style, the delta of a forward contract approaches one with the passage of time to settlement day.

and maturity dates. The question is whether futures are so similar as to be completely interchangeable with forward contracts.

Margrabe (1976) is believed to be the first economist to understand the essential economic distinction between futures and forwards. Margrabe's insight was later incorporated into a classic mathematical treatment by Cox, Ingersoll, and Ross (1981). The origin of the distinction is that an investor in a futures contract—but not an investor in a forward contract—can be materially affected by random changes in short-term interest rates. As described in Chapter 3, currency futures are exchange-traded instruments that are settled up or marked-to-market every trading day. A futures contract pays or receives funds every day, whereas a forward contract creates no intermediate cash flow. Uncertainty exists about the day-to-day interest rates at which the cash gains and losses from the futures position could be invested or need to be financed. Therefore, futures and forwards cannot be perfect substitutes.

The subtle point that Margrabe and Cox, Ingersoll, and Ross made was that the distinction between currency futures and forwards could matter only if there were a systematic tendency for short-term interest rates to correlate, positively or negatively, with exchange rate movements. Otherwise, the marginal uncertainty surrounding the financing of the daily settlement on the futures position would not amount to "economic risk." This being the case, the futures price could not command any risk premium; the futures price would have to be equal to the forward outright. Empirical evidence has yet to find any statistically significant difference between currency futures and forwards. Moreover, Cornell and Reinganum (1981) found no significant correlation between interest rates and exchange rates. This suggests that futures are no more or less risky than forwards in the Margrabe sense.

A Model for the Valuation of Futures Contracts

As described in Chapter 3, the currency futures contracts that are traded on the Chicago Mercantile Exchange's IMM division are quoted American style. The basis of a futures contract is defined as the difference between the future's price and the spot exchange rate. The basis may be positive or negative. Throughout each trading session, futures contracts trade at slight premium or discount to their theoretical value. In turbulent markets, the actual futures basis sometimes can drift away from theoretical fair-value basis but arbitrage between the cash and futures markets usually returns the actual basis to its fair value.

The theoretical fair value basis of a futures contract corresponds to the forward points associated with the forward exchange rate

$$S\left(e^{(R_d - R_f)T} - 1\right)$$

This quantity is greater than zero for $R_d > R_f$, equal to zero for $R_d = R_f$, and less than zero for $R_d < R_f$. This explains why futures on discount currencies have negative bases and futures on premium currencies have positive bases.

Calendar spread is the difference between the price of a far-dated futures contract and the front month contract. Calendar basis is positive for premium currencies and negative for discount currencies, assuming that the spread between the domestic and foreign interest rates is approximately the same at different maturities.

The Linearity Theorem

The Cox, Ingersoll, and Ross paper contained another theorem of practical importance, referred to as the linearity theorem. As applied to foreign exchange derivatives the theorem can be stated as follows:

> The value of a future or forward contract on an index of currencies is equal to the weighted sum of separate futures or forward contracts on the individual currencies, with the weight for each currency being equal to its proportion in the index.

This theorem also works for rates of return:

> The rate of return on a future or forward contract on an index of currencies is equal to the weighted average of the rates of returns on futures or forwards on the individual currencies.

This means that the overall currency exposure of a portfolio can be managed by hedging the individual currency exposures in sum or individually.

What makes the linearity theorem particularly interesting is that it does not hold for currency options. Unlike forwards and futures, options have asymmetric payoff patterns with respect to the underlying exchange rate. This makes an option on an index less valuable than a collection of options on the individual component currencies. An index option can expire as worthless, out-of-the-money, but some of the options on the individual currencies might be in-the-money.

THE VALUATION OF CURRENCY SWAP AGREEMENTS

Introduction to Swaps

A currency swap is an agreement between two parties to exchange currencies on one day and to reexchange the same sums at a later time. Sometimes the initial exchange of currencies is omitted. Customarily, the rate of exchange is set equal to the prevailing spot exchange rate when the first exchange of currencies occurs. Swaps are usually engineered to have a net present value of zero in the first instance. Therefore, intermediate exchanges of currencies are needed to take account of interest rate differentials. These intermediate exchanges can be fixed for the life of the swap (called "fixed-for-fixed"), or one or both sides can be linked to a floating interest rate ("fixed-for-floating" or "floating-for-floating").

The structure of a currency swap is best understood in the context of one of its first important uses, that of an international corporation that finds it economical to borrow in a foreign currency. For example, suppose that a U.S. dollar–based company were able to borrow 100 million British pounds at 7.5 percent with three annual coupon payments plus return of principal at the end of the third year. The cash flow stream of the loan would be as follows.

Beginning of loan	+100 million GBP
End of year one	−7.5 million GBP
End of year two	−7.5 million GBP
End of year three	−107.5 million GBP

The purpose of the swap transaction is to immunize the borrower against changes in the exchange rate. The structure of a hypothetical swap (fixed-for-fixed) is described in Exhibit 4–5. The counterparty to such a swap is typically an investment bank, commercial bank, or corporate treasurer. The initial and final exchanges are based on a spot rate (GBP/USD) of 1.5975. The intermediate exchanges are based on interest rates of 7.5 percent for sterling and 5.7 percent for dollars (annually compounded interest). This swap removes the risk associated with movements in sterling and converts the original sterling loan into a dollar loan.

Other swaps are based on floating interest rates, such as dollar or sterling LIBOR. These swaps are used to immunize the borrower against both exchange rate risk and interest rate risk where a liability is based on a floating rate.

A Model for the Valuation of Swap Agreements[6]

Swaps, like forward contracts, are structured to have an initial net present value equal to zero. Afterward, they gain and lose

EXHIBIT 4–5

Structure of a Fixed-for-Fixed Currency Swap

A. Initial Exchange at Beginning of Swap					
Borrower			**Counterparty**		
Pay	(100,000,000)	GBP	Pay	($159,750,000)	USD
Receive	$159,750,000	USD	Receive	100,000,000	GBP
B. Annual Intermediate Payments—Years 1, 2, and 3					
Borrower			**Counterparty**		
Pay	($9,105,750)	USD	Pay	(7,500,000)	GBP
Receive	7,500,000	GBP	Receive	$9,105,750	USD
C. Reexchange at Conclusion of Swap					
Borrower			**Counterparty**		
Pay	($159,750,000)	USD	Pay	(100,000,000)	GBP
Receive	100,000,000	GBP	Receive	$159,750,000	USD

value as spot exchange rates and interest rates change, and time elapses. As with a forward contract, the value of a swap is determined by the cost or gain to unwind the agreement. There are two methods of swap valuation. One is called the present-value method; the other is the forward-contract method. Both will be demonstrated to determine the value of the fixed-for-fixed swap in Exhibit 4–5 after a lapse of one year.

The Present-Value Method
In the present-value method, the value of a swap is the net present value of its payment streams.

Continuing with the example above, assume that after one year the spot exchange rate (GBP/USD) is 1.5700, the dollar interest rate has risen to 6.5 percent, and the sterling interest rate has risen to 8 percent. These interest rates are applicable for one- and two-year maturities. Exhibit 4–6 demonstrates the present-value method of swap valuation. What remains of the dollar leg of the swap is two annual payments of $9,105,750 plus the final reexchange of $159,750,000. The present value of the dollar payments equals ($157,423,239), where parentheses indicate that the value must be paid by the borrower. On the sterling side, the present value is £99,108,368. At the new spot exchange rate of 1.5700, the dollar equivalent value of the present value of the sterling leg of the swap would be $155,600,137. The net of the two present values is ($1,823,102), which is the value of the swap. In this example, the term structure of interest rates is assumed to be flat for maturities of two years and less.

The Forward-Contract Method of Swap Valuation
The second method of valuation treats each individual exchange of currency as a separate forward contract. Exhibit 4–7 shows this method using forward exchange rates calculated with the annually compounded interest version of the interest parity formula.

As discussed above, the value of a forward contract is equal to the net present value of the cost or gain of unwinding the position. For example, the next remaining exchange of currencies in one year calls for £7,500,000 to be received and $9,105,750 to be paid. Since the forward exchange rate for one year is now

E X H I B I T   4–6

Present-Value Method of Swap Valuation
Beginning of Year 2

Parameters

Domestic interest rate (USD)	6.50%	
Foreign interest rate (GBP)	8.00%	
Spot exchange rate (GBP/USD)	1.5700	

Swap

a. USD cash flow stream

Year	Amount	Present Value
2	($9,105,750)	($8,550,000)
3	($9,105,750)	($8,028,169)
3	($159,750,000)	($140,845,070)
	Total	($157,423,239)

b. GBP cash flow stream

Year	Amount	Present Value
2	7,500,000	6,944,444
3	7,500,000	6,430,041
3	100,000,000	85,733,882
	Total GBP	99,108,368
	Converted to USD	$155,600,137
	Value of swap (USD)	**($1,823,102)**

assumed to be 1.5482, the £7,500,000 could be sold forward for $11,611,458. At the one-year settlement date, the closing transaction would call for £7,500,000 to be paid and $9,105,750 to be received. The difference in dollars between the swap payment and the hypothetical closing transaction, an amount equal to $2,505,708, has a present value of $2,352,778, which is the value of the first currency exchange. Continuing the procedure through the two remaining currency exchanges, the net value of the swap would be ($1,832,102), which matches the value obtained from the present-value method.

E X H I B I T   4–7

Forward-Contract Method of Valuation of a Fixed-for-Fixed
Currency Swap
Beginning of Year 2

Parameters	
Domestic interest rate (USD)	6.50%
Foreign interest rate (GBP)	8.00%
Spot exchange rate (USD/GBP)	1.5700
Forward outright (one year)	1.5482
Forward outright (two years)	1.5267

Swap

a. Forward Contract #1

   (Deliver $9,105,750 and receive 7,500,000 GBP after one year.

Closing Transaction:	
Sell 7,500,000 GBP forward	$11,611,458
Receive $9,105,750	($9,105,750)
Net	$2,505,708
Present value of contract #1	<u>$2,352,778</u>

b. Forward Contract #2

   (Deliver $9,105,750 and receive 7,500,000 GBP after two years.)

Closing Transaction:	
Sell 7,500,000 GBP forward	$11,450,188
Receive $9,105,750	($9,105,750)
Net	$2,344,438
Present value of contract #2	<u>$2,066,996</u>

c. Forward Contract #3

   (Deliver $159,750,000 and receive 100,000,000 GBP in two years.)

Closing Transaction:	
Sell 100,000,000 GBP forward	$152,669,174
Receive $159,750,000	($159,750,000)
Net	($7,080,826)
Present value of contract #3	<u>($6,242,876)</u>
Value of swap (USD)	**($1,823,102)**

Swap Comparative Statics

The present-value method of swap valuation provides an easy framework for analyzing comparative statics of a fixed-for-fixed currency swap. The sign of the change in the value of a swap depends on which currency is being paid and which one is received.

In general terms, the value of a swap, V_t^s at time t equals

$$V_t^s = \sum_{i=1}^{N} \frac{C_i^d}{\left(1+r_d\right)^i} + S_t \sum_{i=1}^{N} \frac{C_i^f}{\left(1+r_f\right)^i}$$

Here the summation operator runs from $i = 1$, for the next exchange of currencies, to N, for the last exchange; and C_d is cash flow in domestic currency, and C_f is cash flow in foreign currency. Cash flow to be received is positive in sign; cash flow to be paid is negative in sign. This formulation leads directly to the sign of the change in the value of a swap were the spot exchange rate or either of the interest rates to change. Swaps can be identified according to the direction of the intermediate payments. The swap in Exhibit 4–5 "pays domestic/receives foreign" currency. The following table summarizes the comparative statics with respect to exchange rates and interest rates. Here again, one must pay attention to the foreign exchange quotation convention.

	Pay Domestic Receive Foreign	Receive Domestic Pay Foreign
Spot rises American convention	Swap rises	Swap falls
Spot rises European convention	Swap falls	Swap rises
Domestic Interest rises	Swap rises	Swap falls
Foreign Interest rises	Swap falls	Swap rises

Swap Duration Analysis

The impact of changes in interest rates on swaps can be analyzed using the concept of duration. Duration is a concept that

Macaulay (1938) invented to link bond price changes to yield changes. It leads to some quick generalizations about the relative sensitivities of swaps to interest rate changes. Since longer-term swaps generally have longer durations than short-term swaps, they are more sensitive to interest rates. Also, the larger the intermediate payment, the smaller the duration of the swap and the less sensitivity to interest rates.

The first term in the swap valuation formula above represents the present value of the entire stream of domestic currency cash flow. The duration is equal to

$$D_d = \frac{\displaystyle\sum_{i=1}^{N} i \frac{C_i^d}{\left(1+r_d\right)^i}}{\displaystyle\sum_{i=1}^{N} \frac{C_i^d}{\left(1+r_d\right)^i}}$$

The duration of the foreign currency leg of the swap is

$$D_f = \frac{\displaystyle\sum_{i=1}^{N} i \frac{C_i^f}{\left(1+r_f\right)^i}}{\displaystyle\sum_{i=1}^{N} \frac{C_i^f}{\left(1+r_f\right)^i}}$$

Modified duration is a related concept. It is equal to duration divided by one plus the interest rate. Exhibit 4–8 calculates duration and modified duration for the dollar and sterling legs of the swap. These measures directly link the change in market value of the swap to a change in interest rates. For example, when the domestic interest rate changes, the value of the swap will change by approximately

$$\frac{-D_d}{\left(1+r_d\right)} \times \begin{bmatrix} \text{Change} \\ \text{in} \\ r_d \end{bmatrix} \times \begin{bmatrix} \text{Present value} \\ \text{domestic currency} \\ \text{cash flows} \end{bmatrix}$$

For example, starting with a domestic interest rate equal to 6.5 percent, the swap is worth a negative $1,823,102. Exhibit 4–8

EXHIBIT 4–8

Duration Analysis of a Fixed-for-Fixed Currency Swap (Beginning of Year 2)

Parameters

Domestic interest rate (USD)	6.50%
Foreign interest rate (GBP)	8.00%
Spot exchange rate (USD/GBP)	1.5700

Duration of Swap

a. Duration of USD cash flow stream

Year	t	Amount	Present Value	$t*$ PV
2	1	($9,105,750)	($8,550,000)	(8,550,000)
3	2	($9,105,750)	($8,028,169)	(16,056,338)
3	2	($159,750,000)	($140,845,070)	(281,690,141)
		Total	($157,423,239)	($306,296,479)
			Duration	1.9457
			Modified duration	**1.8269**

b. Duration of GBP cash flow stream

Year	t	Amount	Present Value	$t*$ PV
2	1	7,500,000	6,944,444	6,944,444
3	2	7,500,000	6,430,041	12,860,082
3	2	100,000,000	85,733,882	171,467,764
		Total GBP	99,108,368	191,272,291
			Duration	1.9299
			Modified duration	**1.7870**

calculates D_d as 1.9457. If the domestic rate rose to 7.5 percent, the change in the value of the swap would be

$$\frac{1.9457}{1.065} \times (.01) \times \$157,423,239 = \$2,876,041$$

using the duration method. The actual change in value is $2,836,387.

A similar formula exists for changes in the foreign interest rate.

$$\frac{-D_f}{(1+r_f)} \times \left[\begin{array}{c} \text{Change} \\ \text{in} \\ r_f \end{array}\right] \times \left[\begin{array}{c} \text{Present value} \\ \text{domestic currency} \\ \text{cash flows} \end{array}\right]$$

Finally, changes in the spot exchange rate operate through the present value of the foreign cash flows

$$\left[\begin{array}{c} \text{Change in} \\ \text{spot exchange rate} \end{array}\right] \times \left[\begin{array}{c} \text{Present value} \\ \text{foreign currency} \\ \text{cash flows} \end{array}\right]$$

In this example, the present value of the foreign currency (pounds) cash flow equals £99,108,368, and each one-cent change in exchange rate causes a change of £991,085, or $1,556,001, in the value of the swap.

Swaps Based on Floating Interest Rates

Currency swaps based on floating interest rates use the conventions of the Eurodollar and London money market. In these markets, interest rates are quoted for fixed-interval time periods, such as one month, three months, and six months. The most important interest rate is LIBOR (London Inter-Bank Offer Rate). LIBOR is an over-the-counter indication of what it would cost a bank of double-A or better credit standing to borrow funds from the bank that supplies the quote. Actually, two quotes are usually given, LIBOR and LIBID, with the latter being the bid side for deposits. Many commercial loans and note instruments in the Eurodollar market are floaters based on LIBOR, plus some margin, that is reset on periodic reference dates. A popular arrangement is to reset and pay interest every six months, although it is possible to get a LIBOR rate for any time period. Take the example of a floating rate note (FRN) paying ¼ of 1 percent over six-month LIBOR. On the reference date, if LIBOR were fixed at 7 percent, the note would pay a coupon equal to

$$\left(\frac{180}{360}\right) \times \left(7.00\% + .25\%\right) = 3.625\%$$

at the next reference date, whereupon a new LIBOR rate would be fixed for the note.

In a popular fixed-for-floating currency swap, the investor agrees to make fixed-amount semiannual payments in the domestic currency. In return, the investor receives payments in the foreign currency, based on a floating interest rate applied to the principal with semiannual reset. This swap is popular with issuers of floating-rate obligations in foreign currencies. The swap immunizes them from currency fluctuations and movements in foreign interest rates. The exchange rate between the two currencies is fixed when the swap is negotiated. For example, based on an exchange rate of 1.6000 for sterling, a swap might call for the investor to pay a fixed 5.50 percent semiannual coupon based on a note amount of $1,600,000 and receive payments in pounds based on six-month sterling LIBOR, applied to a principal amount of £1,000,000. The sterling LIBOR rate would be reset in advance before each six-month period. For example, if sterling LIBOR were fixed at 7.50 percent, the investor would receive

$$\left(\frac{180}{360}\right) \times 7.50\% \times £1 \text{ million} = £37,500$$

and pay

$$\left(\frac{180}{360}\right) \times 5.50\% \times \$1.6 \text{ million} = \$44,000$$

after six months.

Multicurrency Swap Agreements

Currency swaps can be multicurrency agreements that call for several currencies to be paid and received. Exhibit 4–9 is an example of a fixed-for-fixed multicurrency swap that begins

E X H I B I T   4-9

Structure of a Fixed-for-Fixed Multicurrency Swap

Initial Parameters

	Spot	Interest Rate
USD/JPY	84.90	1.10%
GBP/USD	1.5975	7.50%
USD/DEM	1.3950	4.50%
USD		5.70%

A. Initial Exchange at Beginning of Swap

Borrower			Counterparty		
Pay	(200,000,000)	JPY	Pay	($5,386,904)	USD
Pay	(1,000,000)	GBP	Receive	200,000,000	JPY
Pay	(2,000,000)	DEM	Receive	1,000,000	GBP
Receive	$5,386,904	USD	Receive	2,000,000	DEM

B. Annual Intermediate Payments

Borrower			Counterparty		
Pay	($307,054)	USD	Receive	$307,054	USD
Receive	2,200,000	JPY	Pay	($2,200,000)	JPY
Receive	75,000	GBP	Pay	($75,000)	GBP
Receive	90,000	DEM	Pay	($90,000)	DEM

C. Reexchange at Conclusion of Swap

Borrower			Counterparty		
Pay	($5,386,904)	USD	Pay	(200,000,000)	JPY
Receive	200,000,000	JPY	Pay	(1,000,000)	GBP
Receive	1,000,000	GBP	Pay	(2,000,000)	DEM
Receive	2,000,000	DEM	Receive	$5,386,904	USD

with the exchange of U.S. dollars for Japanese yen, German marks, and British pounds. Such a multicurrency swap can be valued using either the present value (see Exhibit 4–10) or forward-contract methods. Multicurrency swaps can also feature floating interest rates.

EXHIBIT 4-10

Present Value of Fixed-for-Fixed Multicurrency Swap
Beginning of Year 2; Annual Compounding

Parameters

	Spot	Interest		Spot	Interest
JPY	87.00	2.00%	DEM	1.4100	6.00%
GBP	1.5700	6.50%	USD	NA	6.00%

Swap

a. USD cash flow

Year	Amount	PV	PV(USD)	PV(USD)
2	($307,054)	($289,674)		
3	($307,054)	($273,277)		
3	($5,386,904)	($4,794,325)		
		Total	($5,357,276)	($5,357,276)

b. JPY cash flow

Year	Amount	PV	PV(JPY)	PV(USD)
2	2,200,000	2,156,863		
3	2,200,000	2,114,571		
3	200,000,000	192,233,756		
		Total	196,505,190	$2,258,680

c. GBP cash flow

Year	Amount	PV	PV(GBP)	PV(USD)
2	75,000	70,423		
3	75,000	66,124		
3	1,000,000	881,659		
		Total	1,018,206	$1,598,584

d. DEM cash flow

Year	Amount	PV	PV(DEM)	PV(USD)
2	90,000	84,906		
3	90,000	80,100		
3	2,000,000	1,779,993		
		Total	1,944,998	$1,379,431
			Value of swap	**($120,580)**

NOTES

1. Grabbe (1986) credits John Maynard Keynes with the discovery of the interest parity theorem. According to Grabbe, Keynes first published his discovery in the *Manchester Guardian Reconstruction* supplement on April 20, 1922. He later expanded it into a key part of his *Tract on Monetary Reform* (1923).

2. The valuation framework presented in this chapter depends on exchange rates, interest rates, and time. No consideration is given to credit issues, meaning that counterparty performance is assumed to be perfect. Suffice it to say that no such assumption is ever made in the real world of finance. As a matter of fact, credit errors have been the root of many financial catastrophes in foreign exchange dealing. Credit issues are ignored here not because they are unimportant but because they are outside the scope of this book.

3. The practice of using continuously compounded interest rates is for mathematical convenience. The continuously compounded analogue, R, of an annually compounded interest rate r is

$$R = \ln(1 + r)$$

and

$$e^{-Rt} = \frac{1}{(1+r)^t}$$

All interest rates in this book are continuously compounded rates unless otherwise noted.

4. See Bilson (1981); Fama (1984); Levitch (1985); Hodrick and Srivastava (1984); Hodrick (1987); Frankel and Froot (1987); Froot and Frankel (1989); Froot and Thaler (1990); and Cavaglia, Verschoor, and Wolf (1994).

5. Equations for the valuation of forward contracts and for their deltas for the other formats that are displayed in Exhibit 4–2 follow. In each case, the opening forward contract buys one unit of foreign exchange. Valuation is in the currency of settlement.

American Convention with Settlement in Foreign Currency

$$V_t = -\frac{1}{S_t} F_0 e^{-R_d(T-t)} + e^{-R_f(T-t)}$$

$$\frac{\partial V_t}{\partial S_t} = \frac{1}{S_t^2} F_0 e^{-R_d(T-t)}$$

European Convention with Settlement in Domestic Currency

$$V_t' = \frac{1}{S_t'} e^{-R_f(T-t)} - \frac{1}{F_0'} e^{-R_d(T-t)}$$

$$\frac{\partial V_t'}{\partial S_t'} = \frac{1}{S_t'^2} e^{-R_f(T-t)}$$

European Convention with Settlement in Foreign Currency

$$V_t' = e^{-R_f(T-t)} - \frac{1}{F_0'} S_t' e^{-R_d(T-t)}$$

$$\frac{\partial V_t'}{\partial S_t'} = -\frac{1}{F_0} e^{-R_f(T-t)}$$

6. This model makes the assumption that the term structures of interest rates are flat, at least in the relevant range of maturities corresponding to the life of the instrument. Where this is not the case, as when yields are steeply rising or inverted with respect to maturity, it is necessary to calculate the present value of each swap payment with a different discount rate (e.g., the yield on a zero coupon bond with matching maturity).

CHAPTER 5

Hedging Foreign Exchange Risk

Investment portfolio managers and corporate treasurers employ a variety of currency hedging techniques to immunize foreign exchange risk. The most simple form of hedging is bilateral hedging that works on a single currency exposure. Multicurrency hedging is a more complicated business. Some of the advanced tools presented in this chapter include basket hedging, hybrid basket hedging, and proxy hedging.

WHAT IS MEANT BY FOREIGN EXCHANGE RATE RISK?

The determination of what constitutes a foreign exchange risk for an investor or corporate treasurer is not always an easy process. For a portfolio manager, currency risk is usually taken to mean the potential foreign exchange translation risk on the stocks, bonds, and other assets that are denominated in a foreign currency. This type of currency risk is independent of the nature of the underlying asset. One million dollars invested in a Japanese government bond has the same currency risk as one million dollars invested in Japanese stocks or real estate. But there can be more subtle forms of risk associated with exchange rates that an investor might want to consider hedging on a case-by-case basis.

111

For example, a rise in the value of the yen might put Toyota at risk as an exporter. But it might not affect at all a Japanese fishing company that sells its catch locally. These less direct currency-related risks are normally not incorporated in the investor's foreign exchange risk management process but rather are included in the security selection process, along with other local market factors.

Corporate treasurers routinely hedge firm commitment foreign currency receivables and payables falling due over one or more quarters in the future, as is indicated in the survey data from Greenwich Associates that was presented in Chapter 1. Some treasurers also hedge anticipated cash flows even though they are not guaranteed ever to materialize. The Greenwich survey also revealed that treasurers hedge balance sheet items to immunize foreign currency assets and liabilities. Although cash flow and balance sheet items are the subject of most corporate hedging, some sophisticated treasurers also hedge foreign exchange–related economic risk. Adler and Dumas (1984) provide a textbook-perfect example of foreign exchange–related economic risk:

> Regional electric utilities are a somewhat extreme case in point. With no foreign currency accounts on their books, they have no accounting exposure to exchange risk. From an economic perspective, however, the story is different. If their customer base is dominated by either importing or exporting firms whose activities and demand for electricity are affected by exchange rate changes, the electric utilities' operations and stock prices themselves will also in principle be exposed to exchange risk. (p. 41)

German automobile manufacturers who export to the United States are a case in point. They benefited from the stronger yen in the early 1990s that handicapped their Japanese competition. In effect, the Germans had an economic interest that was equivalent to a short dollar/yen position, and indeed some companies are believed to have hedged by buying dollars against yen.

Once the portfolio manager or corporate treasurer has isolated the specific foreign exchange risk concern, attention must next turn to the selection of the appropriate type of hedging program.

MECHANICS OF HEDGING A SINGLE FOREIGN CURRENCY EXPOSURE

The discussion will start with an illustration of the basic mechanics of a simple currency hedging program. Consider a U.S. dollar–based investor who owns 100 million pesetas face value worth of a hypothetical Spanish government treasury bill with one year to maturity. The treasury bill is assumed to be a pure discount instrument, meaning that it has no coupon. The investor is worried that the peseta will decline against the dollar and decides to hedge by selling forward for three-month value. Assume that the bill is priced at 7.85 discount, the peseta is trading at 120.00 (USD/ESP), the three-month U.S. dollar interest rate is 5.70 percent, and the three-month peseta interest rate is 8.65 percent. The interest parity forward rate is 120.89

$$120.00 \times e^{(.0865-.057)/4} = 120.89$$

All rates are expressed in their equivalent continuous forms. There are five key decision elements with every hedging program: deciding how much to hedge, funding the hedge, making the term decision, rescaling the hedge, and rolling the hedge.

Deciding How Much to Hedge

The first question is how much foreign currency should be sold on a forward basis to hedge the investment in the Spanish treasury bill? There are two answers, one called a present-value hedge and the other a future-value hedge. In the first, the present value of the investment is hedged. In the other, the future value of the bill out to the hedge horizon is hedged. Exhibit 5–1 shows examples of both types of hedges. The hedge horizon is arbitrarily set equal to three months.

In the case of the present-value hedge, the investor sells the current peseta value of the bills to the forward value date. Quoted at 7.85 discount makes the value of 100 million ESP face equal to 92,150,000

$$100\text{mm ESP} \times \left(\frac{100.00 - 7.85}{100.00} \right) = 92,150,000 \text{ ESP}$$

EXHIBIT 5-1

Basic Hedging with Forward Currency Contracts

Portfolio

Spanish Treasury Bill—Zero Coupon		
Maturity	1 Year	
Quantity	100,000,000	ESP
Price (discount basis)	7.85	
Continuously compounded return	8.1753%	
Market value—Day 0	92,150,000	ESP
Market Value—Day 90	94,052,751	ESP

Exchange Rates and Interest Rates

	Day 0	Case 1	Case 2
		Day 90	Day 90
Spot USD/ESP	120.00	110.00	130.00
USD 3- & 6-month interest	5.70%	5.70%	5.70%
ESP 3- & 6-month interest	8.65%	8.65%	8.65%
Forward 3 months	120.89		

Initial Positions: Day 0

Present-Value Hedge

Sell forward	92,150,000	ESP		
Buy forward	$762,274	USD		

Future-Value Hedge

Sell forward	94,052,751	ESP
Buy forward	$778,014	USD

Bond Portfolio

Value in ESP	92,150,000	
Value in USD	$767,917	

(continued)

Basic Hedging with Forward Currency Contracts (concluded)

Day 90—Case 1: Spot 110

Bond Portfolio

Value in ESP	94,052,751	
Value in USD	$855,025	
Gain in USD	$87,108	

Present-Value Hedge

Buy to close	92,150,000	ESP
Sell to close	$837,727	USD
Gain/loss on hedge	($75,453)	USD
Total return	6.07%	

Future-Value Hedge

Buy to close	94,052,751	ESP
Sell to close	$855,025	USD
Gain/loss on hedge	($77,011)	USD
Total return	5.26%	

Day 90—Case 2: Spot 130

Bond Portfolio

Value in ESP	94,052,751	
Value in USD	$723,483	
Gain in USD	($44,434)	

Present-Value Hedge

Buy to close	92,150,000	ESP
Sell to close	$708,846	USD
Gain/loss on hedge	$53,428	USD
Total return	4.68%	

Future-Value Hedge

Buy to close	94,052,751	ESP
Sell to close	$723,483	USD
Gain/loss on hedge	$54,531	USD
Total return	5.26%	

To construct a present-value hedge, the investor must sell for forward value 92,150,000 pesetas against U.S. dollars. Assuming that the interest parity forward is the market rate, the forward contract would promise to deliver 92,150,000 ESP against $762,274 USD for value in three months.

To construct a future-value hedge, the future value of the bond must be projected to the three-month value date. An assumption must be made as to what will be the rate of return on the bill in the course of the three-month hedge period. Assume that the bill will exactly return its continuously compounded return to maturity over the three-month period. That return is

$$\ln\left[\frac{100,000,000}{92,150,000}\right] = 8.1753\%$$

The future value in one quarter of a year's time is

$$92,150,000 \text{ ESP } e^{.081753/4} = 94,052,763 \text{ ESP}$$

The future-value hedge would sell 94,052,751 ESP against 778,014 USD for value in three months.

In Exhibit 5–1, the gain or loss on both a present-value and a future-value hedge that are closed out on day 90 is compared to the net gain or loss on the bond. Two cases are presented. In the first case, the exchange rate (USD/ESP) has fallen to 110 on day 90. In the other, the exchange rate has risen to 130. In the first case, the gain in dollar terms on the bill is equal to $87,108. The present-value hedge is closed out at a loss of $75,453. The net of the two components is a positive annualized return of 6.07 percent. In the second case, the net return, including the gain on the present-value hedge, is 4.68 percent. This simple experiment demonstrates that a present-value hedge is not neutral with respect to movements in the underlying exchange rate. The reason is that the present-value hedge does not hedge the portion of the total return that represents the promised rate of return on the Treasury bill.

Future-value hedges are neutral with respect to changes in the underlying exchange rate. Exhibit 5–1 shows that the total return is 5.26 percent regardless of whether the exchange rate rises or falls. A simple algebraic paradigm shows why this is true. The total return is equal to the sum of the currency gain or loss on the investment plus the gain or loss on the hedge. Consider a one-year horizon future-value hedge. Denote the present value of a default-free zero coupon bond as P, in foreign currency terms. The future value of the bond, assuming it appreciates by the riskless interest rate R_f will be equal to

$$Pe^{R_f}$$

Denote the spot exchange rates American convention as S_0 and S_1 for the beginning and end of the year, respectively, and the forward rate at the beginning of the year as F_0. The gain or loss on the bond in dollars is equal to

$$S_1 Pe^{R_f} - S_0 P$$

The future value hedge sells forward the future value of the bond against dollars in the amount of

$$Pe^{R_f}$$

in exchange for dollars in the amount

$$F_0 Pe^{R_f}$$

On value day, the gain or loss on the future value hedge will equal

$$F_0 Pe^{R_f} - S_1 Pe^{R_f}$$

which is equal to

$$S_0 Pe^{R_d} - S_1 Pe^{R_f}$$

using the interest parity relationship

$$F_0 = S_0 e^{(R_d - R_f)}$$

The total return is equal to the sum of the gain or loss on the bond plus the gain or loss on the hedge. This is equal to

$$S_0 P\left(e^{R_d} - 1\right)$$

The term

$$e^{R_d} - 1$$

is equal to the interest parity return. Since the level of S_1 is not involved in the expression, the hedged return is neutral with respect to movements in the spot exchange rate.

The obvious obstacle in practice to the construction of a future value hedge is that the future return on investments is not known in advance. A commonsense solution is to use the prevailing level of the foreign interest rate as a proxy for the future return on bond portfolios. In the case of equities, practitioners sometimes use the foreign interest rate plus an estimated equity risk premium.

Funding the Hedge

All hedging programs have cash flow implications. In an invasive program, hedge-related cash is removed from or added to the underlying portfolio immediately. This may require the portfolio manager to sell or buy stocks or bonds. It also complicates the process of performance measurement. Any serious attempt at performance measurement must use the time-weighted rate of return method. Hedge-related cash flows should be regarded as exogenous, the same way a mutual fund treats funds from share purchases and redemptions.

A noninvasive hedging program attempts to isolate hedge-related cash flow to keep from disrupting the underlying investment process. It requires that a pool of liquid assets be set aside to pay and receive funds. If the reserve pool is sufficiently large relative to the needs of the hedging program, the underlying asset portfolio need never be disturbed.

Making the Term Decision

All forms of currency hedging programs use derivative securities, which raises the question of how to decide on the appropriate term of the hedging instruments. If hedging is done with currency futures, liquidity concerns suggest that the front month contract be the investment of choice because it normally is the most actively traded on the calendar.

There is no such clear answer with currency forwards. Forward contracts can be created for any spot value date. The investor can choose between hedging with one single long-term forward or with a series of rolling short-term forwards. If there are no changes in interest rates, a long-term forward hedge will be the same as a series of rolling short-term forward hedges. This point is illustrated in Exhibit 5–2, where a six-month hedge is compared to two consecutive three-month hedges.

However, if the spread between the interest rates changes in the course of the program, material differences can result from the choice between long-term and short-term programs, which makes the choice of the term an active management decision. This decision should be based on the investor's outlook for interest rate spreads.

The effects of the interest rate spread narrowing or widening for the case of a premium currency are shown in Exhibits 5–3 and 5–4. When the spread narrows, the series of short hedges is inferior to the long hedge; when the spread widens, the series of short hedges is superior. The opposite is true for hedging a discount currency. The following table summarizes these rules. (ST means the series of short-term hedges and LT means the long-term hedge.)

	Premium Currency	Discount Currency
Spread narrows	ST < LT	ST > LT
Spread widens	ST > LT	ST < LT

Rescaling the Hedge

The hedging program must be rescaled whenever there has been a significant change in the market value of the underlying secu-

EXHIBIT 5-2

Hedging with Rolling Forwards—Six-Month Horizon, Interest Rate Spread Unchanged

Portfolio

Spanish Treasury Bill—Zero Coupon		
Maturity	1 Year	
Quantity	100,000,000	ESP
Price (discount basis)	7.85	
Continuously compounded return	8.1753%	
Market value—Day 0	92,150,000	ESP
Market value—Day 180	95,994,792	ESP

Exchange Rates and Interest Rates

	Day 0	Day 90	Day 180
Spot USD/ESP	120.00	130.00	140.00
USD 3- & 6-month interest	5.70%	5.70%	
ESP 3- & 6-month interest	8.65%	8.65%	
Forward 3 months	120.89	130.96	
Forward 6 months	121.78		

Initial Positions: Day 0

Bond Portfolio			3-Mo. Future-Value Hedge			6-Mo. Future-Value Hedge		
Value in ESP	92,150,000		Sell forward	94,052,751	ESP	Sell forward	95,994,792	ESP
Value in USD	$767,917		Buy forward	$778,014	USD	Buy forward	$788,244	USD

Hedging with Rolling Forwards—Six-Month Horizon, Interest Rate Spread Unchanged (concluded)

Day 90—Spot Risen to 130

Bond Portfolio		3-Mo. Future-Value Hedge			6-Mo. Future-Value Hedge	
Value in ESP	94,052,751	*Close Out*			No transactions until	
Value in USD	$723,483	Buy to close	94,052,751	ESP	Day 180	
Gain in USD	NA	Sell to close	$723,483	USD		
		Gain on hedge	$54,531	USD		
		New Position				
		Sell forward	95,994,792	ESP		
		Buy forward	$732,996	USD		

Closing Out Day 180—USD/ESP Spot 140

Bond Portfolio		3-Mo. Future-Value Hedge			6-Mo. Future-Value Hedge	
Value in ESP	95,994,792	Buy to close	95,994,792	ESP	Buy to close	95,994,792	ESP
Value in USD	$685,677	Sell to close	$685,677	USD	Sell to close	$685,677	USD
Gain in USD	($82,240)	Gain on hedge	$47,319	USD	Net hedge gain	$102,567	USD
		Previous gain	$55,314	USD	Total return	5.29%	
		Total gain hedging	$102,632	USD			
		Total return	5.31%				

EXHIBIT 5-3

Hedging with Rolling Forwards—Six-Month Horizon, Narrowing Spread

Portfolio

Spanish Treasury Bill—Zero Coupon		
Maturity	1 Year	
Quantity	100,000,000	ESP
Price (discount basis)	7.85	
Continuously compounded return	8.1753%	
Market value—Day 0	92,150,000	ESP
Market value—Day 180	95,994,792	ESP

Exchange Rates and Interest Rates

	Day 0	Day 90	Day 180
Spot USD/ESP	120.00	130.00	140.00
USD 3- & 6-month interest	5.70%	6.70%	
ESP 3- & 6-month interest	8.65%	8.65%	
Forward 3 months	120.89	130.64	
Forward 6 months	121.78		

Initial Positions: Day 0

Bond Portfolio			3-Mo. Future-Value Hedge			6-Mo. Future-Value Hedge		
Value in ESP	92,150,000		Sell forward	94,052,751	ESP	Sell forward	95,994,792	ESP
Value in USD	$767,917		Buy forward	$778,014	USD	Buy forward	$788,244	USD

(continued)

Hedging with Rolling Forwards—Six-Month Horizon, Narrowing Spread (concluded)

Day 90—Spot Risen to 130

Bond Portfolio		3-Mo. Future-Value Hedge			6-Mo. Future-Value Hedge		
		Close Out			No Transactions Until		
Value in ESP	94,052,751	Buy to close	94,052,751	ESP	Day 180		
Value in USD	$723,483 NA	Sell to close	$723,483	USD			
Gain in USD		Gain on hedge	$54,531	USD			
		New Position					
		Sell forward	95,994,792	ESP			
		Buy forward	$734,830	USD			

Closing Out Day 180 — USD/ESP Spot 140

Bond Portfolio		3-Mo. Future-Value Hedge			6-Mo. Future-Value Hedge		
Value in ESP	95,994,792	Buy to close	95,994,792	ESP	Buy to close	95,994,792	ESP
Value in USD	$685,677	Sell to close	$685,677	USD	Sell to close	$685,677	USD
Gain in USD	($82,240)	Gain on hedge	$49,153	USD	Net hedge gain	$102,567	USD
		Previous gain	$55,314	USD	Total return	5.29%	
		Total gain hedging	$104,467	USD			
		Total return	5.79%				

123

EXHIBIT 5-4

Hedging with Rolling Forwards—Six-Month Horizon, Widening Spread

Portfolio

Spanish Treasury Bill—Zero Coupon		
Maturity	1 Year	
Quantity	100,000,000	ESP
Price (discount basis)	7.85	
Bond-equivalent yield	8.1753%	
Market value—Day 0	92,150,000	ESP
Market value—Day 180	95,994,792	ESP

Exchange Rates and Interest Rates

	Day 0	Day 90	Day 180
Spot USD/ESP	120.00	130.00	140.00
USD 3- & 6-month interest	5.70%	4.70%	
ESP 3- & 6-month Interest	8.65%	8.65%	
Forward 3 months	120.89	131.29	
Forward 6 months	121.78		

Initial Positions: Day 0

Bond Portfolio		
Value in ESP	92,150,000	
Value in USD	$767,917	

3-Mo. Future-Value Hedge		
Sell forward	94,052,751	ESP
Buy forward	$778,014	USD

6-Mo. Future-Value Hedge		
Sell forward	95,994,792	ESP
Buy forward	$788,244	USD

(continued)

Hedging with Rolling Forwards—Six-Month Horizon, Widening Spread (concluded)

Day 90—Spot Risen to 130

Bond Portfolio		3-Mo. Future-Value Hedge			6-Mo. Future-Value Hedge	
Value in ESP	94,052,751	*Close Out*			No transactions until	
Value in USD	$723,483	Buy to close	94,052,751	ESP	Day 180	
Gain in USD	NA	Sell to close	$723,483	USD		
		Gain on hedge	$54,531	USD		
		New Position				
		Sell forward	95,994,792	ESP		
		Buy forward	$731,165	USD		

Closing Out Day 180—USD/ESP Spot 140

Bond Portfolio		3-Mo. Future-Value Hedge			6-Mo. Future-Value Hedge	
Value in ESP	95,994,792	Buy to close	95,994,792	ESP	Buy to close	95,994,792	ESP
Value in USD	$685,677	Sell to close	$685,677	USD	Sell to close	$685,677	USD
Gain in USD	($82,240)	Gain on hedge	$45,488	USD	Net hedge gain	$102,567	USD
		Previous gain	$55,314	USD	Total return	5.29%	
		Total gain hedging	$100,802	USD			
		Total return	4.83%				

rities portfolio, as would be the case after a large move in market prices or of an injection or withdrawal of assets. Whatever the cause, the danger is that the face value of the currency hedge may be seriously out of line with the currency exposure of the underlying portfolio, which would create an unintended directional bet on exchange rates.

Rolling the Hedge

Forward and futures positions that approach value date or expiration must be rolled if a hedging program is to continue. The process of rolling a hedge consists of closing the contract that is about to expire and simultaneously establishing a new contract with more distant maturity. In the futures market, calendar rolls can be done as a single order. As expiration nears, a buy/sell market in the roll is quoted in a designated area of the pit. In the case of currency forwards, the roll is usually done two bank business days before value date. As described in Chapter 3, the maturing forward contract is closed with a spot transaction, whereupon a new forward contract is opened. Whatever the instrument, be it futures or forwards, the occasion of a calendar roll is the ideal time to consider rescaling the hedging program.

Discussion of the Relative Merits
of Currency Forwards and Currency Futures

Institutional portfolio managers and corporate treasurers tend to prefer currency forwards to futures for hedging purposes. Forward contracts are more flexible than futures in regard to currency, settlement date, and size. Forward contracts are easier to use because there is no initial or variation margin provided credit lines are in place. The forward market is substantially larger and deeper than futures markets; practically any currency can be traded in the forward market in large size, and trading is conducted virtually around the clock. In contrast, trading in futures is limited to the major currencies, although new currency contracts are listed for trading from time to time.

Futures have two advantages over forwards. One is that the hedger is not required to maintain bank credit lines as is needed for forwards trading; only the initial and variation margin requirements need be met. The other advantage is that futures contracts are guaranteed by the clearinghouse of the exchange, which is widely thought to be equivalent to a triple-A credit–rated counterparty.

HEDGING A MULTICURRENCY EXPOSURE

The previous sections considered how to hedge a single foreign currency exposure. The discussion now turns to the management of not one but multiple foreign currency exposures, a situation that is more relevant to international portfolio managers. Two popular benchmark indices are the FT-Actuaries World Indices for equities (Exhibit 5–5) and the Salomon World Bond Indices for fixed income (Exhibit 5–6). These indices are somewhat representative of the actual country exposures that real institutional portfolios have in place.

Measuring the Foreign Exchange Exposure of a Portfolio

The first step in managing multicurrency risk is to measure the portfolio's exposure to various currencies. Following the earlier discussion in this chapter, the critical factor for each security holding is its currency of denomination. The geographic origin of the security's issuer, where it does business, and where it has markets, property, and plant and equipment are entirely irrelevant. AXA, for example, is an international insurance and financial conglomerate that does business worldwide. AXA is probably affected by movements in all major and minor currencies. But the only currency that matters in the current context of the paradigm exchange rate risk management is the French franc because AXA shares are quoted in French francs.

Exhibits 5–7 and 5–8 illustrate a four-step procedure for measuring the currency exposure of a portfolio. Exhibit 5–9 shows the calculation of the currency exposure of an aggregate portfolio consisting of two subportfolios, each with its own manager. The first is an international equity index fund whose benchmark is the FT-Actuaries World non-USA Index. The second is an

EXHIBIT 5-5

FT-Actuaries World Indices
Country & Regional Market Capitalization Weights
As of December 30, 1994

	Composition		Percentage Weight within Region												
	No. of Secs.	Mkt Cap US$ Bil	Nordic	Europe	Europe ex. U.K.	Pacific Basin	Pacific ex. Japan	North America	Americas	Europe & Pacific	World ex. U.K.	World ex. Japan	World ex. U.S.	World
Australia	68	143.4				4.41	28.38			2.51	1.69	2.16	2.35	1.53
Austria	16	13.1		0.53	0.84					0.23	0.15	0.20	0.22	0.14
Belgium	35	64.8		2.64	4.17					1.13	0.76	0.98	1.06	0.69
Brazil	28	49.6							1.40		0.58	0.75	0.81	0.53
Canada	103	148.2						4.30	4.18		1.75	2.23	2.43	1.58
Denmark	33	34.2	21.48	1.39	2.20					0.60	0.40	0.51	0.56	0.36
Finland	24	28.4	17.87	1.16	1.83					0.50	0.34	0.43	0.47	0.30
France	102	330.5		13.44	21.28					5.79	3.90	4.98	5.43	3.52
Germany	58	339.4		13.81	21.85					5.94	4.00	5.11	5.57	3.62
Hong Kong	56	164.9				5.07	32.62			2.89	1.94	2.48	2.71	1.76
Ireland	14	14.8		0.60	0.95					0.26	0.17	0.22	0.24	0.16
Italy	59	133.2		5.42	8.57					2.33	1.57	2.01	2.19	1.42
Japan	468	2,747.3				84.46				48.10	32.39		45.11	29.27
Malaysia	97	100.7				3.10	19.93			1.76	1.19	1.52	1.65	1.07
Mexico	18	51.6							1.46		0.61	0.78	0.85	0.55
Netherlands	19	181.5		7.38	11.69					3.18	2.14	2.73	2.98	1.93
New Zealand	14	18.9				0.58	3.74			0.33	0.22	0.28	0.31	0.20

(continued)

FT-Actuaries World Indices (concluded)

| | Composition | | | | | | | | | | | | | |
| | | | | | | | Percentage Weight within Region | | | | | | | |
	No. of Secs.	Mkt Cap US$ Bil	Nordic	Europe	Europe ex. U.K.	Pacific Basin	Pacific ex. Japan	North America	Americas	Europe & Pacific	World ex. U.K.	World ex. Japan	World ex. U.S.	World
Norway	23	10.8	6.80	0.44	0.70					0.19	0.13	0.16	0.18	0.12
Singapore	44	56.8				1.75	11.24			0.99	0.67	0.86	0.93	0.61
South Africa	59	130.2									1.54	1.96	2.14	1.39
Spain	38	91.9		3.74	5.92					1.61	1.08	1.38	1.51	0.98
Sweden	36	85.6	53.85	3.48	5.51					1.50	1.01	1.29	1.41	0.91
Switzerland	47	225.1		9.16	14.49					3.94	2.65	3.39	3.70	2.40
Thailand	46	20.7				0.64	4.09			0.36	0.24	0.31	0.34	0.22
United Kingdom	204	905.1		36.82						15.85		13.63	14.86	9.64
United States	513	3,296.0						95.70	92.96		38.86	49.64		35.11
Nordic	116	159.0	100.00											
Europe	708	2,458.5		100.00										
Europe ex. U.K.	504	1,553.3			100.00									
Pacific Basin	793	3,252.7				100.00								
Pacific ex. Japan	325	505.4					100.00							
North America	616	3,444.3						100.00						
Americas	662	3,545.5							100.00					
Europe & Pacific	1501	5,711.2								100.00				
World ex. U.K.	2018	8,481.7									100.00			
World ex. Japan	1754	6,639.6										100.0		
World ex. U.S.	1709	6,090.8											100.00	
World	2222	9,386.9												100.0

Source: Goldman Sachs, FT-Actuaries World Indices™SM.

EXHIBIT 5-6

Salomon Brothers World Government Bond Indices
Country Weightings as of December 1, 1994

	World Govt. Bond Index	Non–U.S. Dollar World Govt. Bond Index	G-7 Index	European Composite Index	Global Composite Index
United States	35.86%		40.70%		35.52%
Japan	20.42%	31.84%	23.18%		20.23%
Germany	10.78%	16.81%	12.24%	26.46%	10.68%
France	6.21%	9.68%	7.05%	15.23%	6.15%
United Kingdom	5.43%	8.46%	6.16%	13.32%	5.38%
Canada	2.83%	4.42%	3.22%		2.81%
Italy	6.57%	10.25%	7.46%	16.13%	6.51%
Australia	0.90%	1.40%			0.89%
Belgium	2.51%	3.92%		6.16%	2.49%
Denmark	0.013%	2.17%		3.41%	1.38%
Netherlands	2.98%	4.64%		7.31%	2.95%
Spain	2.14%	3.33%		5.26%	2.12%
Sweden	1.29%	2.01%		3.16%	1.27%
Austria	0.69%	1.07%		1.68%	0.68%
Ireland				0.85%	0.34%
Switzerland				1.05%	0.42%
New Zealand					0.18%

EXHIBIT 5–7

Measuring the Currency Exposure of a Portfolio

Step 1	Sort the securities by their denomination. *Example: Siemens would be classified as a German mark currency risk.*
Step 2	Measure the market value of each security in the numeraire currency. *Example: The hypothetical portfolio contains 2,500 shares of Siemens. Siemens is quoted at 666 DEM, so the position is worth 1,665,000 DEM. With USD/DEM at 1.3900, the exposure is equivalent to $1,197,842.*
Step 3	Sum across the market values (each measured in the numeraire currency) of all of the securities in each currency to obtain the currency exposure. *Example: The hypothetical portfolio also contains 5,000 shares of AEG. The total USD market value of mark-denominated shares is $1,672,662.*
Step 4	The total market value of the portfolio is the sum of the currency exposure market values and the exposure to each currency is its proportion of the total market value. *Example: Completing steps 1–3 for the other countries results in a total market value of $5,612,836. The weight of the mark is 29.80%.*

actively managed equity portfolio. The third column, on the far right, shows the aggregate exposure to each of the currencies. Once the exposure to each exchange rate has been measured, attention focuses on selecting an appropriate hedging method.

Matched Hedging

Matched hedging is a simple concept. The idea is to use a separate bilateral hedge for each currency exposure. This is easy to implement for a limited number of currencies. Otherwise, if the number of currency exposures is large, a matched hedge may not be efficient because managing a large number of separate hedges is cumbersome, and opening and closing forward contracts on minor currencies can be expensive. Matched hedging is

Hypothetical International Portfolio
Currency Exposure Calculations

	Shares	Local Price	Local Market Value	Total Local MV	USD Total MV	Currency Exposure
Australia 0.7400						
ANZ Bank	50,000	5.02	251,000			
Placer Dome	50,000	31.50	1,575,000			
News Corp	50,000	6.68	334,000	2,160,000	$ 1,598,400	28.48%
Germany 1.3900						
AEG	5,000	132	660,000			
Siemens	2,500	666	1,665,000	2,325,000	$ 1,672,662	29.80%
Hong Kong 7.7325						
Cathay Pacific	100,000	11.65	1,165,000			
Hutchison Whampo	100,000	33.70	3,370,000	4,535,000	$ 586,486	10.45%
Japan 83.80						
JAL	50,000	585	29,250,000			
NEC	35,000	900	31,500,000			
Toyota	25,000	1740	43,500,000	104,250,000	$ 1,244,033	22.16%
U.K. 1.6100						
British Air	25,000	4.05	101,250			
Glaxo	30,000	7.21	216,300			
Racal Electronics	25,000	2.45	61,250	317,550	$ 511,256	9.11%
				Total portfolio	$ 5,612,836	100.00%

mentioned here to show how a sledgehammer can be used to open the currency hedging nut. It is meant to increase appreciation for basket and hybrid basket hedging, two techniques that are more economical and that will now be introduced.

Basket Hedging

Basket hedging is an important tool in currency risk management. The idea is to combine a handful of major currencies into a basket that can be used to hedge the entire currency exposure of an entire portfolio. The latter is referred to as the index. Basket hedging is an application of portfolio theory and quadratic programming.

The first step in basket hedge construction is the estimation of the standard deviations of currency rates of return and their correlations. A sample correlation matrix for the currency returns in the FT-Actuaries World non-USA index countries is displayed in Exhibit 5–10. Annualized standard deviations are displayed on the diagonal. This matrix was estimated using the BARRA World Markets Model™ on daily currency returns. The estimation procedure applies exponential weights favoring the most recent observations (the half-life is 69 days). More elaborate techniques for estimating correlations and standard deviations incorporate macroeconomic variables and even observed option implied volatility.

Next for consideration is the actual optimization methodology. The objective of optimization is to produce a set of weightings for the basket currencies that makes the basket track the index as closely as possible. Two techniques are discussed in the appendix to this chapter. Both approaches assume that the expected rates of return on all currencies are zero. The first method is called constrained optimization because the sum of the basket weightings is constrained to equal one. This method produces the error-minimizing basket currency, but it does not address the question of the appropriate size of the basket relative to the index. In fact, the constrained optimization method tends to produce a basket that is fractionally more or less volatile than the index. Therefore, it is necessary to adjust the size of the basket relative to the market value of the underlying portfolio by a

EXHIBIT 5-9

Multiple International Equity Managers
Determining the Currency Exposure of the Aggregate Portfolio

Country	Manager 1 FT-Actuaries ex-USA		Manager 2 Active International Equity		Total Portfolio International Equity	
Australia	$ 607,500	2.43%			$ 607,500	1.22%
Austria	$ 55,000	0.22%			$ 55,000	0.11%
Belgium	$ 275,000	1.10%			$ 275,000	0.55%
Canada	$ 627,500	2.51%			$ 627,500	1.26%
Denmark	$ 145,000	0.58%			$ 145,000	0.29%
Finland	$ 120,000	0.48%			$ 120,000	0.24%
France	$ 1,397,500	5.59%	$ 2,500,000	10.00%	$ 3,897,500	7.80%
Germany	$ 1,435,000	5.74%	$ 6,250,000	25.00%	$ 7,685,000	15.37%
Hong Kong	$ 697,500	2.79%	$ 1,250,000	5.00%	$ 1,947,500	3.90%
Ireland	$ 62,500	0.25%			$ 62,500	0.13%

(continued)

134

Multiple International Equity Managers (concluded)

Country	Manager 1 FT-Actuaries ex-USA		Manager 2 Active International Equity		Total Portfolio International Equity	
Italy	$ 562,500	2.25%			$ 562,500	1.13%
Japan	$ 11,620,000	46.48%	$ 6,250,000	25.00%	$ 17,870,000	35.74%
Malaysia	$ 425,000	1.70%	$ 500,000	2.00%	$ 925,000	1.85%
Mexico	$ 217,500	0.87%			$ 217,500	0.44%
Netherlands	$ 767,500	3.07%			$ 767,500	1.54%
New Zealand	$ 80,000	0.32%			$ 80,000	0.16%
Norway	$ 45,000	0.18%			$ 45,000	0.09%
Singapore	$ 240,000	0.96%	$ 1,250,000	5.00%	$ 1,490,000	2.98%
Spain	$ 387,500	1.55%			$ 387,500	0.78%
Sweden	$ 362,500	1.45%			$ 362,500	0.73%
Switzerland	$ 952,500	3.81%	$ 3,750,000	15.00%	$ 4,702,500	9.41%
Thailand	$ 87,500	0.35%	$ 750,000	3.00%	$ 837,500	1.68%
U.K.	$ 3,830,000	15.32%	$ 2,500,000	10.00%	$ 6,330,000	12.66%
Total	$ 25,000,000	100.00%	$ 25,000,000	100.00%	$ 50,000,000	100.00%

Correlations and Standard Deviations (Along Diagonal)
Estimation with BARRA World Markets Model (5.0a) Using Two Years of Daily Data, Exponentially Weighted (69-Day Half-Life)

	AUD	ATS	BEF	CAD	DKK	FIM	FRF	DEM	HKD	IEP	ITL	JPN
Australia	0.065	-0.087	-0.122	0.015	-0.122	-0.096	-0.102	-0.111	0.021	-0.018	-0.096	-0.169
Austria		0.090	0.918	-0.260	0.909	0.682	0.898	0.937	0.059	0.769	0.503	0.583
Belgium			0.085	-0.226	0.961	0.742	0.955	0.968	0.129	0.804	0.551	0.621
Canada				0.040	-0.212	-0.154	-0.223	-0.251	0.029	-0.137	-0.129	0.141
Denmark					0.081	0.774	0.972	0.969	0.133	0.829	0.615	0.610
Finland						0.087	0.749	0.738	0.100	0.664	0.598	0.471
France							0.082	0.965	0.122	0.839	0.626	0.623
Germany								0.087	0.106	0.829	0.540	0.626
Hong Kong									0.007	0.146	0.136	0.150
Ireland										0.072	0.543	0.507
Italy											0.092	0.411
Japan												0.082
Malaysia												
Mexico												
Netherlands												
Norway												
New Zealand												
Singapore												
Spain												
Sweden												
Switzerland												
Thailand												
U.K.												

(continued)

Correlations and Standard Deviations (Along Diagonal) (concluded)

	MYR	MXM	NLG	NOK	NZD	SGD	ESP	SEK	CHF	THB	GBP
Australia	0.023	-0.066	-0.116	-0.096	0.650	-0.038	-0.117	-0.090	-0.111	-0.152	-0.013
Austria	0.170	-0.161	0.930	0.903	0.081	0.322	0.758	0.568	0.893	0.121	0.742
Belgium	0.193	-0.060	0.971	0.949	0.037	0.358	0.835	0.631	0.910	0.138	0.749
Canada	-0.043	0.195	-0.244	-0.219	-0.049	-0.083	-0.144	-0.100	-0.224	0.055	-0.125
Denmark	0.189	-0.052	0.971	0.964	0.024	0.367	0.852	0.696	0.920	0.165	0.781
Finland	0.173	-0.020	0.741	0.770	0.032	0.292	0.725	0.779	0.699	0.134	0.622
France	0.193	-0.034	0.965	0.960	0.022	0.376	0.868	0.668	0.916	0.176	0.796
Germany	0.181	-0.093	0.991	0.960	0.051	0.357	0.825	0.627	0.946	0.168	0.770
Hong Kong	0.116	0.145	0.110	0.134	-0.021	0.193	0.188	0.175	0.073	0.073	0.178
Ireland	0.171	-0.032	0.822	0.847	0.102	0.366	0.754	0.586	0.790	0.143	0.882
Italy	0.176	0.025	0.555	0.639	-0.038	0.309	0.638	0.640	0.538	0.113	0.566
Japan	0.186	0.022	0.619	0.626	-0.045	0.384	0.554	0.409	0.581	0.169	0.496
Malaysia	0.029	0.006	0.188	0.195	0.048	0.391	0.202	0.168	0.175	0.135	0.149
Mexico		0.551	-0.072	-0.044	-0.159	0.021	-0.004	0.013	-0.135	0.116	0.010
Netherlands			0.086	0.961	0.046	0.361	0.829	0.634	0.941	0.170	0.765
Norway				0.080	0.065	0.377	0.842	0.684	0.918	0.146	0.799
New Zealand					0.052	-0.040	-0.017	0.007	0.057	-0.076	0.112
Singapore						0.032	0.405	0.264	0.344	0.455	0.347
Spain							0.081	0.653	0.776	0.197	0.702
Sweden								0.088	0.588	0.121	0.601
Switzerland									0.097	0.147	0.749
Thailand										0.048	0.155
U.K.											0.069

rescaling factor. The second optimization method is called the unconstrained method. It does not force the sum of the basket weightings to equal one. No rescaling adjustment is needed. The unconstrained method is actually a multiple regression of the index returns on the basket currency returns. Either of the two methods, constrained optimization with rescaling or the unconstrained approach, produces useable baskets. Experience shows it is hard to choose between them because there is often no significant difference in tracking error.

Exhibits 5–11 and 5–12 show basket hedges from a U.S. dollar–based investor's perspective for the FT-Actuaries World non-U.S.A. Index and for the Salomon Brothers World Government Bond Index ex-U.S.A. Each basket is composed of marks, pounds, and yen. These baskets were constructed using the BARRA World Markets Model™. The technique is the same one described as constrained optimization with rescaling in the appendix to this chapter.

The FT-Actuaries World non-U.S.A. Index basket is concentrated in USD/JPY as should be expected given the sizable weight that Japan has in the index. The projected tracking error is 1.044 percent, annualized. In the implementation of the basket hedge, yen, marks, and pounds are sold against the dollar forward for value in one year's time. Two of these currencies, marks and yen, happened to have been at premium to the USD on April 12, 1995, when this exhibit was prepared. The result is that the basket hedge has a net forward pickup equal to 2.68 percent, annualized.

The basket hedge for the Salomon World Government Bond Index ex-U.S.A. (Exhibit 5–12) has an estimated tracking error equal to 1.234 percent, annualized. Consideration can be given to adding a fourth basket currency, a candidate being the French franc. In basket 2, the four-currency basket projects a smaller tracking error but there is a sacrifice of yield pickup. Deciding on the correct number of currencies to include in the basket raises the difficult issue of whether it is proper to think of there being a risk–return trade-off between tracking error and yield pickup. This idea is fundamentally flawed because it is hard to imagine that tracking error is true economic risk in the Markowitz–Sharpe–Lintner sense.

EXHIBIT 5-11

Basket Hedge for FT-Actuaries World Index World Ex-USA, as of March 31, 1995
BARRA World Markets Model (5.0a). Database March 1995. Market Prices April 12, 1995

Index (As of Dec 30, 1994)

Country	Percentage
Australia	2.43
Austria	0.22
Belgium	1.10
Canada	2.51
Denmark	0.58
Finland	0.48
France	5.59
Germany	5.74
Hong Kong	2.79
Ireland	0.25
Italy	2.25
Japan	46.48
Malaysia	1.70
Mexico	0.87
Netherlands	3.07
New Zealand	0.32
Norway	0.18
Singapore	0.96
Spain	1.55
Sweden	1.45
Switzerland	3.81
Thailand	0.35
U.K.	15.31
Total	**99.99**

Basket

Currency	Raw Weight	Scaling	Adjusted Weight	Spot	Points	Outright	Give up Pickup
GBP/USD	31.17%	0.9926	30.94%	0.6289	0.0047	0.6336	–0.74%
USD/DEM	16.39%	0.9926	16.27%	1.4040	–0.0218	1.3822	1.58%
USD/JPY	52.44%	0.9926	52.05%	83.77	–4.03	79.74	5.05%
Total	**100.00%**		**99.26%**			**Weighted average**	**2.68%**

Estimated tracking error: 1.044%

EXHIBIT 5-12

Basket Hedges for Salomon World Government Bond Index Ex-U.S.A.
BARRA World Markets Model (5.0a). Database March 1995. Market Prices April 12, 1995

Index (As of Dec 30, 1994)

Country	Percentage
Australia	1.40
Austria	1.07
Belgium	3.92
Canada	4.42
Denmark	2.17
France	9.68
Germany	16.81
Italy	10.25
Japan	31.84
Netherlands	4.64
Spain	3.33
Sweden	2.01
U.K.	8.46
Total	**100.00**

Basket 1

Currency	Raw Weight	Scaling	Adjusted Weight	Spot	Points	Outright	Give up Pickup
GBP/USD	25.19%	0.9859	24.83%	0.6289	0.0047	0.6336	-0.74%
USD/DEM	37.51%	0.9859	36.98%	1.4040	-0.0218	1.3822	1.58%
USD/JPY	37.30%	0.9859	36.77%	83.77	-4.03	79.74	5.05%
Total	**100.00%**		**98.59%**			Weighted average	**2.29%**

Estimated tracking error: 1.234%

Basket 2

Currency	Raw Weight	Scaling	Adjusted Weight	Spot	Points	Outright	Give up Pickup
GBP/USD	19.06%	0.9914	18.90%	0.6289	0.0047	0.6336	-0.74%
USD/DEM	9.33%	0.9914	9.25%	1.4040	-0.0218	1.3822	1.58%
USD/JPY	35.98%	0.9914	35.67%	83.77	-4.03	79.74	5.05%
USD/FRF	35.63%	0.9914	35.32%	4.8900	0.0150	4.9050	-0.31%
Total	**100.00%**		**99.14%**			Weighted average	**1.72%**

Estimated tracking error: 0.990%

EXHIBIT 5-13

Hybrid Basket Hedge for Salomon World Government Bond Index Ex-U.S.A.

BARRA World Markets Model (5.0a). Database March 1995. Market Prices April 12, 1995
Hybrid consists of a Matched Hedge for USD/ITL Plus a Basket Hedge for Remainder of Index

Index (As of Dec 30, 1994)

Country	Percentage
Australia	1.40
Austria	1.07
Belgium	3.92
Canada	4.42
Denmark	2.17
France	9.68
Germany	16.81
Italy	10.25
Japan	31.84
Netherlands	4.64
Spain	3.33
Sweden	2.01
U.K.	8.46
Total	**100.00**

Basket

Currency	Raw Weight	Scaling	Adjusted Weight	Spot	Points	Outright	Give up Pickup
GBP/USD	20.78%	0.9958	20.69%	0.6289	0.0047	0.6336	−0.74%
USD/DEM	39.91%	0.9958	39.74%	1.4040	−0.0218	1.3822	1.58%
USD/JPY	39.31%	0.9958	39.15%	83.77	−4.03	79.74	5.05%
Total	**100.00%**		**99.58%**			**Weighted average**	**2.46%**

Estimated tracking error: 0.772%

Hybrid

Currency	Raw Weight	Scaling	Adjusted Weight	Spot	Points	Outright	Give up Pickup
BASKET	89.75%	1.0000	89.75%				2.46%
USD/ITL	10.25%	1.0000	10.25%	1724.00	78.50	1802.50	−4.36%
Total	**100.00%**		**100.00%**			**Weighted average**	**1.76%**

Estimated tracking error: 0.693%

Implementation of a basket hedge follows all of the same steps as a bilateral hedge. Consideration must be given to rolling and rescaling the hedge and to management of the ensuing cash flow. In addition, the basket composition must be refreshed over time as the index composition changes and as standard deviations and correlation coefficients change.

Hybrid Basket Hedging

A hybrid basket hedge consists of a matched hedge for one or more of the index currencies plus a separately optimized basket for the other currency exposures. Exhibit 5–13 shows a hybrid basket hedge for the Salomon World Government Bond Index ex-U.S.A. The hybrid is formed using a matched hedge for the Italian lira exposure and a basket hedge comprised of yen, marks, and pounds for the remainder of the index exposure. Note that the tracking error is lower for the hybrid basket hedge.

Why use a hybrid basket hedge? The answer depends on one's expectations concerning the stochastic behavior of a currency. In the case of Italy, 1994 and the beginning of 1995 were periods of heightened political and economic uncertainty. By taking the lira out of the index and hedging it separately, the portfolio manager is implicitly saying that the correlation between the lira and the index is unstable.

The Limitations of Basket Hedging

Several potential problems with optimization need to be considered. First and foremost, there is the question of the reliability of the estimated standard deviations and correlation coefficients. If these are unreliable, the basket hedge can be expected to experience large tracking errors. On a more theoretical level, it is possible that one or more of the basket weightings might turn out to be negative. If this is objectionable, then the optimization can be constrained to find the best basket that has nonnegative weightings. More importantly, the basket weightings may be very different from the actual portfolio weightings. For example, German securities may not be in the portfolio, but the basket might use the mark to hedge the risk of EMS country securities.

Proxy Hedging

Proxy hedging is fundamentally different from any of the hedging techniques that have been discussed, in that in reality it is a form of active currency management. Proxy hedging refers to the use of a substitute, or proxy, currency. Interbank currency traders use proxy hedging all the time. Suppose a trader wants to close a long dollar/Swiss position but that conditions are not opportune at the moment to make a sale. An alternative is to sell the more liquid dollar/mark as a proxy. This would convert the position to an exposure in the mark/Swiss cross rate. The mark/Swiss cross is considerably less risky than dollar/Swiss, so the original position is hedged, in a manner of speaking. Later, in more favorable conditions, the trader might choose to unwind the entire position.

Proxy hedging began to attract a following among global fixed-income managers during the final portion of the exchange rate mechanism's narrow-band period, roughly from 1989 to the middle of 1992. Before the first ERM crisis in September 1992, a substantial speculative position began to accumulate in what became known as the convergence play (IMF 1993). The basic view was that the high interest rates in the weaker ERM currencies (for example, Italy and Spain) would fall and that the low interest rates in the stronger currencies (for example, Germany) would rise—hence the origin of the term convergence play. To take an example, suppose a dollar-based investor wanted to capture the relatively high interest rates in Spain. Initially, she would have had to sell dollars and buy pesetas, in order to purchase the Spanish bonds, leaving her with an effective position short dollar/peseta (USD/ESP). She might choose to use dollar/mark as a proxy currency hedge. The result of the substitution of dollar/mark as the hedge would be that she would be short mark/peseta (i.e., long Spain and short marks) and long the interest rate differential between Spanish and German interest rates. Some of the enthusiasm for trades like this was based on the mistaken belief that the ERM would be capable of preventing a sharp drop in the value of the weaker currencies. In the end, proxy hedging and the convergence play fell out of favor following the two disastrous European currency crises in September 1992 and August 1993.

The Mathematics of Creating a Proxy Currency Basket

The objective is to find a combination or basket of currencies that will minimize the tracking error with respect to a targeted currency index. Two approaches will be discussed. The first, the constrained optimization approach, solves for a set of weights for the basket currencies that by constraint sum to unity. Baskets made with this approach need to be scaled up or down to match the volatility of the index. The second approach, the unconstrained optimization approach, does not constrain the sum of the basket weights and is identical to classical multiple linear regression.

The Constrained Optimization Approach

Assume that three currencies will be utilized. The weights on the three currencies are designated as x_1, x_2, and x_3. The index itself is given a weight of -1 and is designated as x_4. The problem is to choose x_1, x_2, and x_3 so as to

$$\text{Min}\{\text{var}(\text{proxy} - \text{index})\} = \sum_{i=1}^{4}\sum_{j=1}^{4} x_i x_j \sigma_{ij}$$

subject to the constraints

$$\sum_{i=1}^{3} x_i = 1$$

and

$$x_4 = -1$$

The symbol σ_{ij} represents the covariance between the rates of return on currencies i and j (where $i = j$, it represents the currency's own variance). This formulation is the standard one from portfolio theory. To find the variance of the portfolio (the "portfolio" here being the basket minus the index), sum all of the N^2 elements of the variance–covariance matrix, each having first been multiplied by the respective weights of their pairwise components (see Fama and Miller 1972 or Francis and Archer 1979). Using the method of Lagrange multipliers, let the variable Z equal

$$Z = \sum_{i=1}^{4} \sum_{j=1}^{4} x_i x_j \sigma_{ij} + \lambda_1 \left(\sum_{i=1}^{3} x_i - 1 \right) + \lambda_2 (x_4 + 1)$$

To minimize Z, and therefore solve for the component weights that minimize the tracking error subject to the two constraints, set the six first-order partial derivatives equal to zero

$$\frac{\partial Z}{\partial x_1} = 2x_1\sigma_1^2 + 2x_2\sigma_{12} + 2x_3\sigma_{13} + 2x_4\sigma_{14} + \lambda_1 = 0$$

$$\frac{\partial Z}{\partial x_2} = 2x_2\sigma_2^2 + 2x_3\sigma_{23} + 2x_4\sigma_{24} + 2x_1\sigma_{12} + \lambda_1 = 0$$

$$\frac{\partial Z}{\partial x_3} = 2x_3\sigma_3^2 + 2x_1\sigma_{13} + 2x_2\sigma_{23} + 2x_4\sigma_{34} + \lambda_1 = 0$$

$$\frac{\partial Z}{\partial x_4} = 2x_4\sigma_4^2 + 2x_1\sigma_{14} + 2x_2\sigma_{24} + 2x_3\sigma_{34} + \lambda_2 = 0$$

$$\frac{\partial Z}{\partial \lambda_1} = x_1 + x_2 + x_3 - 1 = 0$$

$$\frac{\partial Z}{\partial \lambda_2} = x_4 + 1 = 0$$

This can be written in matrix algebra as

$$\mathbf{Ax = B}$$

where

$$\mathbf{A} = \begin{bmatrix} \sigma_1^2 & \sigma_{12} & \sigma_{13} & \sigma_{14} & 1 & 0 \\ \sigma_{21} & \sigma_2^2 & \sigma_{23} & \sigma_{24} & 1 & 0 \\ \sigma_{31} & \sigma_{32} & \sigma_3^2 & \sigma_{34} & 1 & 0 \\ \sigma_{41} & \sigma_{42} & \sigma_{42} & \sigma_4^2 & 0 & 1 \\ 1 & 1 & 1 & 0 & 0 & 0 \\ 0 & 0 & 0 & 1 & 0 & 0 \end{bmatrix}$$

$$\mathbf{x} = \begin{bmatrix} x_1 \\ x_2 \\ x_3 \\ x_4 \\ \lambda_1 \\ \lambda_2 \end{bmatrix}$$

$$\mathbf{B} = \begin{bmatrix} 0 \\ 0 \\ 0 \\ 0 \\ 1 \\ -1 \end{bmatrix}$$

The solution is

$$\mathbf{x} = \mathbf{A}^{-1}\mathbf{B}$$

which involves multiplying the inverse of the 6×6 matrix $\mathbf{A}$ by the column vector $\mathbf{B}$. The first three elements of the matrix $\mathbf{X}$ are the values x_1, x_2, and x_3 that solve the optimization problem. However, because of the constraint that they sum to unity, the basket may not track the index with minimum tracking error. A "quick and dirty fix" involves scaling the exposure to the optimized basket (without changing the x's) to the index. Regressing the index on the basket

$$R_{\text{index},t} = b_0 + b_1 R_{\text{proxy},t} + \tilde{e}_t$$

provides an estimate of the rescaling coefficient b_1

$$x_i^{\text{adj}} = \hat{b}_1 x_i \qquad (i = 1, 2, 3)$$

Some notes of caution are in order. First the solution may contain values of the x's that are negative. This means that the investor would have to extend the position in the currency with the negative weight beyond the exposure in the portfolio. If this is not allowed, a different methodology that constrains the proxy weights to be nonnegative must be used. Second, if the matrix **A** is ill-conditioned, it may have no inverse. Typically, this arises because the variance–covariance matrix contains elements that are mutually inconsistent. In a larger sense, one should always remember that output from any optimization technique is never better than the quality of the data.

The Unconstrained Optimization Approach

In the second approach, the constraint that the sum of the x_i's be unity is dropped. The optimization problem becomes to solve for the x's and λ to minimize

$$Z = \sum_{i=1}^{4}\sum_{j=1}^{4} x_i x_j \sigma_{ij} + \lambda(x_4 + 1)$$

which can be written in matrix terms as

$$\mathbf{Ax = B}$$

where

$$\mathbf{A} = \begin{bmatrix} 2\sigma_1^2 & 2\sigma_{12} & 2\sigma_{13} & 2\sigma_{14} & 0 \\ 2\sigma_{21} & 2\sigma_2^2 & 2\sigma_{23} & 2\sigma_{24} & 0 \\ 2\sigma_{31} & 2\sigma_{32} & 2\sigma_3^2 & 2\sigma_{34} & 0 \\ 2\sigma_{41} & 2\sigma_{42} & 2\sigma_{43} & 2\sigma_4^2 & 1 \\ 0 & 0 & 0 & 1 & 0 \end{bmatrix}$$

$$\mathbf{x} = \begin{bmatrix} x_1 \\ x_2 \\ x_3 \\ x_4 \\ \lambda \end{bmatrix}$$

$$\mathbf{B} = \begin{bmatrix} 0 \\ 0 \\ 0 \\ 1 \\ -1 \end{bmatrix}$$

Note that the unconstrained optimization method is identical to estimating the parameters in

$$R_{\text{index},t} = b_1 R_{1,t} + b_2 R_{2,t} + b_3 R_{3,t} + \tilde{e}_t$$

using classical linear regression estimation (with no intercept term). Also note that in the unconstrained approach, no rescaling is necessary because the sum of the weights does not have to equal unity.

CHAPTER 6

Currency Options

The currency option market is one of the world's largest option markets and the only option market that is open 24 hours per day. The vast majority of trades are executed over-the-counter alongside the interbank market for spot and forward foreign exchange. There are also currency options and currency futures options that trade on listed exchanges.

OPTION BASICS

Currency options are derivative securities; that is, they are derived from another asset, namely underlying positions in foreign exchange, and cannot exist on their own. Derivatives trading is a zero-sum game by definition because the total position of the entire market is flat. For every buyer of an option there must be a seller.

As in all option markets, there are two basic varieties of currency options, calls and puts. A currency call option is the right, but not the obligation, to buy a fixed face amount of foreign exchange at a fixed exchange rate, called the strike, on or possibly before the option's expiration date. A currency put is the right, but not the obligation, to sell a fixed face amount of foreign exchange at a fixed strike exchange rate on or possibly before the option's expiration date. Put and call options can be held as either long or short positions. A call on one currency is also a put on the other currency. For example, an option to buy dollars in exchange for marks rightfully could be called either a dollar call or a mark put. Mistakes can be avoided by making reference to both currencies, for example, by writing dollar call/mark put (or USD call/DEM put). The face amount of an option can be specified in either currency; the strike converts one face currency to the other. The USD/DEM options in Exhibit 6–1 that are struck at 1.4081 have equivalent face amounts of 10 million USD and 14,081,000 DEM.

Options that can be exercised only on the expiration date are called European options. They constitute the bulk of the options that are traded in the interbank market. American options can be exercised at any time before expiration. The distinction between American and European exercise conventions turns out to be nontrivial in the valuation of currency options, as will be discussed in Chapter 8.

E X H I B I T   6–1

Put and Call Options on USD/DEM

Parameters		
Face in USD		$10,000,000
Face in DEM		14,081,000
Spot exchange rate		1.4100
Strike		1.4081
Days to expiration		32
USD interest rate		6.00%
DEM interest rate		4.46%
Implied volatility		14.75%
Option Valuation	**USD Put /DEM Call**	**USD Call/DEM Put**
USD pips	0.0123084	0.0123072
Total USD	$173,315	$173,298
DEM pips	0.0244	0.0244
Total DEM	244,374	244,350
Percentage of face	1.73%	1.73%

An option is said to be at-the-money forward if its strike is equal to the prevailing forward outright for value at option expiration. The USD/DEM put and call options in Exhibit 6–1 are struck at-the-money forward outright, 1.4081. At-the-money spot means that the option is struck at the prevailing spot exchange rate.

The price of an option is called the premium. Premium can be expressed in a number of ways. Usually, it is quoted in terms of domestic currency per one unit of foreign currency face amount. In Exhibit 6–1, a USD put/DEM call on 10 million USD face is quoted at 0.0123084 dollars per mark of face. The aggregate dollar premium is equal to $173,315 (with some allowance for small rounding error) because

$$\$0.0123084(USD/DEM) \times 14,081,000(DEM) = \$173,315$$

Alternatively, this option can be quoted in terms of marks per one dollar of face, or 0.0244374 DEM (equal to 244,374 DEM in aggregate). This convention is preferred when it matches the way that currency is quoted in the spot market (i.e., dollar/mark is quoted in marks per dollar). In spot terms, the option costs 2.44 "big figures," and the purchaser of the option needs spot USD/DEM to be below 1.3837 (equal to 1.4081 minus .0244) in order to break even.

Premium also can be quoted as a percentage of face amount. The premium on the USD put/DEM call is equal to 1.73 percent of face because

$$\frac{\$173,315}{\$10,000,000} = 1.73\%$$

The expiration value of an option is solely a function of the spot exchange rate in relation to the option strike. The USD put/DEM call in Exhibit 6–1 would be in-the-money by 2.81 "big figures" at spot equal to 1.3800 given that the option is struck at 1.4081. The expiration value of this option can be found using

$$\text{Max}\left[0, \frac{K - S_T}{S_T} \times \text{USD FACE}\right]$$

where K is the option strike and S_T is the spot exchange rate at expiration time T. In the example, the expiration value is

$$\text{Max}\left[0, \frac{1.4081 - 1.3800}{1.3800} \times \$10,000,000\right] = \$203,623$$

The expiration value for the USD call/DEM put is

$$\text{Max}\left[0, \frac{S_T - K}{S_T} \times \text{USD Face}\right]$$

The profit or loss at expiration is defined as the option expiration value minus the original cost of the option. Exhibit 6–2 shows diagrams of the net profit or loss at expiration for long and short positions in the one-month USD put/DEM call. Premium and

E X H I B I T   6–2A

Long USD Put/DEM Call
32 Days; Strike = 1.4081

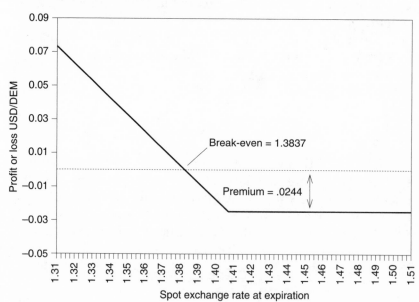

net profit or loss in the exhibit are measured in units of mark pips per dollar of face. The maximum possible loss associated with buying an option is the original premium. That is not the case with short option positions. The potential loss associated with a short option position is unbounded.

The break-even level for an option trade is defined as the spot level for which the expiration value of the option is equal to the original premium. For a long position in a USD put/DEM call, the break-even level is equal to the strike minus the premium. This would be

$$S_T^{BE} = K - P = 1.4081 - .0244 = 1.3837$$

where S_T^{BE} is the break-even level of spot at expiration time T, and P is the put premium, using the USD put/DEM call in Exhibit 6–1 as an example. The break-even level for a long

EXHIBIT 6–2B

Long USD Call/DEM Put
32 Days; Strike = 1.4081

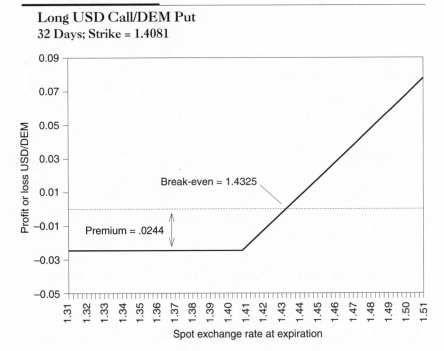

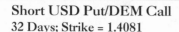

E X H I B I T   6–2C

Short USD Put/DEM Call
32 Days; Strike = 1.4081

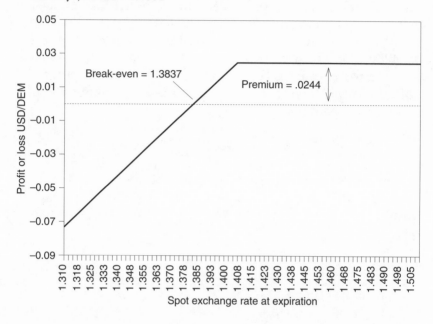

position in a USD call/DEM put from Exhibit 6–1 is equal to the strike plus the premium

$$S_T^{BE} = K + C = 1.4081 + .0244 = 1.4325$$

where C is the option premium.

The intrinsic value, or parity value, of an in-the-money option is the absolute value of the difference between the spot exchange rate and the option strike. The intrinsic value of an out-of-the-money or at-the-money option is zero. The difference between premium and intrinsic value is called the time value.

ELEMENTARY OPTION STRATEGIES

Currency options used alone or in combination can achieve a wide variety of investment objectives. Some objectives are directed at risk-control strategies. Others intend to express direc-

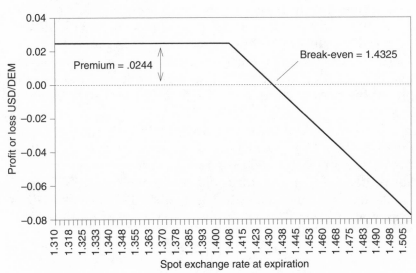

Spot exchange rate at expiration

tional views on foreign exchange rates. These trades are designed to profit from correctly anticipating when, by how much, and in what direction exchange rates will move. Volatility strategies are more complex and are unique to option trading. In its most elementary form, the view expressed by a long volatility position is that the future up or down moves in exchange rates will be sufficiently large to cover the cost of the option premium. Short volatility trades hope for tranquil market conditions.

Basic Strategies for Risk Management

As was described in Chapter 5, foreign exchange risk derives from any actual or implied long or short exposure to foreign currency. The exposure could come from a position in spot or forward foreign exchange, or from a portfolio of foreign stocks and bonds or from other assets, or it could be based on future receipts of foreign currency, such as would be the case for an overseas exporter. The techniques that were presented in Chapter 5 use forward currency contracts to hedge exposure to foreign exchange. Hedging with forward currency contracts provides effective protection against foreign exchange risk but precludes participating in upside gains. Options provide an alternative way to manage foreign exchange risk. The basic difference is that option-based programs can provide downside risk protection while preserving a chance of upside participation in foreign currency gains. Two option strategies that are popular for managing foreign exchange risk are the protective currency put and the currency collar (also referred to as a range forward).

Exhibit 6–3A shows a long USD/DEM cash position that is protected by a USD put/DEM call. Suppose that a U.S. dollar–based investor established the position at the spot level of 1.4100. For protection, the investor could buy a one-month USD put/DEM call. The at-the-money forward strike (1.4081) with 32 days to expiration costs .0244 mark pips. The protected position has a

EXHIBIT 6–3A

Long USD with Put Protection
32 Days to Expiration

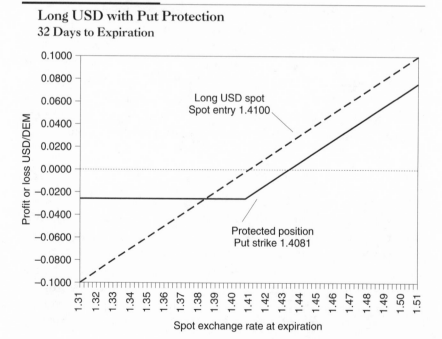

Spot exchange rate at expiration

maximum loss at expiration equal to the option strike less the cash entry level less the cost of the option.

Option strike	1.4081
Cash entry level	(1.4100)
Cost of put	(0.0244)
	(0.0263)

It is important to note that the purchase of the put in no way compromises the upside potential if the dollar were to appreciate against the mark. In a symmetrical fashion, a USD call/DEM put could be used to protect a short USD/DEM position.

The second strategy, Exhibit 6–3B, is called a collar. It consists of a long position in a USD put/DEM call (struck at 1.3800),

EXHIBIT 6–3B

Long USD/DEM with Protective Collar
32 Days to Expiration

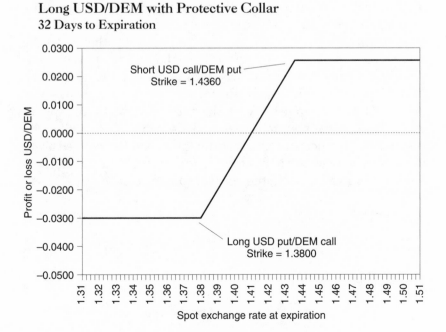

a short position in a USD call/DEM put (struck at 1.4360), and an underlying cash position, which is long USD/DEM. The collar establishes a floor for the long USD/DEM position equal to the strike on the USD put/DEM call minus the net cost of the two options plus the mark-to-market on the cash position. The collar also creates a cap or maximum gain on the position because of the short USD call/DEM put. The cap is equal to the strike of the short USD call/DEM put minus the net cost of the two options plus any mark-to-market on the cash position. Collars can be constructed so that the cost of the long option exactly equals the cost of the short option, a strategy called a zero cost collar. This will be discussed further in Chapter 7.

Strategies to Express Directional Views

Currency options can be used to make leveraged bets on the future direction of foreign exchange movements. Two popular combination strategies are the vertical spread and the risk reversal.

Traders often prefer vertical spreads to buying a single call or put. A vertical spread is a combination of two calls or two puts held in opposite direction with different strikes but the same expiration date. In a vertical put spread (also called a bear spread), the investor buys one put and sells another with the same expiration date. The second put has a lower strike and therefore a lower premium. It serves to reduce the cost of the overall position and establish a more favorable break-even point. Within the range between the two strike prices, the spread gains value as the spot falls. Below the second, lower strike, the position is "capped out"; no further gains can be realized were the spot exchange rate to fall to even lower levels. In the example depicted in Exhibit 6–3C, the vertical spread consists of

Long USD put/DEM call ($K_1 = 1.4081$); $P_1 = .0244$ mark pips

Short USD put/DEM call ($K_2 = 1.3881$); $P_2 = .0158$ mark pips

The net cost of the spread is

$$C_1 - C_2 = .0244 - .0158 = .0086$$

EXHIBIT 6–3C

USD Put/DEM Call Spread
32 Days; Strikes at 1.4081 and 1.3881; Net Cost .0086 USD/DEM

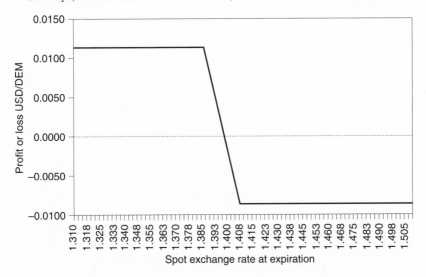

The cost of the spread is less than the cost of buying the long USD put/DEM call by itself. The spread also has a higher break-even point

$$S_T^{BE} = K_1 + (C_1 - C_2) = 1.3995$$

than the stand-alone option (break-even = 1.3837).

The opposite directional view could be expressed by entering into a USD call/DEM put spread (this would be a bull spread). A long position in a vertical spread can never lose more than its original net premium.

A more aggressive directional play is the risk reversal. A bearish risk reversal consists of buying an out-of-the-money USD put/DEM call and selling an out-of-the-money USD call/DEM put (see Exhibit 6–3D). This trade is usually established at a set of strikes designed to make the trade zero cost. Risk reversals can be very profitable when the directional view is correct—the profitable long option is obtained "free of charge." But if the directional view turns out to be wrong, there is a

E X H I B I T   6–3D

Bearish USD/DEM Risk Reversal
32 Days; Strikes at 1.3800 and 1.4360; Net Premium Zero

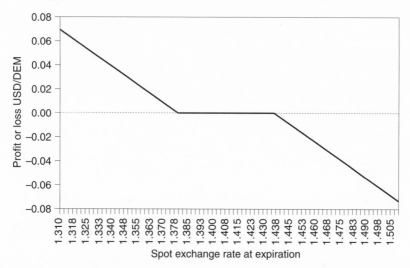

chance of a very large and unbounded loss on the short option position. Risk reversals are important in option trading; further discussion follows in Chapter 7.

Strategies to Express Volatility Views

Options give traders the ability to express views not only on the future direction of exchange rates but also on their future volatility. It is possible to be either "long volatility" or "short volatility." Straddles and strangles are commonly employed in relatively simple volatility trading.

A straddle consists of a put and a call having the same strike and expiration date. In a long straddle (Exhibit 6–3E), the investor buys both the put and the call, usually struck at-the-money forward. The view is that exchange rates will be volatile enough to push either the put or the call in-the-money by more than the cost of the straddle. The straddle in Exhibit 6–3E costs .0489 mark pips and has two break-even levels,

E X H I B I T   6–3E

USD/DEM Straddle
32 Days; Strike at 1.4081; Total Premium .0489 USD/DEM

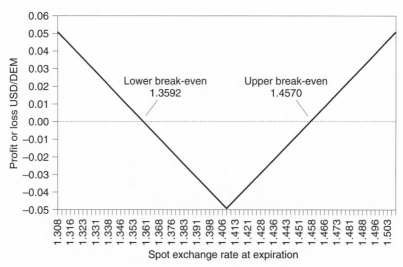

Spot exchange rate at expiration

$$\text{Upper } S_T^{BE} = K + (C + P) = 1.4570$$

$$\text{Lower } S_T^{BE} = K - (C + P) = 1.3592$$

The upper break-even level is where spot at expiration exceeds the strike by the total cost of the put and the call. The lower break-even level is where spot is lower than the strike by the total cost of the put and the call.

A strangle consists of an out-of-the-money put and an out-of-the-money call. Exhibit 6–3F shows a long position in a 1.4281/1.3881 strangle on USD/DEM. Because both options are out-of-the-money, the strangle costs less than the straddle does. The strangle in the exhibit costs .0315 mark pips. Its break-even points are

$$\text{Upper } S_T^{BE} = K_{\text{call}} + (C + P) = 1.4596$$

$$\text{Lower } S_T^{BE} = K_{\text{put}} - (C + P) = 1.3566$$

USD/DEM Strangle
32 Days; Strikes at 1.4281 and 1.3881; Net Cost .0315 USD/DEM

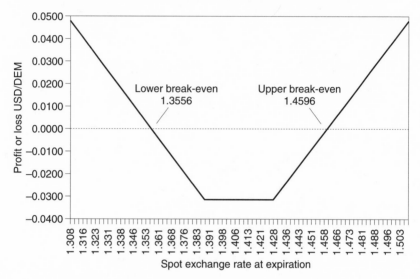

The writer of a straddle (i.e., short the put and short the call) hopes that the proceeds of the sale of the options will cover the amount by which either option is in-the-money at expiration. A less aggressive short volatility bet can be established by selling a strangle. Either way, the view is that exchange rates will not be volatile. Both the short straddle and short strangle have unlimited risk. More complex volatility strategies are discussed in Chapter 7.

PUT–CALL PARITY
FOR CURRENCY OPTIONS

European calls and puts having a common expiration and strike are linked by what is known as the put–call parity theorem. It assumes a perfect market for currency options and foreign exchange. This means there are no taxes or transactions costs, and all market participants are price takers. Additionally, arbitrageurs can borrow and lend domestic and foreign currency at the prevailing interest rates. These assumptions, plus the proposition that any profitable arbitrage opportunities will be cleared from the market, bring about put–call parity. The relationship states the difference between the price of a European put and a call having the same strike and the same expiration is equal to the difference between the present value of the face amount of domestic currency and the present value (using the foreign currency's interest rate) of the face amount of foreign currency. Put–call parity holds at every moment of time in an option's life.

There is a trick to understanding put–call parity. Assume that a trader were to buy a put and sell a call. At expiration, he would have a short position in the face amount of foreign currency and also a long position in cash equal to the strike, no matter which option finishes in the money. If the put finishes in-the-money, he would exercise. This means he would deliver the face amount of foreign exchange and receive the strike. If the call finishes in-the-money, it would be exercised against him. He would be required to deliver the face amount of currency in exchange for the strike. If both options finish at-the-money, they both would be worthless. On the other hand, the short position in foreign exchange would exactly be the long position in the domestic currency (the strike). Exhibit 6–4 contains a numerical example of put–call parity.[1] The put–call parity relationship for European exercise can be written algebraically as

$$P - C = Ke^{-R_d\tau} - Se^{-R_f\tau}$$

where

C is the price of the currency call.
P is the price of the currency put.
K is the strike.
R_d is the domestic interest rate.
R_f is the foreign interest rate.
S is the spot exchange rate, American quotation convention.
τ is the time remaining until expiration in years.

E X H I B I T   6–4

Demonstration of Put–Call Parity for European Currency Options

Parameters			
Domestic currency:	$10,000,000 USD	Standard deviation	14.75%
Foreign currency:	14,081,000 DEM	Horizon (days)	32
Spot exchange rate	1.4100	Strike price	1.4081
Interest rate USD	6.00%	Price of put	
Interest rate DEM	4.46%	on 10 MM USD	$173,315
		Price of call	
		on 10 MM USD	$173,298

Options Portfolio

		Payoff Matrix: Day 365	
	Initial Cost	**S > K**	**S < K**
Buy a call on 10 MM USD Strike = 1.4081	($173,298)	−14.081 MM DEM + $10 MM USD	0
Sell a put on 10 MM USD Strike = 1.4081	$173,315	0	−14.081 MM DEM + $10 MM USD
		Net payoff in either state:	
Net cost of options portfolio	$17	−14.081 MM DEM + $10 MM USD	

Bond Portfolio

	Initial Cost	**Payoff Matrix: Day 32**
Buy a bill with FV = 10MM USD to mature in 32 days (USD interest rate)	($9,947,535)	$10,000,000 USD
Borrow DEM FV = 14.081MM DEM to mature in 21 days (DEM interest rate) Convert to USD at spot	$9,947,552	(14,081,000) DEM
Net cost of bond portfolio	$17	−14.081 MM DEM + $10 MM USD

Put–call parity suggests ways that one option can be used to replicate the other. In a conversion, a synthetic put is created by doing the following:

Buying a call at the same strike and expiration as the put to be synthesized.

Investing in a noncoupon discount bill that pays the strike on expiration day.

Borrowing the present value of the face amount of foreign currency with repayment due on expiration day.

In a reversal, a synthetic call is created by doing the following:

Buying a put with the same strike and expiration date as the call to be synthesized.

Borrowing the present value of the strike with repayment due at expiration day.

Investing in a discounted bill that pays the face amount of foreign currency on expiration day.

Put–call parity can be thought of as

$$[\text{Put} + \text{Long foreign currency}]$$

equals

$$[\text{Call} + \text{Long domestic currency}]$$

Put–call parity cannot hold as an equality for American currency options because of the possibility of optimal early exercise. A less binding parity relationship does exist in the form of an inequality (Gibson 1991, DeRosa 1991).

Put–Call Parity American Exercise

$$C + K - S^{-R_f \tau} \geq P \geq C + Ke^{-R_d \tau} - S$$

A SHORT HISTORY OF OPTION PRICING THEORY

Black and Scholes (1973) created a revolution in thought about option pricing. They addressed the problem of how to value a

European exercise option on shares of a non-dividend-paying common stock. Their paper assumed a standard set of perfect market assumptions. They also assumed that the price of the underlying shares follows a random walk in continuous time with variance proportional to the square of the stock price. Given these conditions, they were able to derive a key partial differential equation that governs the pricing of options, as well as the valuation of other derivative securities. Under the constraint of European exercise, Black and Scholes solved the equation to arrive at the value of option.

Merton (1973) modified the Black–Scholes approach for the case of an option on shares of a hypothetical company that pays a continuous—i.e., not discrete—dividend over time. Much later, Garman and Kohlhagen (1983) adapted the Merton continuous dividend approach for European exercise options on foreign exchange. Their approach was to substitute the interest rate spread between the domestic currency and the foreign currency in place of Merton's continuous dividend.

The Black–Scholes solution is restricted to European exercise options, but it could include any American options that would never be optimally exercised before expiration. A theoretical breakthrough, called the binomial model, was introduced by Cox, Ross, and Rubinstein (1979). The binomial model is applicable to all types of options, including currency options, for both European and American exercise conventions. The drawback with the binomial model is that it is somewhat cumbersome in practice. MacMillan (1986) and Barone-Adesi and Whaley (1987) introduced a quadratic approximation method, which provides reasonably precise estimates of binomial solutions with substantially reduced computational effort.

On another front, Black (1976) derived a model for European exercise futures options. Currency future options of both European and American varieties can be valued with binomial models as well as with the quadratic approximation model.

VALUATION OF EUROPEAN CURRENCY OPTIONS

Garman and Kohlhagen's model for European options on foreign currencies will be referred to as the BSGK (Black–Scholes–

Garman–Kohlhagen) model in this text. Some initial simplifying assumptions are required:

1. There are no taxes or transactions costs, and all currency option and foreign exchange market participants are price-takers.
2. Foreign and domestic interest rates are riskless and constant over the option's life. Borrowing and lending are permitted at these rates without limitation.
3. Instantaneous changes in spot foreign exchange rates are generated by a diffusion process of the form

$$\frac{d\tilde{S}}{\tilde{S}} = \mu dt + \sigma d\tilde{z}$$

   where $\tilde{S}$ is the spot exchange rate, quoted American convention, $d\tilde{S}$ is the differential in $\tilde{S}$, μ is a drift term, dt is the differential in time, σ is the standard deviation of the log returns in spot rates, and $d\tilde{z}$ is the differential of a stochastic variable. $d\tilde{z}$ is normally distributed having zero expectation and standard deviation equal to the square root of dt.

The first assumption is the standard frictionless market condition found in many financial models. The inclusion of the foreign currency interest rate in the second assumption was Garman and Kohlhagen's principal modification to the earlier models. The interest rate spread between the domestic and foreign rates plays a role analogous to the continuous dividend in the Merton model. The third assumption directly implies that spot exchange rates are distributed lognormally[2] and that the log return series

$$\ln \frac{S_t}{S_{t-1}}$$

is normally distributed.

The heart of the model is the idea that a position in a currency option can be locally hedged by taking an opposite position in spot foreign exchange. By definition, a local hedge is supposed to operate on small, short-run price fluctuations. In Exhibit 6–1, the 10 million USD face USD put/DEM call struck at 1.4081 is worth $173,315 when spot is trading at 1.4100. As a matter of fact, this option would fall in value to $156,000 (a drop of $17,315) if the spot exchange rate were to rise to 1.4150. Suppose that one were to construct a local hedge with cash by going long dollars/short marks. If the spot exchange rate were to rise, on one hand, the option would fall in value; but, on the other hand, the long dollar position would rise in value. The opposite would happen if the spot exchange rate were to fall; the option would become more valuable, but the spot hedge would lose value. The size of the short dollar position that is needed to hedge the option varies with the level of the spot exchange rate. At a higher spot rate, a smaller cash position would be sufficient to hedge this particular option, it being a USD put/DEM call. But at a lower spot level, a larger cash position would be required.

Suppose the size of the cash hedge were continuously adjusted in response to exchange rate movements. The option position would be perfectly hedged; the aggregate position consisting of the option plus the cash hedge would constitute a riskless investment. According to first principles of financial theory, this position must earn exactly the riskless rate of interest.

The percentage of the option face that is required to correctly hedge movements in the spot exchange rate is called the delta (δ) of the option. An alternate definition is that delta is the absolute amount by which the premium of the option rises or falls when the exchange rate changes by one unit. Delta is bounded by zero and one for a call option, and by minus one and zero for a put option. Traders have adopted the convention of multiplying call deltas by 100 and put deltas by –100. As a rule of thumb, the delta of an at-the-money option is approximately 50 (i.e., 0.5 for calls and –0.5 for puts). Out-of-the-money deltas are small, perhaps even zero. This is because a unit change in the spot rate doesn't matter for an option that is apt to expire worthless. At the other extreme, in-the-money deltas are large and can approach 100. An option with delta equal to 100 moves up and down in equal unit value with the spot rate.

Garman and Kohlhagen, following the Black–Scholes methodology, used an important lemma from stochastic calculus, called Ito's lemma, to derive the following partial differential equation

$$\frac{1}{2}\sigma^2 S^2 \frac{\partial^2 C}{\partial S^2} - R_d C + \left(R_d S - R_f S\right)\frac{\partial C}{\partial S} - \frac{\partial C}{\partial \tau} = 0$$

that governs the pricing of a currency call. This derivation requires that a perfect hedge can be operated between the option and spot positions in currency.

Garman and Kohlhagen solved the partial differential equation to obtain the value of the call by imposing the expiration day payoff function

$$C_T = \text{MAX}[0, S_T - K]$$

as a boundary condition. They repeated the same approach to arrive at the value of a put option.

The Model in Spot Exchange Rates[3]

The exact BSGK equations for puts and call are

$$C = e^{-R_f \tau} S N\left(x + \sigma\sqrt{\tau}\right) - e^{-R_d \tau} K N(x)$$

$$P = e^{-R_f \tau} S \left(N\left(x + \sigma\sqrt{\tau}\right) - 1\right) - e^{-R_d \tau} K \left(N(x) - 1\right)$$

$$x = \frac{\ln\left(\dfrac{S}{K}\right) + \left(R_d - R_f - \dfrac{\sigma^2}{2}\right)\tau}{\sigma\sqrt{\tau}}$$

where

C	is the premium on a European currency call.
P	is the premium on a European currency put.
S	is the spot exchange rate, American convention.
K	is the strike.
τ	is the time in years to expiration.
R_f	is the foreign currency interest rate.
R_d	is the domestic interest rate.

σ   is the standard deviation in the diffusion process that
      generates currency returns.
$N(\ )$ is the cumulative normal distribution function.

Graphs of BSGK European USD put/DEM call option theoretical premiums before expiration are displayed in Exhibit 6–5.
The horizontal axis is the spot exchange rate. The vertical axis is
the option premium. Premium is measured in units of dollars
per marks of face. Each curvilinear line represents the value of
the option given a fixed amount of time remaining to expiration.
In general, the option curve shifts downward and becomes more
convex as time elapses. The curve finally collapses onto the expiration locus at expiration.
      The cumulative normal distribution is given in Exhibit 6–6.[4]
Exhibit 6–7 shows numerical examples of the calculation of
European call and put premiums using the model.

E X H I B I T   6–5

BSGK Value of European USD Put/DEM Call
90 Days, 30 Days, and 7 Days; Strike = 1.4081

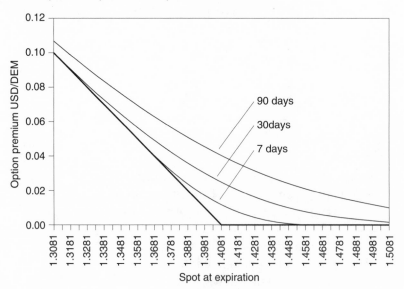

The Model in Forward Exchange Rates

Garman and Kohlhagen also provided a formulation of their model in terms of the forward exchange rate

$$C = e^{-R_d \tau}\left(FN\left(y + \sigma\sqrt{\tau}\right) - KN(y)\right)$$

$$P = e^{-R_d \tau}\left(F\left(N\left(y + \sigma\sqrt{\tau}\right) - 1\right) - K\left(N(y) - 1\right)\right)$$

$$y = \frac{\ln\left(\dfrac{F}{K}\right) - \dfrac{\sigma^2}{2}\tau}{\sigma\sqrt{\tau}}$$

where F is the forward exchange rate as derived from the interest parity theorem

$$F = Se^{(R_d - R_f)\tau}$$

The Risk-Neutrality Approach

Cox and Ross (1976) suggested an insightful way to understand option pricing theory by calling attention to the fact that option values are independent of investor attitudes towards risk. This follows from the primary BSGK postulate that it is theoretically possible to remove all directional risk from a currency option by dynamic hedging with positions in spot foreign exchange. Hence, the value of an option should be equal in the eyes of a risk-averse investor and a risk-neutral investor. The value of an option to the latter, who by definition is indifferent to risk, is equal to the present value of the mathematical expectation of the payoff values at expiration. Consider different cases or *states* at option expiration. The states wherein the option expires at- or out-of-the-money are worthless. The state wherein the option is in-the-money at expiration is worth the present value of the con-ditional expectation of the future spot exchange rate minus the strike. The mathematical expectation is conditional on the option being in-the-money at expiration. The probability of the option being in-the-money at expiration as well as the expected value of the spot exchange rate at expiration can be derived from the

Cumulative Normal Distribution

Z	0.00	0.01	0.02	0.03	0.04	0.05	0.06	0.07	0.08	0.09
0.0	0.500	0.504	0.508	0.512	0.516	0.520	0.524	0.528	0.532	0.536
0.1	0.540	0.544	0.548	0.552	0.556	0.560	0.564	0.567	0.571	0.575
0.2	0.579	0.583	0.587	0.591	0.595	0.599	0.603	0.606	0.610	0.614
0.3	0.618	0.622	0.626	0.629	0.633	0.637	0.641	0.644	0.648	0.652
0.4	0.655	0.659	0.663	0.666	0.670	0.674	0.677	0.681	0.684	0.688
0.5	0.691	0.695	0.698	0.702	0.705	0.709	0.712	0.716	0.719	0.722
0.6	0.726	0.729	0.732	0.736	0.739	0.742	0.745	0.749	0.752	0.755
0.7	0.758	0.761	0.764	0.767	0.770	0.773	0.776	0.779	0.782	0.785
0.8	0.788	0.791	0.794	0.797	0.800	0.802	0.805	0.808	0.811	0.813
0.9	0.816	0.819	0.821	0.824	0.826	0.829	0.831	0.834	0.836	0.839
1.0	0.841	0.844	0.846	0.848	0.851	0.853	0.855	0.858	0.860	0.862
1.1	0.864	0.866	0.869	0.871	0.873	0.875	0.877	0.879	0.881	0.883
1.2	0.885	0.887	0.889	0.891	0.893	0.894	0.896	0.898	0.900	0.901
1.3	0.903	0.905	0.907	0.908	0.910	0.911	0.913	0.915	0.916	0.918
1.4	0.919	0.921	0.922	0.924	0.925	0.926	0.928	0.929	0.931	0.932
1.5	0.933	0.934	0.936	0.937	0.938	0.939	0.941	0.942	0.943	0.944

(continued)

Cumulative Normal Distribution (concluded)

Z	0.00	0.01	0.02	0.03	0.04	0.05	0.06	0.07	0.08	0.09
1.6	0.945	0.946	0.947	0.948	0.949	0.951	0.952	0.953	0.954	0.954
1.7	0.955	0.956	0.957	0.958	0.959	0.960	0.961	0.962	0.962	0.963
1.8	0.964	0.965	0.966	0.966	0.967	0.968	0.969	0.969	0.970	0.971
1.9	0.971	0.972	0.973	0.973	0.974	0.974	0.975	0.976	0.976	0.977
2.0	0.977	0.978	0.978	0.979	0.979	0.980	0.980	0.981	0.981	0.982
2.1	0.982	0.983	0.983	0.983	0.984	0.984	0.985	0.985	0.985	0.986
2.2	0.986	0.986	0.987	0.987	0.987	0.988	0.988	0.988	0.989	0.989
2.3	0.989	0.990	0.990	0.990	0.990	0.991	0.991	0.991	0.991	0.992
2.4	0.992	0.992	0.992	0.992	0.993	0.993	0.993	0.993	0.993	0.994
2.5	0.994	0.994	0.994	0.994	0.994	0.995	0.995	0.995	0.995	0.995
2.6	0.995	0.995	0.996	0.996	0.996	0.996	0.996	0.996	0.996	0.996
2.7	0.997	0.997	0.997	0.997	0.997	0.997	0.997	0.997	0.997	0.997
2.8	0.997	0.998	0.998	0.998	0.998	0.998	0.998	0.998	0.998	0.998
2.9	0.998	0.998	0.998	0.998	0.998	0.998	0.998	0.999	0.999	0.999
3.0	0.999	0.999	0.999	0.999	0.999	0.999	0.999	0.999	0.999	0.999

Note: For variates less than zero, $F(z) = 1 - F(-z)$.

Valuation of European Currency Calls and Puts Using the BSGK Model

Parameters

$S = 1.4100$ Volatility = 14.75%

$K = 1.4081$ Days to expiration = 32

$R_d = 6.00\%$ Face = 14.081 MM DEM

$R_f = 4.46\%$ Face = 10 MM USD

The Model

$$C = e^{-R_f \tau} SN\left(x + \sigma\sqrt{\tau}\right) - e^{-R_d \tau} KN(x)$$

$$P = e^{-R_f \tau} S\left(N\left(x + \sigma\sqrt{\tau}\right) - 1\right) - e^{-R_d \tau} K\left(N(x) - 1\right)$$

$$x = \frac{\ln\left(\dfrac{S}{K}\right) + \left(R_d - R_f - \dfrac{\sigma^2}{2}\right)\tau}{\sigma\sqrt{\tau}}$$

Convert Spot Rates to American Convention

$$S' = \frac{1}{1.4100} = 0.70922$$

$$K' = \frac{1}{1.4082} = 0.71018$$

Calculate τ, x, and $x + \sigma\sqrt{\tau}$

$$\tau = \frac{32}{365} = 0.087671$$

$$x = \frac{\ln\left(\dfrac{.70922}{.71018}\right) + \left(6.00\% - 4.46\% - \dfrac{14.75\%^2}{2}\right)\tau}{14.75\%\sqrt{\tau}} = -.02180$$

$$x + \sigma\sqrt{\tau} = .02188$$

Find Cumulative Normal Densities

$$N(x) = .4913046156$$

$$N\left(x + \sigma\sqrt{\tau}\right) = .5087266272$$

Calculate Values for the Call and Put

$$C = e^{-0.0446\tau} \times (.70922) \times N\left(x + \sigma\sqrt{\tau}\right) - e^{-0.06\tau} \times (.71018) \times N(x)$$

$$= .0123084 \text{ (USD/DEM)}$$

$$P = e^{-0.0446\tau} \times (.70922) \times \left(N\left(x + \sigma\sqrt{\tau}\right) - 1\right) - e^{-0.06\tau} \times (.71018) \times \left(N(x) - 1\right)$$

$$= .0123072 \text{ (USD/DEM)}$$

cumulative lognormal distribution. Following Gemmill (1993) and Jarrow and Rudd (1983), the option model can be decomposed into the following parts

$$\left[e^{-R_d\tau}\right]\left[N(x)\right]\left[e^{(R_d-R_f)\tau}S\frac{N(x+\sigma\sqrt{\tau})}{N(x)}-K\right]$$

The first term in brackets is the present value factor. The second is the probability that the option will finish in-the-money. The third term is the expected payoff at expiration conditional on the option finishing in-the-money.

THE SENSITIVITY OF OPTION PREMIUMS TO PARAMETERS

Once the theoretical premium on an option is known, it is natural to want to know how sensitive the model is to the various input parameters. The following table summarizes the direction of the effect that an increase in each of the BSGK variables has on the values of European calls and puts on foreign currency (spot quoted American convention).

	Calls	Puts
$\dfrac{\partial}{\partial S}$	↑	↓
$\dfrac{\partial}{\partial K}$	↓	↑
$\dfrac{\partial}{\partial \sigma}$	↑	↑
$\dfrac{\partial}{\partial R_d}$	↑	↓
$\dfrac{\partial}{\partial R_f}$	↓	↑

The expressions in the left-hand column of the table, being partial derivatives, are the changes in the value of an option when a single factor changes, holding all other factors constant. Partials operate in the theoretical world of infinitesimal changes.

The change in the value of an option given a change in one parameter, designated as y, is given by

$$dC = \frac{\partial C}{\partial y} dy$$

where dc and dy are differentials in c and y. In practice, traders work with discrete changes in parameters. The change in an option price can be approximated as

$$\Delta C \cong \frac{\partial C}{\partial y} \Delta y$$

where ΔC and Δy represent discrete changes. This relationship holds only in an approximate sense because a sufficiently large Δy might induce a change in the partial derivative, $\partial C / \partial y$.

Delta and Gamma

The single most important factor influencing a currency option's value is the level of the spot exchange rate. Currency calls rise and currency puts fall with increases in the spot exchange rate (working with the American convention of spot quotation). Delta is defined as the magnitude of the change in the option's value with respect to a change in the spot exchange rate. The deltas of calls and puts are given by the partial derivatives

$$\delta_{call} \equiv \frac{\partial C}{\partial S} = e^{-R_f \tau} N\left(x + \sigma\sqrt{\tau}\right)$$

$$\delta_{put} \equiv \frac{\partial P}{\partial S} = e^{-R_f \tau} \left[N\left(x + \sigma\sqrt{\tau}\right) - 1\right]$$

The deltas of calls and puts are bounded as follows

$$0 \le \delta_{call} \le 1$$

$$-1 \le \delta_{put} \le 0$$

The delta of the USD put/DEM call in Exhibit 6–1 is equal to .5067. In practice, traders convert delta into units of one or the other face currencies, such as 5.067 million USD. In other words, given small moves in the spot rate, the value of the USD put/DEM call should behave like a short spot position of approximately five million USD/DEM. For example, if the spot exchange rate were to move up from 1.4100 to 1.4150, the value of the option should fall by $17,905, since

$$\frac{(1.4100 - 1.4150)}{1.4150} \times \$5.067 \text{ MM} = -\$17,905$$

This approximates the actual theoretical change in the option's value of minus $17,315.

Exhibit 6–8 shows the delta of currency call graphed against the spot exchange rate. The S-shaped appearance is due to the presence of the cumulative normal distribution function in the equation for delta.

E X H I B I T   6–8

Delta of USD Puts/DEM Calls

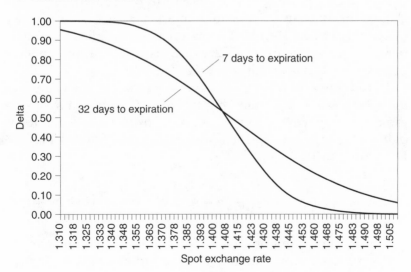

Delta itself is a function of the spot exchange rate. Its partial derivative with respect to spot is called gamma (γ)

$$\gamma \equiv \frac{\partial \delta}{\partial S} = \frac{\partial^2 C}{\partial S^2}$$

Gamma is very important to option traders; it is analogous to the concept of convexity in fixed-income analysis. Differentiating the equation for delta yields a formulation for gamma that is the same for both puts and calls

$$\gamma \equiv \frac{\partial^2 C}{\partial S^2} = \frac{e^{-R_f \tau} N'\left(x + \sigma\sqrt{\tau}\right)}{S\sigma\sqrt{\tau}}$$

$N'(\ )$ is the probability density function for the normal distribution. In the case of variable z defined to have zero mean and unit standard deviation

$$N'(z) = \frac{1}{\sqrt{2\pi}} e^{-z^2/2}$$

The gamma for the USD put/DEM call of Exhibit 6–1 is equal to 12.83. If the spot rate moved from 1.4100 to 1.4150, the change in spot in American quotation terms would equal -0.00251 (i.e., .70671 – .70922). This amount multiplied by gamma (equal to 12.83) gives –0.0322, which is in fact approximately equal to the change in delta from .5067 to .4745.

It is common practice to express gamma as the change in delta associated with one "big figure" of change in spot. For example, if spot were to rise to 1.4200 from 1.4100, the dollar delta of the option would fall from 5.074 MM USD to 4.433 MM USD, or by $640,795, since

$$\gamma_{1\,\text{Big Figure}} = \left(\frac{1}{1.4200} - \frac{1}{1.4100}\right) \times 12.83 \times \$10 \text{ MM USD} \cong -\$640,795$$

Short-dated options have the greatest levels of gamma (Exhibit 6–9A). At-the-money options are also rich in gamma (Exhibit 6–9B).

EXHIBIT 6–9A

Gamma of USD Put/DEM Call
32 Days to Expiration; Strike = 1.4081

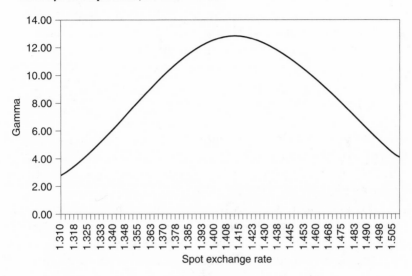

EXHIBIT 6–9B

Gamma of USD Put/DEM Call
At-the-Money Forward Strike

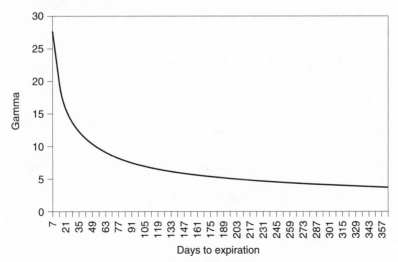

Time Decay

In almost every case, a European option falls in value with the passage of time. This is called time decay. Time decay is given by the partial derivative of the option value with respect to time remaining to expiration. This partial derivative is called theta (θ). For a currency call, theta is given by

$$\theta_{call} \equiv \frac{\partial C}{\partial \tau} = -R_f e^{-R_f \tau} SN\left(x + \sigma\sqrt{\tau}\right) + R_d e^{-R_d \tau} KN(x) + \frac{e^{-R_d \tau}\sigma}{2\sqrt{\tau}} KN'(x)$$

To figure one day's worth of decay, divide theta by 365 and multiply by the face of the option. For the USD put/DEM call in Exhibit 6–1, the one day's worth of time decay (going from day 32 to day 31) is equal to $2,892.

It is possible for some European options to experience positive time decay. Normally, this does not occur except in the case of deep in-the-money, low-volatility options, given a sufficiently large spread between the domestic and foreign interest rates.

Options with little time to expiration proportionately decay the fastest (Exhibit 6–10). Out-of-the-money options decay faster than in-the-money options because time value, rather than intrinsic value, accounts for their value.

The Relationship between Theta and Gamma

Delta, theta, and gamma are related through the BSGK partial differential equation. This equation for a currency call can be written

$$\frac{1}{2}\sigma^2 S^2 \gamma - R_d C + \left(R_d S - R_f S\right)\delta - \theta = 0$$

where the symbols γ, δ, and θ replace the partial derivatives, with no change in meaning. At a given level of delta, gamma and theta are related. This explains why traders call theta the "rent on gamma." It also demonstrates that options with high levels of gamma have fast time decay.

EXHIBIT 6–10A

One Day of Time Decay on USD Put/DEM Call
32 Days to Expiration; Strike = 1.4081

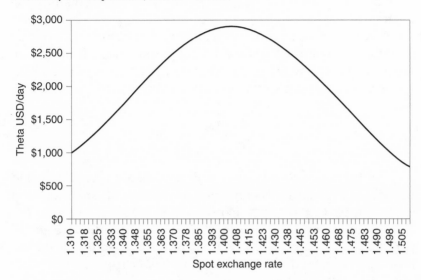

EXHIBIT 6–10B

One Day of Time Decay on USD Put/DEM Call
At-the-Money Forward Strike

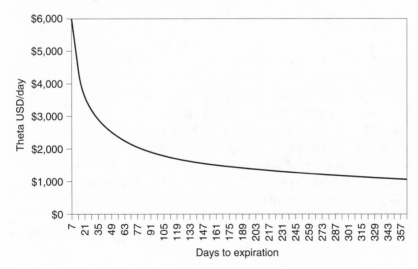

Volatility[5]

An increase in volatility leads to increases in the value of all European options. This is because the greater the level of volatility, the greater the probability that any option will expire in-the-money. The fact that it also means a greater probability that the option will expire out-of-the-money is less important because the option holder's maximum loss is the premium. The partial derivative of the option price with respect to volatility is given by

$$\kappa_{call} \equiv \frac{\partial C}{\partial \sigma} = e^{-R_d \tau} K \sqrt{\tau} N'(x)$$

In this text, we will refer to this as kappa (κ), but it is called elsewhere by many other names, including omega, tau, and vega. Kappa in the above expression gives the change in the value of an option for a 1 percent change in volatility (i.e., 14.75 percent to 15.75 percent). This must be multiplied by the option face in marks and divided by 100. The kappa of the USD put/DEM call in Exhibit 6–1 is $11,748.

Kappa is greatest for long-dated options. It is also relatively larger in the case of options that are at-the-money (Exhibit 6–11).

Interest Rate Partials

Currency calls (e.g., USD put/DEM call) are a positive function of the domestic interest rate and a negative function of the foreign interest rate. The opposite is true for currency puts (e.g., USD call/DEM put). This is because a rise in the foreign currency interest rate depresses the present value of the face amount of foreign currency. This will lower the value of a currency call—which receives the face amount of foreign currency upon exercise—and will increase the value of a currency put— which delivers foreign currency upon exercise. Similarly, when the domestic interest rate rises, the present value of the face amount of domestic currency falls. By the same logic, the value of a currency call will rise and the value of a currency put will fall.

E X H I B I T 6–11A

Kappa of USD Put/DEM Call
32 Days to Expiration; Strike = 1.4081

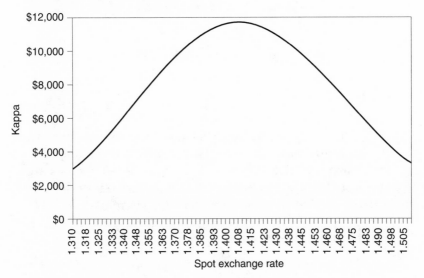

E X H I B I T 6–11B

Kappa of USD Put/DEM Call
At-the-Money Forward Strike

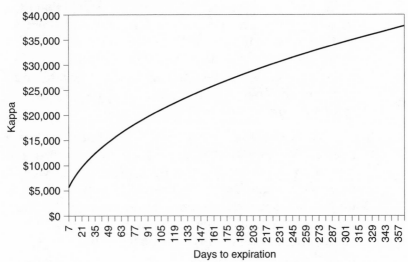

The interest rate partial derivatives for currency calls are

$$\frac{\partial C}{\partial R_d} = \tau e^{-R_d \tau} KN(x)$$

$$\frac{\partial C}{\partial R_f} = -\tau e^{-R_f \tau} SN\left(x + \sigma\sqrt{\tau}\right)$$

NOTES

1. Put–call parity requires that an at-the-money forward put must have the same value as an at-the-money forward call. The put and call in Exhibits 6–1 and 6–4 are struck at-the-money forward rounded to four decimal digits. The effect of the rounding is to make the USD put/DEM call ever-so-slightly more expensive than the USD call/DEM put.

2. The original Black–Scholes formulation specified that the stochastic process governing stock prices is a random walk in continuous time with variance rate proportional to the square of the stock price. This makes the distribution of possible stock prices at the end of any finite interval lognormal. Also, it was specified that the variance of the return on the stock is constant. Later theoreticians chose to work with a diffusion process— sometimes called a generalized Wiener process. In other texts, it is merely assumed that spot exchange rates are generated by an unspecified stochastic process that results in normally distributed log returns.

3. The BSGK model can also be used in the valuation of cross-currency options, meaning puts and calls whose premiums are quoted in a third currency. An example would be a variant of the USD put/DEM call with the option premium quoted in Japanese yen. DeRosa (1992), following a proof by Margrabe, demonstrates that the value of this cross-currency option can be calculated in two stages. First, the value of the option should be calculated as a USD

put/DEM call with the premium in either USD or DEM. Next, that premium is converted at the spot exchange rate to yen to get the value of the cross-currency option.

4. Abramowitz and Stegun's (1972) *Handbook of Mathematical Functions* (paragraph 26.2.17) gives the following polynomial approximation for the cumulative normal density function for variable x

$$y = \frac{1}{1 + .2316419x}$$

$$N(x) = 1 - Z(x)(b_1 y + b_2 y^2 + b_3 y^3 + b_4 y^4 + b_5 y^5) + e(x)$$

where

$b_1 = .319381530$
$b_2 = -.356563782$
$b_3 = 1.781477937$
$b_4 = -1.821255978$
$b_5 = 1.330274429$

If x is less than zero, the $N(x)$ is equal to $1 - N(x)$. The absolute value of the error term should be less small (i.e., $e(x)$ less than 7.5×10–8). The value of $Z(x)$ is given by

$$Z(x) = \frac{1}{\sqrt{2\pi}} e^{-x^2/2}$$

5. Strictly speaking, the BSGK theoretical value for a currency option is a function of only two variables, namely, the spot exchange rate and time to expiration. Volatility and interest rates play the role of "state variables," and it is in that context that one can speak of partial derivatives.

The BSGK Model

The Black–Scholes–Garman–Kohlhagen model for European currency call and put options is as follows

$$C = e^{-R_f \tau} S N(x + \sigma \sqrt{\tau}) - e^{-R_d \tau} K N(x)$$

$$P = e^{-R_f \tau} S(N(x + \sigma \sqrt{\tau}) - 1) - e^{-R_d \tau} K(N(x) - 1)$$

$$x = \frac{\ln\left(\dfrac{S}{K}\right) + \left(R_d - R_f - \dfrac{\sigma^2}{2}\right)\tau}{\sigma \sqrt{\tau}}$$

where:

C is the premium on a European currency call.
P is the premium on a European currency put.
S is the spot exchange rate, American quotation convention.
K is the strike, American quotation convention.
τ is the time in years to expiration.
R_f is the foreign currency interest rate.
R_d is the domestic interest rate.
σ is the standard deviation of currency returns.
$N(\ )$ is the cumulative normal distribution function.

Partial derivatives are as follows.

Delta

$$\delta_{\text{call}} \equiv \frac{\partial C}{\partial S} = e^{-R_f \tau} N(x + \sigma \sqrt{\tau})$$

$$\delta_{\text{put}} \equiv \frac{\partial P}{\partial S} = e^{-R_f \tau}\left(N(x + \sigma \sqrt{\tau}) - 1\right)$$

Gamma

$$\gamma_{\text{call}} = \gamma_{\text{put}} \equiv \frac{\partial^2 C}{\partial S^2} = \frac{e^{-R_f \tau} N'\left(x + \sigma\sqrt{\tau}\right)}{S\sigma\sqrt{\tau}}$$

Kappa

$$\kappa_{\text{call}} = \kappa_{\text{put}} \equiv \frac{C}{\partial \sigma} = e^{-R_d \tau} K\sqrt{\tau} N'(x)$$

Strike

$$\frac{\partial C}{\partial K} = -e^{-R_d \tau} N(x)$$

$$\frac{\partial P}{\partial K} = -e^{-R_d \tau}\left(N(x) - 1\right)$$

Time Decay

$$\theta_{\text{call}} \equiv \frac{\partial C}{\partial \tau} = -R_f e^{-R_f \tau} S N\left(x + \sigma\sqrt{\tau}\right) + R_d e^{-R_d \tau} K N(x) + \frac{e^{-R_d \tau}\sigma}{2\sqrt{\tau}} K N'(x)$$

$$\theta_{\text{put}} \equiv \frac{\partial P}{\partial \tau} = R_f e^{-R_f \tau} S\left(N\left(x + \sigma\sqrt{\tau}\right) - 1\right) - R_d e^{-R_d \tau} K\left(N(x) - 1\right)$$

$$- \frac{e^{-R_d \tau}\sigma}{2\sqrt{\tau}} K N'(x)$$

Domestic Interest Rate

$$\frac{\partial C}{\partial R_d} = \tau e^{-R_d \tau} K N(x)$$

$$\frac{\partial P}{\partial R_d} = \tau e^{-R_d \tau} K\left(N(x) - 1\right)$$

Foreign Interest Rate

$$\frac{\partial C}{\partial R_f} = -\tau e^{-R_f \tau} SN\left(x + \sigma\sqrt{\tau}\right)$$

$$\frac{\partial P}{\partial R_f} = -\tau e^{-R_f \tau} S\left(N\left(x + \sigma\sqrt{\tau}\right) - 1\right)$$

CHAPTER 7

Currency Option Applications

This chapter covers some common uses of currency options, beginning with a discussion of option implied volatility and a look at how options are quoted in the interbank market. Next, practical uses of currency options for risk management will be covered. Uses of options in trading with directional and volatility views will be presented. Finally, risk monitoring with applications from option pricing theory will be introduced.

THE NATURE OF CURRENCY OPTION VOLATILITY

Implied Volatility

In the discussion of the BSGK model in the preceding chapter, the volatility parameter, σ, was defined as the standard deviation of the log return of the spot exchange rate. This parameter is not directly observable in the marketplace, unlike the spot exchange rate and the interest rates on the domestic currency and foreign currency, all of which are quoted in the market. However if there is a quoted price for an option, the model can be used in reverse to reveal the market level of "implied volatility." No mathematical inverse to the BSGK equation is known to exist. Iterative procedures, such as Newton's method,[1] can be used to estimate implied volatility. The routine is as follows. First, assume a trial implied volatility and calculate the theoretical value for the option. Next, select a new candidate implied volatility based on the size of the "error" (defined as being equal to the difference between the known actual value of the option and the theoretical value). The size of the revision to the candidate implied volatility is generated by

$$\sigma_{n+1} = \sigma_n - \frac{C - C(\sigma_n)}{g'(\sigma_n)}$$

$$g'(\sigma_n) = -e^{-R_d \tau} K \sqrt{\tau} N'(x)$$

where

σ_{n+1} is the next candidate implied volatility on the $(n + 1)^{\text{th}}$ trial.

σ_n is the current candidate implied volatility.

C is the known value of the option.

$C(\sigma_n)$ is the theoretical value of the option priced at σ_n volatility.

$g'(\sigma_n)$ is a function of known BSGK parameters.

Next, a new theoretical option price is calculated along with its error. The process continues until the size of the error is judged too small to matter, whereupon the last candidate value is taken to be the implied volatility.

How Options Are Traded in the Interbank Market

Implied volatility plays a key role in the way currency options are traded in the interbank market. In the exchange-traded market for currency options, contract size, strike, and expiration are all standardized. This makes it is easy to identify options and to quote their prices in terms of cents and fractions thereof per contract. In contrast, little is standardized in the interbank option market. Options on practically every exchange rate exist. There is flexibility on the size of face and strike. Expiration can be set for any nonbank holiday. The process by which options are identified has been greatly simplified with the help of concepts from option pricing theory. In fast-moving markets, option traders need only specify the expiration date, the approximate delta, the exchange rate, whether the option is a put or a call, and the face amount. Quotations are made in terms of implied volatility, called "volatility" for short. There is a bid volatility and an ask volatility.

Straddles comprise the largest volume of trading in the interbank market. A straddle consists of a put and a call with the same strike, expiration date, and face amount. Straddle strikes are usually at-the-money forward. Exhibit 7–1 shows quotations for straddles on various exchange rates for terms to expiration ranging from one week to one year. Other expirations, even as short as overnight and as long as five years, are available in the market under normal conditions. The quote on one-month dollar/mark (USD/DEM) is 14.25 – 14.75. Some quotes are given "over" or in reference to dollar/mark. Examples in Exhibit 7–1 include the Swiss franc (USD/CHF) and British pound (GBP): One-month Swiss volatility in Exhibit 7–1 is quoted at 1.80 "over," meaning 16.05 – 16.55; one month sterling volatility is quoted as –5.45 "under," meaning 8.80 – 9.30.

To take a practical example, imagine a conversation between a customer and an option dealer concerning the straddle from Exhibit 6–1:

> *Customer:* One-month dollar/mark on 10 dollars a leg, please.
>
> *Dealer:* 14.25 to 14.75.
>
> *Customer:* Mine at 14.75.
>
> *Dealer:* At 14.75 I sell one-month dollar/mark, 10 dollars a leg.

The customer bought the straddle when he said "mine." As is the convention in the interbank market, "10 dollars" means 10 million dollars. Had he said "yours," it would have indicated that he was selling the straddle to the dealer. The straddle will be

EXHIBIT 7-1

Sample Currency Option Implied Volatility Quotations
Straddles, At-the-Money Forward Strikes, As of June 19, 1995

Exchange Rate	1-Week	1-Month	3-Month	1-Year	1-Month 25 Delta Risk Reversal
USD/DEM	14.00–16.00	14.25–14.75	13.75–14.25	12.70–13.00	.50–1.50 DEM calls over
USD/JPY	13.50–15.50	14.00–14.50	14.00 –14.50	13.60–14.00	2.00–3.00 JPY calls over
USD/CHF (over)	2.00	1.80	1.40	1.00	.50–1.50 CHF calls over
GBP (under)	–5.50––6.00	–5.45	–3.95––4.05	–1.95	Around
AUD	7.40–8.40	7.90–8.40	8.20–8.70	8.35–8.85	.20–.80 AUD puts over
USD/CAD	5.40–6.40	5.60–6.10	5.65–6.05	5.90–6.20	.00–.30 CAD puts over
DEM/JPY	7.75–9.75	8.90–9.40	9.50–10.00	10.10–10.50	.30–1.30 DEM puts over
DEM/CHF	3.50–5.00	4.00–4.50	4.00–4.50	4.00–4.50	.40–.85 DEM puts over
GBP/DEM	9.00–11.00	9.80–10.20	9.50–10.10	9.10–9.70	.60–1.20 GBP puts over
DEM/ITL	13.50–15.50	14.20–15.20	13.50–14.10	12.50–3.50	.75–1.75 DEM calls over
DEM/FRF	3.00–5.00	4.10–4.60	4.70–5.30	4.80–5.40	.60–1.50 DEM calls over

struck at-the-money forward automatically because no other strike was mentioned. As a consequence, the straddle will have little if any net delta.[2] This means that the dealer can buy or sell the straddle without having altered the exposure of his book to spot exchange rate risk.

Straddles are not the only thing traded in the interbank market. Consider the following conversation:

Customer: One-month 50 delta USD put/DEM call on 10 dollars, please.

Dealer: 14.25 to 14.75.

Customer: Mine at 14.75.

Dealer: Done at 14.75. I sell a one-month 50 delta mark call on 10 dollars at 14.75. One moment for details.

This trade by itself would impact the dealer's delta position. By selling the 50 delta USD put/DEM call on 10 dollars, the dealer would gain approximately 5 dollars of spot exposure. This is why it is the custom in the interbank market for option trades to nearly always come packaged with a spot currency (or "cash") hedge in an amount equal to the delta of the option.[3] In other words, every option trade consists of two trades, one for the option and one for the spot hedge. There is an implied commitment in this conversation for the customer to buy the USD put/DEM call plus do a spot currency transaction with the dealer to buy approximately five million of spot USD/DEM. Seen from the other perspective, the dealer commits to sell the option to the customer plus sell to the customer approximately five USD/DEM spot. The function of the spot currency trade is to make the option trade a "delta neutral" event for both parties.

It is customary for the dealer to work out the details (or "deets" in market slang) and present them to the customer for approval as soon as is practical after the commitment to do the trade is made. First, the exact expiration date is set. The expiration date must be a valid spot value date, so bank holidays are excluded. Next, the spot level and forward points are fixed, usually at midmarket levels (i.e., the mean of the bid and ask). Then the exact strike price is established. Now, the exact delta can be calculated. This could turn out to be significantly different from the approximate delta that was presumed when the customer asked for the quotation. In some cases, the strike is changed. Other times, the dealer may ask for or offer to adjust the implied volatility. When the dealer and the customer agree on all of these items, the option trade and the spot hedge trade are booked.

Customers can buy and sell options outright, that is, with no accompanying spot hedge, which is called trading on a "live" basis. In practice, dealers never trade on a live basis for their own book—dealers in the interbank market never buy and sell options without their accompanying spot hedges. When a customer wishes to buy or sell an option on a live basis, the dealer turns to the alternative of executing a cash hedge for himself in the interbank spot or forward market.

Currency options are also dealt in a whole variety of strategy packages. An example is the put spread discussed in the previous chapter. The spread consists of a long (or short) position in a USD put/DEM call plus a short (or long) position in a USD put/DEM call having the same expiration but different strike. For example, a one-month USD put/DEM call spread might consist of a long position in a 50 delta option plus a short position in a 25 delta option. The strike on the 50 delta from Exhibit 6–1 is 1.4081. The strike on the 25 delta option is 1.3650. A trading conversation might be as follows:

Customer: One-month USD put/DEM call spread, 50 delta by 25 delta on 10 dollars a leg, please.

Dealer: 14.50 choice for the 50 delta option and 15.20 to 15.80 for the 25 delta option

Here "14.50 choice" means that the 50 delta option is quoted "flat," meaning no bid–ask spread, at 14.50 – 14.50. This is a way of simplifying the quotation; a dealer's spread is applied only to the 25 delta option.

Another strategy that gets special quotation treatment is the risk reversal. A risk reversal consists of a long (or short) position in a call and a short (or long) position in a put having approximately the same delta, in absolute value terms. The rough equivalence of the option prices with symmetric deltas hints at the appeal of this strategy: it can easily be structured to have a zero up-front cost. There is a well-developed market for risk reversals of one-month and three-month expiration at 25 and 15 deltas in all the major exchange rates. For example, the one-month 25 delta risk reversal market could be quoted as follows:

> *Customer:* One-month USD/DEM 25 delta risk reversal on 10 dollars, please.

> *Dealer:* I am .50 to 1.50 for the mark calls over mark puts.

In the risk-reversal market, prices are quoted above and below some midlevel volatility. Assuming a midlevel volatility of 14.50, the dealer's quote means that he would (1) buy the USD put/DEM call for 15.00 and sell the USD call/DEM put for 14.50 or (2) sell the USD put/DEM call for 16.00 and buy the USD call/DEM put for 14.50. Said another way, the dealer is 14.50 choice for mark puts and 15 to 16 for mark calls. Note that the sterling risk reversal is quoted "around," which is a trader's term meaning no bias for either calls or puts.

THE BEHAVIOR OF IMPLIED VOLATILITY

As can be seen in Exhibit 7–1, option volatility varies across term to expiration. Volatility for a specific expiration date can be greatly influenced by the future calendar of economic events. Dates for the release of important economic data or when international trade talks, elections, central bank meetings, and economic and political summits are scheduled are apt to command comparatively higher levels of implied volatility.

Changes in implied volatility are not affected through parallel shifts in the volatility term structure. Short-dated volatilities are the most volatile, as can be seen by comparing the behavior of one-week (Exhibit 7–2) and six-month dollar/mark (Exhibit 7–3). The term structure of implied volatility can have practically any shape; it can be positive sloping, negative sloping, or flat. Xu and Taylor (1994) study the term structure of implied volatility using daily data on pounds, marks, Swiss francs, and yen

EXHIBIT 7-2

USD/DEM One-Week Implied Volatilities
January 1, 1994 to January 1, 1996

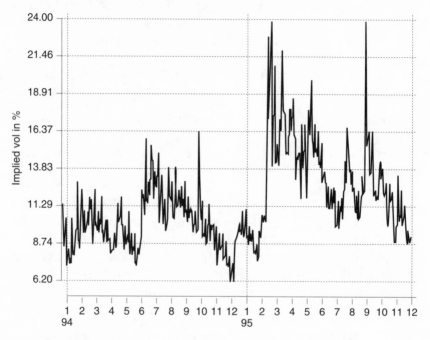

© Swiss Bank Corporation, 1995.

options that traded on the Philadelphia Stock Exchange from 1985–1989. They report:

> The term structure sometimes slopes upwards, sometimes downward, and its direction (up or down) frequently changes. The direction changes, on average, approximately once every two or three months. . . . The term structures of the pound, mark, Swiss franc, and yen at any moment in time have been very similar. (p. 73)

As a general rule, implied volatility rises whenever there is a good reason to believe that a sharp movement in spot rates is probable. Short-dated options are usually well bid in such an environment because they are rich in gamma. But when the excitement fades, short-dated volatility has been known to come

EXHIBIT 7–3

USD/DEM Six-Month Implied Volatilities
January 1, 1994 to January 1, 1996

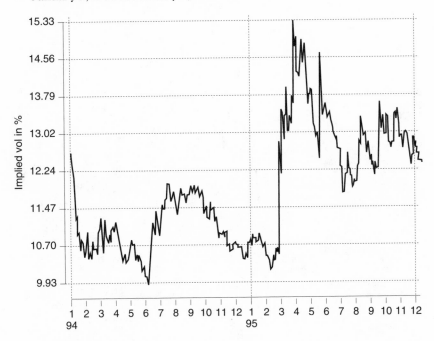

© Swiss Bank Corporation, 1995.

down quickly. A dramatic example of this is found in the behavior of dollar/mark volatility during the autumn 1992 European exchange rate mechanism crisis (Exhibit 7–4).

Implied volatility can possess subtle but usually ephemeral relationships with the level of the spot exchange rate. For example, consider the case of dollar/yen in 1994 when the spot rate broke down below the 100 level for the first time. The Bank of Japan publicly expressed its concern that the yen had appreciated too much against the dollar. The view in the market was that if the dollar were to sink any lower, the Bank of Japan, and possibly other central banks, would intervene to buy dollars against yen. These concerns were reflected in the pricing of dollar/yen options. The level of implied volatility rose for short-dated expi-

EXHIBIT 7–4

USD/DEM Implied Volatility During the 1992 ERM Crisis
One-Week and Three-Month Options

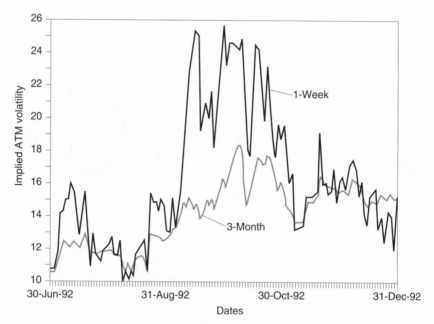

rations. More interesting was the fact that a relationship between the level of the spot rate and implied volatility became built into the market. Implied volatility rose whenever the dollar fell against the yen and fell back whenever the dollar rose.

Implied Volatility and Strike: Smiles and Skews

A well-known empirical finding, commonly referred to as the "smile," is that out-of-the-money currency options often trade for higher implied volatilities than at-the-money options. This is the case for 25 delta puts and calls for all but one currency on June 19, 1995, as shown in Exhibit 7–1.

What is the reason for the smile? The best answer is that it is an artifact of the leptokurtic nature of currency returns, as was described in Chapter 1. Where there is an abundance of outliers, as with the leptokurtic distribution of currency returns, low delta options are particularly interesting to traders seeking to make low-cost, high-leverage speculative bets.

The smile in currency implied volatility is sometimes non-symmetrical (i.e., a "crooked smile"). This phenomenon is called the skew.[4] Traders measure the skew by comparing the volatility of same delta calls and puts, in other words, by examining the risk-reversal market. Some skew is evident in the quotations in Exhibit 7–1, as of June 19, 1995, but it varies by currency. Sterling, being quoted "around," has no skew on that day. Dollar/mark is skewed .50 – 1.50 for mark calls over mark puts. Dollar/yen is heavily skewed in favor of yen calls; the risk-reversal market is quoted 2.00 – 3.00 for yen calls over yen puts. Skew can change from one day to the next. Skew can also be a function of institutional factors. In the case of dollar/yen, there normally is a preference for yen calls, which is alleged to result from the situation of the Japanese exporters. The exporters are naturally long dollars, which they intend to convert to yen at some time. One favorite trade of theirs is to buy out-of-the-money dollar puts/yen calls and to sell dollar calls/yen puts for zero or near zero cost. The combination of this risk reversal with their long dollars creates a "collared" long dollar position.

Empirical Volatility and the Validity of the BSGK Model

The BSGK model assumes the volatility of spot exchange rates in log returns to be a known constant. From the preceding discussion, there should be no doubt that neither actual nor implied volatility is constant. In fact, a large part of option trading is trying to forecast movements in implied volatility and changes in volatility smiles and skews—yet practitioners apply the BSGK model with little or no modification. Traders treat implied volatility as a variable, despite the potentially serious theoretical contradiction that nonconstant volatility represents. How big of a problem is this? In the context of quoting and trading options, it is not serious. On the most basic level, the BSGK model is a language for quoting options: Dealers make bid and ask quotes in terms of volatility, which the BSGK formula transforms into real money prices. The issue becomes serious in the realm of risk management. The question is whether the model's risk parameters, meaning delta, gamma, and kappa, are biased because of the misspecification of volatility as a constant. Financial theoreticians have recently given attention to two new classes of option models that do not require constant variance assumption.

One of the new of option models, called the stochastic volatility model, explicitly treats volatility as a random variable. Key works are by Chesney and Scott (1989), Hull and White (1987), Scott (1987), Stein and Stein (1991), Heston (1983), and Ball and Roma (1994). Part of the appeal for treating volatility as a random variable is the obvious compatibility with the empirical finding that sample currency returns are leptokurtic. In addition, recent empirical work by Jacquier, Polson, and Rossi (1994) demonstrated that stochastic volatility models successfully describe time series behavior of the underlying exchange rates.

Stochastic volatility models postulate that option prices must satisfy a fundamental partial differential equation in two state variables, the asset price and volatility (Garman 1976). Unlike the asset price, volatility is not traded in the marketplace. This means that a risk premium on volatility must explicitly enter the partial differential equation. Finding solutions to the equation has been difficult. Hull and White were able to derive a power series technique to value stochastic volatility options by assuming that increments to volatility and the underlying asset prices are uncorrelated. Stein and Stein developed an analytical approach using Fourier inversion methods, also assuming zero correlation. Heston proposed using Fourier methods but does not require the zero correlation assumption. Chesney and Scott formulated a stochastic volatility model for currency options under the premise that volatility is mean-reverting. Using Monte Carlo simulation, they tested their model on dollar/Swiss option and spot exchange rates. The results were somewhat disappointing because the stochastic volatility model seems to have no better explanatory power than the BSGK model refreshed daily with current estimates of volatility.

A second option model specifies log currency returns as a mixed jump–diffusion process. In a mixed jump–diffusion process, the time series follows some orderly stochastic process, such as a diffusion process, but is subject to random jumps. The jump component itself is specified as a separate stochastic process, usually as the Poisson process. The mixed jump–diffusion process is compatible with leptokurtic currency returns, as is the random variance model. This is because the random jumps are a possible source for the relatively abundant outliers. Early in the development of option theory, Merton (1976) derived an option pricing model based on the mixed jump–diffusion process. Jorion (1988) adapted Merton's model for currency options. Jorion's empirical work showed that the Merton model can contribute to the understanding of low-delta currency options beyond the capacity of the BSGK model.

One central interest is whether either of the two new models can explain the observed volatility smile. In theory, either the stochastic volatility model (see Ball and Roma 1994) or the jump–diffusion model could account for the phenomenon of a symmetrical smile. Taylor and Xu (1994) were able to trace a portion of the smile effect to stochastic volatility. Taking the process to the next logical step, Bates (1994b) proposed a "nested" stochastic-volatility/jump–diffusion process model that he tested with trading data on the IMM deutschemark futures options. He reported:

> The stochastic volatility model cannot explain the "volatility smile" evidence of implicit excess kurtosis, except under parameters implausible given the time series properties of implied volatilities. Jump fears can explain the "volatility smile," and are consistent with an 8% jump in the $/DM futures price observed over 1984–91.

In spite of all of the new theoretical developments, not many practitioners have made use of the new models. The common sentiment is that the new models that have appeared to date are all too complicated or too costly or not marginally worthwhile to implement in the crush and stress of the option trading environment. One complaint surrounds the need to quantify the new parameters. Examples are the speed to which stochastic volatility reverts to its mean in the random variance model and the probability of a noncontinuous jump taking place in the Merton model. None of these parameters are easy to estimate; the associated errors in measurement may induce potentially dangerous biases that could be even more pernicious than the problem of forcing nonconstant variance into the BSGK framework.

OPTION APPLICATIONS
FOR RISK CONTROL

One practical use of the BSGK model is for the determination of strike levels for put protection and collar protection strategies of the sort that were discussed in Chapter 6. European exercise options are preferred for use in risk-control strategies because early exercise is not deemed important.

Put Protection Programs

Suppose the objective of the program is to protect a U.S. dollar–based investor who has a long exposure to the German mark by virtue of owning a portfolio of German securities. The maximum foreign exchange translation loss that can be tolerated is denoted as d, which is a fraction of the total exposure. Another way to express this is to say that the floor is equal to $(1 - d)$. A maximum tolerable loss of 5 percent corresponds to a floor equal to 95 percent. If put options were free, a strike set at 95 percent would guarantee the floor. Options are never free, so most investors count the premium as part of the floor. The problem is how to find the strike that guarantees the floor, counting the cost of the put.

Another question concerns the source of the funds used to pay for the put option. Externally funded programs use outside funds to pay for the put. Internally funded programs meet the cost of the put with resources taken from the portfolio. This introduces a circular element to the problem: The greater the desired level of protection, the more expensive the put; since the put premium comes out of the portfolio, the more expensive the put, the less there is of underlying exposure to protect.

Externally Funded Put Programs

Even though the cost of the put is not taken out of the portfolio, it is still counted against the floor (Black and Rouhani 1987). Define the following terms:

S_0 is the spot exchange rate (American quotation convention) at the start of the program.

S_T is the spot exchange rate at the expiration of the program.

V_0 is the initial value of the portfolio measured in the domestic currency; the initial value of the portfolio measured in foreign currency is equal to V_0/S_0.

V_T is equal to the initial value of the portfolio, V_0, revalued at time T for exchange rate movements—but not for local market price changes. V_T can be expressed as

$$V_T = V_0 \frac{S_T}{S_0}$$

The relationship of V_T to d is:

$$\frac{V_T - V_0}{V_0} > -d$$

or

$$V_T - V_0 > -dV_0$$

Define $P_0(K^*)$ as the initial value of the currency put, which grants the right, but not the obligation, to sell V_0/S_0 units of foreign currency in exchange for strike K^* units of domestic currency. The expiration value of the put is given by:

$$\mathrm{MAX}\left[0, K^* - V_0 \frac{S_T}{S_0}\right] = \mathrm{MAX}[0, K^* - V_T]$$

The program is a success if the following floor condition is satisfied at expiration:

Floor Condition

$$V_T - V_0 + \mathrm{MAX}[0, K^* - V_T] - P_0(K^*) > -dV_0$$

$P_0(K^*)$ is a function of only one variable, K^*, because all of the other option parameters can be taken as constants. Newton's method can be used to iteratively search for the value of K^* that satisfies the floor constraint.

For example, suppose that a U.S. dollar investor desires protection for an exposure to the German mark. The horizon is one year and the maximum loss due to foreign exchange, d, is set to 5 percent, making the floor 95 percent. Assume implied volatility equal to 13 percent, U.S. dollar interest rate of 5.88 percent, and German mark interest rate of 4.56 percent. The program can be accomplished with a put having a strike equal to 98.78 percent of the initial spot exchange rate. The put should cost 3.78 percent of the exposure to the mark. To check the results, work in terms of an exposure to 100 DEM when spot is equal to 1.4100. This would make the initial value of the portfolio equal to $70.9220 and the floor equal to $67.3759. The put would cost $2.6809 and be struck at 1.4274. If, one year later, the dollar has risen to 1.6000, the value of the protected portfolio would equal the following:

1. Value of the portfolio (100 DEM)		$62.5000
2. Payoff from put		$ 7.5574
3. Less cost of put		($ 2.6809)
	Total	$67.3766

This confirms that the program would be effective.

Exhibit 7–5 shows sample results from this method (see "externally funded put") for a variety of volatilities, floors, and interest rates for one-year programs. These put programs are expressed in terms of percentages of the initial value of the portfolio to be protected. Strikes are percentages of the initial spot exchange rate.

Internally Funded Put Programs

Internally funded put programs subtract the cost of the put from the exposure that is to be protected. The analysis is more difficult because the more that is spent to protect the foreign exchange exposure, the less there is to protect. Define the following terms:

A_0 is the initial value of a portfolio A, which contains foreign securities denominated in foreign currency. (If the put program were not implemented, 100 percent of the initial funds would go into A.)

EXHIBIT 7-5

Basic Strategies for Risk Control
One-Year Programs

Option Parameters				Externally Funded Put		Internally Funded Put			Zero-Cost Collar Program			
Sigma	Floor	R_d	R_f	Premium	Strike	Premium	Strike	N	Put Premium	Put Strike	Call Premium	Call Strike
10.0%	90%	7%	9%	1.2%	91.2%	1.2%	91.0%	0.988	1.0%	90.0%	1.0%	107.3%
10.0%	90%	8%	8%	0.8%	90.8%	0.8%	90.7%	0.993	0.7%	90.0%	0.7%	111.7%
10.0%	90%	9%	7%	0.5%	90.5%	0.5%	90.4%	0.995	0.4%	90.0%	0.4%	116.3%
10.0%	95%	7%	9%	4.3%	99.3%	4.0%	98.8%	0.961	2.4%	95.0%	2.4%	101.4%
10.0%	95%	8%	8%	2.7%	97.7%	2.5%	97.4%	0.975	1.7%	95.0%	1.7%	105.6%
10.0%	95%	9%	7%	1.7%	96.7%	1.6%	96.6%	0.984	1.3%	95.0%	1.3%	110.0%
12.5%	90%	7%	9%	2.2%	92.2%	2.1%	91.9%	0.979	1.6%	90.0%	1.6%	107.5%
12.5%	90%	8%	8%	1.6%	91.6%	1.5%	91.3%	0.985	1.2%	90.0%	1.2%	111.9%
12.5%	90%	9%	7%	1.1%	91.1%	1.0%	90.9%	0.990	0.9%	90.0%	0.9%	116.6%
12.5%	95%	7%	9%	6.3%	101.3%	5.9%	100.6%	0.945	3.2%	95.0%	3.2%	101.4%
12.5%	95%	8%	8%	4.2%	99.2%	4.0%	98.8%	0.961	2.5%	95.0%	2.6%	105.7%
12.5%	95%	9%	7%	2.9%	97.9%	2.8%	97.7%	0.973	2.0%	95.0%	2.0%	110.2%
15.0%	90%	7%	9%	3.5%	93.5%	3.2%	92.9%	0.969	2.3%	90.0%	2.3%	107.6%
15.0%	90%	8%	8%	2.6%	92.6%	2.4%	92.2%	0.977	1.9%	90.0%	1.9%	112.2%
15.0%	90%	9%	7%	1.9%	91.9%	1.8%	91.6%	0.982	1.5%	90.0%	1.5%	116.9%
15.0%	95%	7%	9%	8.6%	103.6%	7.8%	102.4%	0.927	4.1%	95.0%	4.1%	101.5%
15.0%	95%	8%	8%	6.0%	101.0%	5.6%	100.3%	0.947	3.4%	95.0%	3.4%	105.8%
15.0%	95%	9%	7%	4.4%	99.4%	4.1%	98.9%	0.960	2.8%	95.0%	2.8%	110.4%

N represents fractional units of portfolio A.

A_T is the value of portfolio A_0 revalued for movements in exchange rates as of the expiration of the program

$$A_T = A_0 \frac{S_T}{S_0}$$

$P_0(K^*)$ is the initial value of the currency put that grants the right but not the obligation to sell A_0/S_0 units of foreign currency for K^* units of domestic currency. At expiration, the put will be worth

$$\text{MAX}\left[0, K^* - A_0 \frac{S_T}{S_0}\right] = \text{MAX}[0, K^* - A_T]$$

The program must satisfy two conditions:

1. As required by the budget constraint, the initial total assets, V_0, must be invested in the N fractional units of portfolio A. To protect that investment, N fractional put units will be purchased. The total cost must not exceed the value of the total assets:

$$V_0 = N \times A_0 + N \times P_0(K^*)$$

2. The floor constraint requires that the program keep the investment above the desired floor:

$$N\left[(A_T - A_0) + \text{MAX}[0, K^* - A_T] - P_0(K^*)\right] > -dV_0$$

Using the same parameters from the previous example, an internally funded 95 percent floor program can be implemented with $P_0(K^*)$ = 3.5839 percent, K^* = 98.40459 percent, and N = .9654. Spot dollar/mark is assumed to be 1.4100. The prices of the put and its strike are

$$P_0(K^*) = 100 \times \frac{1}{1.4100} \times (.035839) = \$2.5418$$

$$K^* = \frac{1}{1.4100} \times .9840459 = .697905$$

The strike is equal to 1.43286, European quotation. At the spot exchange rate 1.4100 (.70922 American convention), the 95 percent floor equates to a spot rate of 1.4842 (or .673759 American convention). The budget constraint is satisfied because

1. Invest in portfolio $100 \times (.9654) \times (.70922)$ = 68.4681
2. Invest in put $100 \times (.9654) \times (.025418)$ = 2.4538
                                                   Total   70.9219

To check the floor constraint, assume that at expiration, the exchange rate has moved up sharply, say to 1.6000. That would make the whole portfolio worth $62.50, the whole put worth $7.2905, and the protected portfolio worth

.9654 shares in A $(.9654) \times \$62.500$ = \$60.3375
.9654 put options $(.9654) \times \$7.2905$ = \$ 7.0382
                                       Total   \$67.3757

This meets the desired floor of 95 percent.

Exhibit 7–5 shows values for $P_0(K^*)$, K^*, and N for various implied volatilities, levels of interest rates, and two floors, 95 percent and 90 percent for one-year programs. These can be generated from a Newton algorithm constructed to find strikes, put prices, and values of N that satisfy both the budget constraint and floor condition within a specified margin of error. As can be seen in Exhibit 7–5, the cost of a put protection program is higher for discount currencies. This is a simple fact of interest parity. The market incorporates the interest rate spread in option prices just as it does in forward exchange rates.

Zero-Premium Collar Programs

In a protective collar program, the cost of a currency put is offset in whole or in part by the sale of a currency call. Where the premiums of the put and call exactly match, the program is called a zero-premium collar. Although such a strategy has a net cash flow of zero at inception, there is an opportunity cost to consider since the upside profit potential in the zone above the call's strike is forfeited. The zero premium dollar is therefore not truly costless.

Using the same parameters as in the above example, a put struck at 95 percent can be purchased for the same premium as a call struck at 108.68 percent. At a spot rate of 1.4100, the USD call/DEM put would be struck at 1.4842, and the USD put/DEM call would be struck at 1.2974. This example assumes that the put and the call can be priced with the same volatility; in other words, that there is no smile or skew. Moreover, the dealer spread is ignored.

The right-hand block of Exhibit 7–5 contains call strikes for zero-premium collar programs. These collars are priced using a flat volatility structure, meaning that the same implied volatility is applied to both the put and the call. The presence of a skew in implied volatility can have important implications for collar pricing. If calls are bid over puts, the purchaser of a collar will benefit from being able to set a higher strike on the call, thereby giving up less upside profit potential. But if low delta puts are expensive relative to calls, the collar will look less attractive because the call strike will have to be lowered to make the premium equal to zero.

Zero-premium collars may seem to have minimal cash flow implications. This is because there is no initial premium, since the put premium is covered by the sale of the call. No portion of the investment in the underlying portfolio need be sacrificed, as had to happen with the internally funded put program. Assuming that any foreign exchange gains or losses on the underlying foreign currency exposure are accrued but not realized, one of the following cases must apply at expiration:

1. The spot exchange rate is below the put strike. The put expires in-the-money, which provides positive cash flow that offsets all or at least a portion of the accrued but unrealized foreign exchange loss on the portfolio.

2. The spot exchange rate is above the put strike but below its initial level. The put is worthless, and there is an unprotected, accrued (but unrealized) foreign exchange rate loss on the portfolio.

3. The spot exchange rate is above its initial level but below the call strike. There is an accrued (but unrealized) exchange rate gain on the portfolio, and both the put and the call are worthless.

4. The spot exchange rate is above the call strike. There is an accrued (but unrealized) gain on the portfolio and a realized loss on the short call, which expires in-the-money. Consequently, some portion of the underlying portfolio may have to be liquidated.

EXPRESSING DIRECTIONAL VIEWS USING CURRENCY OPTIONS

While not everyone wants to be in the business of speculating in foreign exchange, some knowledge about how directional bets are made can be useful in the context of understanding the foreign exchange market. A directional bet in foreign exchange is any position that seeks to profit from correctly anticipating the direction of future movements in the exchange rate. Directional trading is actively pursued by commercial and investment banks, hedge funds, futures and options floor traders, and private speculators. Some corporate treasurers conduct active hedging programs that should be classified as directional trading.

Cash Markets Trading

Trading to express directional views on foreign exchange is conventionally done by taking positions in the cash market. A trader who is bearish on the dollar with respect to the mark could sell dollars/buy marks on a spot basis. For example, a trader might sell 10 million dollars (or equivalently buy 14.1 million marks) at 1.4100. Once established, a spot position may be held indefinitely, provided that it is possible to roll the position, for example, with spot/next or tom/next swaps.

What happens if the trader is wrong about the direction? Losses on an unprotected spot position can mount up quickly. It is not unheard of for dollar/mark to move by two big figures in brief periods of time. A move of this size would equate to a loss of $139,860 on the 10 million dollar spot position (and by today's standards of speculation in foreign exchange, 10 million dollars is a small position). For purposes of risk control, spot positions are rarely established without some companion stop-loss order. Such a stop might be at 1.4150 in the example. If the dollar rallies and the stop is executed at trigger level, the loss on the position would be limited to only 50 DEM pips (about $35,335).

It is worth noting that in practice, stop-losses are executed in moving markets. Specifically defined, a stop-loss order is an order to buy (or sell) at the market rate if the market trades at or above the stop-loss rate for a buy stop (at or below for a sell stop). In the above example, if 1.4150 is paid in the market, the buy stop would be "elected," or become a live order to buy at the market rate. If the next price in the market is 1.4155 bid, 1.4160 offer, there would be a slippage of 20 percent, which would create an incremental loss of $7,038 over the intended loss of $35,335.

Option Trades

Options provide different ways to trade directional views. In the most simple case, a bearish directional view can be expressed with a put, such as the USD put/DEM call in Exhibit 6–1 and Exhibit 6–2A.

From the perspective of a cash trader, exercise of the put would provide an advantageous short-dollar position on expiration day, provided that the exchange rate is below the strike. If the exchange rate is actually above the strike at expiration, no short position would be initiated because the option would expire out-of-the-money. The trader in effect would have been protected by the option; the worst-case scenario is that the premium would be lost.

An option trader's perspective is multidimensional. He is interested not only in directional moves but also in volatility, the passage of time, and option dynamics. Consider the example of the one-month USD put/DEM call analyzed in Exhibit 7–6. Because the strike is set to the at-the-money forward level (1.4081), the option has high levels of gamma, theta, and kappa, given its term to expiration. The option premium is .012294 USD pips per one unit of mark face, for a total of $173,115, or equivalently, 0.024409 DEM pips per USD of face. The delta of the option is approximately equal to 50, which means that the option behaves like a short five million USD cash position in response to local spot exchange rate movements. Spot movements also affect the delta. If the value of the dollar moves up, the delta will fall. For instance, at

USD Put/DEM Call, 32 Days to Expiration

	Units	Option	Comparative Statics		Comparative Statics	
			USD Down 2%	USD Down 1%	USD Up 1%	USD Up 2%
Face	USD	$10,000,000	$10,000,000	$10,000,000	$10,000,000	$10,000,000
Face	DEM	14,081,000	14,081,000	14,081,000	14,081,000	14,081,000
Spot	European	1.4100	1.3824	1.3960	1.4242	1.4388
Strike	European	1.4081	1.4081	1.4081	1.4081	1.4081
Parameters						
Volatility		14.75%	14.75%	14.75%	14.75%	14.75%
Days to expiry		32	32	32	32	32
Interest rate DEM		4.46%	4.46%	4.46%	4.46%	4.46%
Interest rate USD		6.00%	6.00%	6.00%	6.00%	6.00%
Pricing						
Unit price	USD pips	0.012294	0.020752	0.016222	0.009037	0.006401
Unit price	DEM pips	0.024409	0.040394	0.031889	0.018124	0.012969
Total price	USD	$173,115	$292,215	$228,421	$127,255	$90,136
Price change	Percent		68.80%	31.95%	−26.49%	−47.93%
Risk Measures						
Delta	USD	($5,067,194)	($6,800,609)	($5,962,514)	($4,158,559)	($3,283,877)
Gamma	USD	$649,865	$592,353	$636,447	$629,638	$577,922
Kappa	USD (1% vol)	$11,749	$10,708	$11,506	$11,384	$10,450
Theta	USD/day	$2,888	$2,708	$2,864	$2,772	$2,525

spot level of 1.4388, the delta is 33. If the value of the dollar falls, the delta will rise. At spot level of 1.3824, the delta is equal to 68. Changes in delta can be approximated by knowing the gamma of the option. The initial value of gamma is equivalent to $649,865, corresponding to a big-figure move in spot. Kappa, the measure of the risk associated with changes in implied volatility, is initially equal to $11,769 for a one percentage point rise (e.g., from 14.75 percent to 15.75 percent). Theta, the measure of daily time decay, indicates that the cost of holding the option for one extra day, specifically from day 32 to day 31, is $2,888.

Convexity is also evident, which is another way to say that the option has positive gamma. The middle and right-hand panels of Exhibit 7–6 show the comparative statics for plus and minus 1 percent and 2 percent movements in the value of the dollar relative to the mark. One way to understand convexity is to look for asymmetry in up and down moves. A 1 percent down move (USD/DEM falling from 1.4100 to 1.3960) adds 31.95 percent to the value of the option. But a 1 percent up move (USD/DEM rising from 1.4100 to 1.4242) produces smaller absolute value loss equal to 26.49 percent. This is magnified in the case of 2 percent moves: The down move enhances the option price by 68.80 percent, but the up move lowers it by 47.93 percent.

The behavior of an option changes as it ages. Exhibit 7–7 displays at-the-money USD puts/DEM calls for differing terms to expiration. All of the options have deltas approximately equal to 50, but gamma is significantly greater for short-dated options. Theta is smaller for the long-dated options, as one would expect given the mathematical relationship between gamma and theta (see Chapter 6). Exhibit 7–7 shows that sensitivity to implied volatility, measured by kappa, rises with term to expiration. Although short-dated options experience only small price movements when implied volatility rises or falls, the price movement for long-dated options can be quite substantial. This is a little tricky because implied volatility for the far dates does not fluctuate nearly as much as for the near dates.

Sometimes being correct about direction is not enough. Timing of execution and choice of expiration are crucial elements to success in option trading. If the spot move takes place immediately, a short-dated option will be a success—the high level of

EXHIBIT 7-7

USD Put/DEM Call, Various Terms to Expiration
At-the-Money Forward; As of June 19, 1995

	Units	1 Week USD Put/ DEM Call	1 Month USD Put/ DEM Call	3 Months USD Put/ DEM Call	1 Year USD Put/ DEM Call
Face	USD	$10,000,000	$10,000,000	$10,000,000	$10,000,000
Face	DEM	14,096,000	14,081,000	14,045,000	13,915,000
Spot	European	1.4100	1.4100	1.4100	1.4100
Strike (ATMF)	European	1.4096	1.4081	1.4045	1.3915
Parameters					
Volatility		16.00%	14.75%	14.25%	13.00%
Days to expiry		7	32	92	365
Interest rate DEM		4.56%	4.46%	4.50%	4.56%
Interest rate USD		6.06%	6.00%	6.06%	5.88%
Pricing					
Unit price	USD pips	0.006251	0.012294	0.020004	0.035102
Unit price	DEM pips	0.012424	0.024409	0.039614	0.068871
Total price	USD	$88,110	$173,115	$280,951	$488,444
Risk Measures					
Delta	USD	($5,040,273)	($5,067,194)	($5,086,418)	($5,029,885)
Gamma	USD	$1,284,891	$649,865	$393,729	$209,326
Kappa	USD (1% vol)	$5,518	$11,749	$19,721	$37,597
Theta	USD/day	$6,496	$2,888	$1,691	$763

gamma will leverage the trade. However, the trader could be correct about the future direction of the exchange rate but be wrong as to when the market actually moves. In particular, the move might very well occur after the short-dated option expires. Buying a longer-dated option increases the probability of capturing the move. However, longer-dated options are more expensive, and they have less gamma than short-dated options. If the anticipated move happens early on, the profit on the trade will be considerably less with the long-dated option than what could have been achieved with a short-dated, high-gamma option.

Suppose the trader proves to be correct about the move in the exchange rate. Now a new set of decisions must be addressed. Should the option be sold, or should it be held to expiration? Should the trader hedge the paper profit by doing cash trades? In the example of the dollar put, the trader might try to lock up some of the gain if spot falls below the strike by buying some dollars (i.e., long dollars/short marks). If the entire face of the option is cash hedged, no further participation in downward dollar moves would be possible. But further gains could be realized in the event of a reversal in spot direction, meaning the situation where the exchange rate were to rise back up above the strike.

This is because at prices below the strike, the long cash position would be exactly offset by the identical short cash position behavior of the in-the-money USD put. At spot prices above the strike, however, the put would not be exercised. The long cash position initiated below the strike would no longer be neutralized by an in-the-money USD put and would therefore provide profit at all spot prices above the strike. The act of covering the full face amount of the USD put in the cash market effectively changes the USD put into a USD call.

Spread Trades

Spreads are popular directional trades. A bear spread consists of a long position in a put plus a short position in a lower delta put. A bull spread consists of a long position in a call and a short position in a lower delta call.

The USD put/DEM call spread in Exhibit 7–8 provides an alternative way to express the dollar bearish view. This spread

EXHIBIT 7-8

USD Put/DEM Call Spread, 32 Days to Expiration
As of June 19, 1995

	Units	Components		Spread	Comparative Statics	
		Long USD Put/ DEM Call	Short USD Put/ DEM Call	USD Put/ DEM Call Spread	Spot Down 2%	Spot Up 2%
Face	USD	$10,000,000	($10,000,000)			
Face	DEM	14,081,000	(13,650,000)			
Spot	European	1.4100	1.4100		1.3818	1.4382
Strike	European	1.4081	1.3650			
Parameters						
Volatility		14.50%	15.80%			
Days to expiry		32	32			
Interest rate DEM		4.46%	4.46%			
Interest rate USD		6.00%	6.00%			
Pricing						
Unit price	USD pips	0.012098	−0.005090	0.007008	0.010814	0.003970
Unit price	DEM pips	0.024020	−0.009796	0.014224	0.021632	0.008185
Total price	USD	$170,352	($69,473)	$100,879	$156,551	$56,911
Price change	Percent				55.19%	−43.59%
Risk Measures						
Delta	USD	($5,065,710)	$2,596,878	($2,468,831)	($2,705,065)	($1,857,431)
Gamma	USD	661,075	(494,036)	167,039	(7,915)	250,852
Kappa	USD (1% vol)	$11,749	($9,275)	$2,474	($747)	$4,121
Theta	USD/day	$2,843	($2,381)	$462	($304)	$873

consists of a long position in the 50 delta put (struck at 1.4081) and a short position in a 25 delta put (struck at 1.3650). Exhibit 7–9A shows the behavior of the spread one month before expiration. Selling the 25 delta option limits the possible gains were the dollar to fall below the strike. For a cash market trader, selling the 25 delta option represents a view that the strike level of 1.3650 is the furthest level to which the dollar could drop during the course of the option.

A spread trade is more conservative than an outright option purchase because the premium cost, and therefore the maximum loss, is lower. The maximum loss on the dollar put spread is .014224 DEM pips (or $100,879) compared to .0244 DEM pips (or $173,289), with the latter representing the cost of buying the 50 delta option.

Seen from another view, the proceeds from selling the low delta option in a spread pay for part of the cost of buying the

EXHIBIT 7–9A

USD Put/DEM Call Spread, 32 Days to Expiration
Strikes at 1.4081 and 1.3650

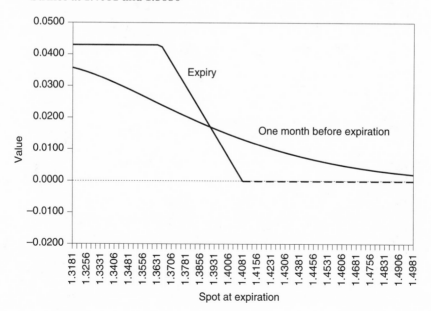

high delta option. Lowering the entry cost of the position gives the trader some additional leverage.

Before expiration, the spread will behave differently from an outright position in an option. Exhibit 7–8 shows that the spread has a smaller gamma and kappa, and a diminished rate of time decay compared to owning the 50 delta option outright, all of which are consequences of the short position in the 25 delta option.

Risk Reversals

A risk reversal is a more aggressive strategy than either an outright option or a spread. An example is the 25 delta risk reversal (see Exhibit 7–9B and Exhibit 7–10), which is composed of a long position in a 25 delta USD put/DEM call and a short position in a 25 delta USD call/DEM put. In a risk reversal, the

E X H I B I T 7–9B

USD/DEM 25 Delta Risk Reversal, 32 Days to Expiration

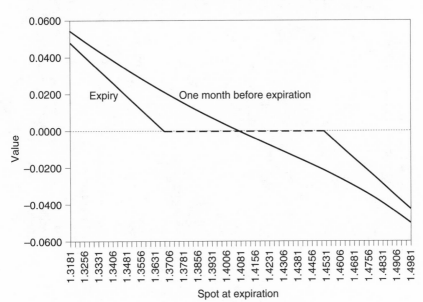

E X H I B I T 7-10

USD/DEM 25 Delta Risk Reversal, 32 Days to Expiration
As of June 19, 1995

| | Units | Components | | USD/DEM Risk Reversal | Comparative Statics | |
		Long USD Put/ DEM Call	Short USD Call/ DEM Put		Spot Down 2% Risk Reversal	Spot Up 2% Risk Reversal
Face	USD	$10,000,000	($10,000,000)			
Face	DEM	13,675,000	(14,525,000)			
Spot	European	1.4100	1.4100		1.3824	1.4388
Strike	European	1.3675	1.4525			
Parameters						
Volatility		14.50%	16.00%			
Days to expiry		32	32			
Interest rate DEM		4.46%	4.46%			
Interest rate USD		6.00%	6.00%			
Pricing						
Unit price	USD pips	0.00454	−0.00508	−0.0005	0.0069	−0.0077
Unit price	DEM pips	0.00875	−0.01040	−0.0017	0.0127	−0.0164
Total price	USD	$62,027	($73,736)	($11,709)	$91,871	($114,017)
Risk Measures						
Delta	USD	$2,536,107	($2,476,940)	($5,013,048)	(5,554,193)	(5,274,697)
Gamma	USD	531,750	(475,926)	55,824	326,336	(226,882)
Kappa	USD (1% vol)	$9,178	($9,628)	($450)	$4,637	($5,606)
Theta	USD/day	$2,170	($2,285)	($115)	$1,110	($1,300)

218

deltas of the put and call are approximately equal in absolute value, by definition. The initial delta of the 25 delta risk reversal is actually equal to 50 because it gets 25 delta from each option. Risk reversals are usually dealt at close to zero cost—the premiums on the two options net each other out—except where there is a pronounced volatility skew.

Exhibit 7–10 analyzes the risk reversal. Initially, the trade has virtually no gamma, no kappa, and no theta. This is because the long and short options are effectively mirror images that serve to cancel each other. If spot moves decidedly in the direction of one or the other strikes, the risk profile of the risk reversal will be dominated by the personality of whichever option then has the greater delta. Risk reversals are popular because they are big winners if the trader's directional view is correct. They are zero-cost strategies that can produce unlimited gains. But if the directional view is wrong, and the spot rate approaches the short strike, major losses may be in the offing.

EXPRESSING VIEWS ON VOLATILITY

Option strategies can be devised to express views on either future levels of implied volatility or on the actual volatility of exchange rates. What makes trading volatility complicated is the subtle interplay between these two concepts. There is no simple or direct relationship between actual and implied volatility. For example, a high level of actual volatility does not imply that options should be trading at high levels of implied volatility. On the other hand, some periods of high implied volatility have been associated with market crises, where there has been the potential for a large move in exchange rates. On a more subtle note, periods of high implied volatility can be especially dangerous because they tend to end abruptly once a large move in exchange rates has taken place.

Straddles and Strangles

Straddles and strangles were presented in Chapter 6 as simple ways to trade volatility. Long positions in straddles and strangles are long actual volatility as well as long implied volatility.

The actual volatility bet is that the spot exchange will move in either direction by a sufficient amount to recover the cost of the position. Straddles and strangles are also long implied volatility because they are positive kappa. If the value of implied volatility rises, the value of both the straddle and strangle will rise. Exhibit 7–11 shows the effect of 1 percent up and down moves in implied volatility on the value of the straddle.

The ideal situation for a long straddle or long strangle position is a sharp move in the spot level accompanied by a rise in implied volatility. This sometimes happens when a currency suddenly becomes the target of speculative attention. But some caution is warranted, as has already been mentioned: Implied volatility has been known to drop following a large move in the spot rate. This was the case in the 1992 exchange rate mechanism crisis. Implied volatility immediately fell once the mark crosses had moved and sterling and the lira had departed from the ERM (see Exhibit 7–4).

A short position in a straddle or a strangle is short actual volatility. The seller hopes that the damage done by movement in the spot exchange rate will not exceed the premium that was collected. The position is also short implied volatility because it is short kappa.

Gamma Trades

A gamma trade consists of a long position in a short-term option with an accompanying cash hedge (or "delta hedge") that makes the total position initially delta-neutral. Exhibit 7–12 shows an example of a gamma trade that uses a one-week, at-the-money forward USD put/DEM call on 10 dollars of face. The cash hedge is a long dollar/short mark position of approximately five million dollars in size.

A gamma trade is usually thought of as a pure bet on actual volatility. The view is that there will be a move in spot in either direction that will more than cover the value lost in time decay. Although delta-neutral in the first instance, the gamma trade is directionally sensitive because any movement in the spot exchange rate will cause the delta of the option to change. The trade makes money because the net delta of the option plus cash

USD/DEM Straddle, One Year to Expiration
Movements in Implied Volatility

	Units	Components			Comparative Statics	
		Long USD Put/ DEM Call	Long USD Call/ DEM Put	USD/DEM Straddle	Volatility Up	Volatility Down
Face	USD	$10,000,000	$10,000,000			
Face	DEM	13,915,000	13,915,000			
Spot	European	1.4100	1.4100		1.4100	1.4100
Strike	European	1.3915	1.3915			
Parameters						
Volatility		13.00%	13.00%		14.00%	12.00%
Days to expiry		365	365		365	365
Interest rate DEM		4.56%	4.56%		4.56%	4.56%
Interest rate USD		5.88%	5.88%		5.88%	5.88%
Pricing						
Unit price	USD pips	0.035143	0.035207	0.070350	0.075753	0.065897
Unit price	DEM pips	0.068951	0.069076	0.138027	0.148628	0.129292
Total price	USD	$489,014	$489,900	$978,914	$1,054,097	$916,962
Price change	USD				$75,182	($61,952)
Risk Measures						
Delta	USD	($5,029,885)	$4,539,439	($490,446)	($528,929)	$602,629
Gamma	USD	$209,326	$209,326	$418,652	$388,617	$451,511
Kappa	USD (1% Vol)	$37,597	$37,597	$75,195	$75,169	$74,859
Theta	USD/Day	$763	$423	$1,186	$1,277	$1,130

221

A Gamma Trade: USD Put/DEM Call with Delta Hedge, One Week to Expiration
As of June 19, 1995; One Day of Decay

| | Units | USD Put/ DEM Call | No Spot Movement | Comparative Statics | |
				Spot Down 0.84%	Spot Down 1.00%
Face	USD	$10,000,000	$10,000,000	$10,000,000	$10,000,000
Face	DEM	14,096,000	14,096,000	14,096,000	14,096,000
Spot	European	1.4100	1.4100	1.3983	1.3960
Strike	European	1.4096	1.4096	1.4096	1.4096
Parameters					
Volatility		16.00%	16.00%	16.00%	16.00%
Days to expiry		7	6	6	6
Interest rate DEM		4.56%	4.56%	4.56%	4.56%
Interest rate USD		6.06%	6.06%	6.06%	6.06%
Pricing and Risk Measures					
Unit price	USD pips	0.00626	0.00579	0.00925	0.01003
Unit price	DEM pips	0.01245	0.01150	0.01823	0.01973
Total price	USD	$88,304	$81,563	$130,367	$141,328
Theta	USD/day	$6,496	$7,003	$6,553	$6,352
Kappa	USD (1% vol)	$5,518	$5,110	$4,728	$4,569
Cash hedge	USD	$5,040,273			
P&L option	USD		($6,742)	$42,063	$53,024
P&L cash hedge	USD		$0	($42,211)	($50,403)
Net P&L	USD		($6,742)	($148)	$2,621

hedge rises and falls along with the spot exchange rate. The greater the gamma, the more valuable a movement in the spot exchange rate (hence the term *gamma trade*). Exhibit 7–12 shows a one-week gamma trade under three scenarios. With no movement in spot, the full time decay of $6,742 must be absorbed. In the second case, spot moves but not by enough to pay for the daily time decay. Finally, in the third case, there is a 1 percent move in spot, which proves sufficient to make the gamma trade profitable.

Hedged Volatility Trades

Hedged volatility trades are designed to extract the difference between implied volatility and subsequently experienced actual volatility. Unlike the gamma trade, the cash hedge is frequently adjusted to bring the net position back to being delta-neutral. Exhibits 7–13 and 7–14 show hedged volatility trades using a 92-day USD put/DEM call. The size of the cash hedge is adjusted once per week over a period of four weeks. The net profit or loss on the trade is the sum of the profit or loss on the adjusted cash hedge plus the profit or loss on the option.

If the option were held to expiration and if the cash hedge were rebalanced continuously, the profit or loss on the entire trade would depend on whether the experienced actual volatility did in fact exceed, equal, or fall short of the implied volatility that was paid to buy the option, absent consideration of transactions costs. If actual exceeds implied, there should be a profit. If actual equals implied, there should be no profit or loss. But if actual is less than implied, the program should end in a loss. Exhibit 7–13 shows the performance of the hedged volatility trade in a calm market, with spot movements never exceeding 1 percent per week in absolute value. This program loses money. In Exhibit 7–14, the same trade is subjected to volatile spot movements, ranging between 2 percent and 4 percent per week. This market environment is more kind to the trade and allows it to quickly amass substantial profits.

Exhibits 7–13 and 7–14 arbitrarily execute weekly rebalancing trades. There is in fact no optimal rule for how to operate the cash hedge with the real-world transactions costs. Some

EXHIBIT 7-13

A Hedged Volatility Trade: USD Put/DEM Call with Delta Hedge, 92 Days to Expiration Calm Market Conditions; Weekly Rehedging

	Units	USD Put/DEM Call	Week 1 Spot Down 0.50%	Week 2 Spot Down 0.75%	Week 3 Spot Up 1.00%	Week 4 Spot Down 0.50%
Face	USD	$10,000,000	$10,000,000	$10,000,000	$10,000,000	$10,000,000
Face	DEM	14,045,000	14,045,000	14,045,000	14,045,000	14,045,000
Spot	European	1.4100	1.4030	1.3924	1.4064	1.3993
Strike	European	1.4045	1.4045	1.4045	1.4045	1.4045
Parameters						
Volatility		14.25%	14.25%	14.25%	14.25%	14.25%
Days to expiry		92	85	78	71	64
Interest rate DEM		4.50%	4.50%	4.50%	4.50%	4.50%
Interest rate USD		6.06%	6.06%	6.06%	6.06%	6.06%
Pricing and Risk Measures						
Unit price	USD pips	0.02002	0.02101	0.02311	0.01826	0.01919
Unit price	DEM pips	0.03964	0.04140	0.04520	0.03607	0.03771
Total price	USD	$281,118	$295,106	$324,612	$256,515	$269,508
Theta	USD/week	$11,837	$12,355	$12,848	$13,431	$14,147
Kappa	USD (1% vol)	$19,721	$18,979	$18,012	$17,395	$16,484
Cash hedge	USD	$5,086,418	$5,355,294	$5,794,105	$5,188,770	
P&L option	USD		$13,988	$29,506	($68,098)	$12,993
P&L cash hedge	USD		($25,560)	($40,468)	$57,367	($26,074)
Net P&L	USD		($11,572)	($10,962)	($10,730)	($13,081)
Cumulative P&L	USD		($11,572)	($22,534)	($33,265)	($46,345)

224

EXHIBIT 7-14

A Hedged Volatility Trade: USD Put/DEM Call with Delta Hedge, 92 Days to Expiration
Volatile Market Conditions; Weekly Rehedging

	Units	USD Put/DEM Call	Week 1 Spot Down 2.00%	Week 2 Spot Down 3.00%	Week 3 Spot Up 4.00%	Week 4 Spot Down 2.00%
Face	USD	$10,000,000	$10,000,000	$10,000,000	$10,000,000	$10,000,000
Face	DEM	14,045,000	14,045,000	14,045,000	14,045,000	14,045,000
Spot	European	1.4100	1.3818	1.3403	1.3940	1.3661
Strike	European	1.4045	1.4045	1.4045	1.4045	1.4045
Parameters						
Volatility		14.25%	14.25%	14.25%	14.25%	14.25%
Days to expiry		92	85	78	71	64
Interest rate DEM		4.50%	4.50%	4.50%	4.50%	4.50%
Interest rate USD		6.06%	6.06%	6.06%	6.06%	6.06%
Pricing and Risk Measures						
Unit price	USD pips	0.02002	0.02732	0.04222	0.02172	0.03010
Unit price	DEM pips	0.03964	0.05303	0.07947	0.04252	0.05774
Total price	USD	$281,118	$383,754	$592,910	$305,042	$422,694
Theta	USD/week	$11,837	$12,187	$10,665	$13,443	$13,109
Kappa	USD (1% vol)	$19,721	$18,382	$13,982	$17,234	$14,731
Cash hedge	USD	$5,086,418	$6,206,406	$7,788,307	$5,740,814	
P&L option	USD		$102,636	$209,156	($287,868)	$117,652
P&L cash hedge	USD		($103,804)	($191,951)	$299,550	($117,159)
Net P&L	USD		($1,169)	$17,206	$11,682	$492
Cumulative P&L	USD		($1,169)	$16,037	$27,719	$28,211

traders rebalance according to their short-run directional view. Others trade only after spot makes a move of some predetermined size, such as one or two big figures. Still others do one trade per day at a set time, such as 3 P.M. Whatever the rule, it is clear that doing too many cash trades is not desirable because of transactions costs. Each rebalancing trade has an implied cost equal to the bid–offer spread on the spot exchange rate.

Finally, there is the question of the behavior of implied volatility over the course of the trade. If the program is operated right up to the option expiration date, movements in implied volatility are irrelevant (except possible interim negative marks-to-market if implied volatility drops). But a good case can be made for early liquidation of the trade if implied volatility rises to the level of the trader's original targeted actual volatility.

RISK MONITORING

The success of the derivatives revolution has meant that many institutions and corporations manage large, complex portfolios containing positions in foreign exchange and related instruments. These institutions are dependent on having accurate assessments of risk in a multicurrency environment that include exposure to options and other complex contingent claim instruments. Risk-monitoring technology is in priority demand because of the significant scale of the risk exposure that is known to exist.

The Dollars-at-Risk Concept

Industry practice has focused around a dollars-at-risk methodology that is essentially an application in portfolio risk analysis. (The most prominent example is RiskMetrics™ [J. P. Morgan 1995].) In the dollars-at-risk approach, each risk exposure is estimated as a daily shock loss in present-value, home-currency terms. The daily dollars-at-risk of exposure is defined as the estimated daily loss associated with an extremely low-probability, adverse market movement. This can be quantified in probability terms. A popular assumption in risk monitoring is that daily currency returns are multivariate normal. This makes it possible to speak in terms of a price movement not expected to occur more than 10 percent of the time, which is equivalent to 1.65 normal standard deviations. The size of the daily dollars-at-risk (DaR) for asset x is given as

$$\text{DaR}_x = V_x \times \frac{dV_x}{dp} \times \Delta p_{\text{day}}$$

where V_x is the value of asset x, the derivative is the sensitivity of asset x to price movement, and the third term is shock-loss movement in price. Under the assumption of normality, a 10 percent shock-loss movement is

$$\Delta p_{\text{day}} = p \times \frac{1}{\sqrt{220}} \times 1.65 \times \sigma$$

where it is assumed there are 220 trading days in one year, and σ is the annualized standard deviation. For example, assuming an the annualized standard deviation for dollar/mark of 13 percent, the 10 percent shock-loss daily price change is equal to

$$\Delta p = 1.4100 \times \left[\frac{1}{\sqrt{220}} \times 1.65 \times (.13) \right] = .0204$$

The reference spot level here is taken to be 1.4100. This calculation can be interpreted to mean that there is a 5 percent chance that dollar/mark will fall by more than 2.04 pfennigs and a 5 percent chance that dollar/mark will rise by more than 2.04 pfennigs in one day, given a 13 percent annualized standard deviation. The daily dollars-at-risk on a long position in $10,000,000 USD/DEM is equal to

$$\text{DaR} = \$10,000,000 \times \left(\frac{.0204}{1.4100 + .0204} \right) = \$142,617$$

Obviously, careful attention must be paid to the reliability of the estimated standard deviation, as the volatility of markets can be subject to sudden changes.

Computing the daily shock loss for forward contracts is slightly more complicated because some allowance must be made for the risk of movements in the interest rates. A foreign exchange forward contract is an agreement to exchange at some time in the future a sum of one currency for a sum of another currency at a specified forward rate. Interest rate risk can be analyzed by treating each currency leg of the forward like a zero coupon bond.

The risk associated with a currency option is a far more complicated affair. There are at least three methods. The first uses the delta of the option. DaR is equal to the delta multiplied by the shock-loss movement in the exchange rate. The problem is that the delta of the option is a function of the spot exchange rate. The second method is called the delta–gamma approach. The approximate change in the value of the option is given by

$$dV = \delta dS + \frac{1}{2}\gamma(dS)^2$$

where dV is the differential of the option value, and dS is the differential of the spot exchange rate. Even this method may be unsatisfactory in the case of large changes in spot, such as would have to be presumed for shock-loss movements. The third and most accurate method is called the secant, or full recalculation, approach. The DaR of the option in this method is simply the change in its value recalculated after a shock-loss movement in the exchange rate.

Portfolio Dollars-at-Risk

The dollars-at-risk for a portfolio is a function of the individual dollars-at-risk corresponding to the separate positions as well as the correlations among the positions. Denote the 3×3 correlation matrix, $\mathbf{P}$, as

$$\mathbf{P} = \begin{bmatrix} 1 & \rho_{1,2} & \rho_{1,3} \\ \rho_{2,1} & 1 & \rho_{2,3} \\ \rho_{3,1} & \rho_{3,2} & 1 \end{bmatrix}$$

where the ρ terms are the correlations. The portfolio dollars-at-risk is then computed as

$$\left[\mathbf{V} \times \mathbf{P} \times \mathbf{V}^T \right]^{\frac{1}{2}}$$

where $\mathbf{V}$ and $\mathbf{V}^T$ are the vector and transposed vector of daily dollars-at-risk for individual positions:

$$\mathbf{V} = \left[\mathrm{DaR}_1 \quad \mathrm{DaR}_2 \quad \mathrm{DaR}_3 \right]$$

and

$$\mathbf{V}^T = \begin{bmatrix} \mathrm{DaR}_1 \\ \mathrm{DaR}_2 \\ \mathrm{DaR}_3 \end{bmatrix}$$

Some risk-monitoring systems look at risk not on a daily basis but over longer periods of time, to allow for greater flexibility for the unwinding of positions. This requires a slight modification to the equation for the daily shock loss to incorporate the square root of the unwind period.

How Good Is the Dollars-at-Risk Approach?

The dollars-at-risk approach is obviously flawed in several ways, but it is a contribution of practical importance. Over time, more sophisticated approaches are sure to appear.

The Achilles heel of the approach is its fundamental reliance on the estimated standard deviations and correlations and on the maintained assumption that exchange rate returns are distributed multivariate normal. Empirical evidence contradicts the latter assumption and points to leptokurtic samples in assessing returns. In a leptokurtic sample, there is a relative abundance of observations that are outliers by comparison to a normal sample. The danger with the normal assumption is in underestimating the probability of a large movement in prices. The problem can be arbitrarily corrected by inflating the defined size of what is considered a shock-loss price movement. Instead of using 10 percent events, one could use 5 percent or even 2.5 percent events to estimate the dollars-at-risk. A more sophisticated alternative is to construct a leptokurtic "population" from experimental exchange rate movements for use in simulation analysis.

There are, of course, multiple alternative approaches in the estimation of correlations and standard deviations. Some techniques rely exclusively on historical price data. A popular approach is to give greater proportionate weight to the observations in the recent past. One such technique assigns exponentially declining weights to observations on the basis of their age of occurrence. Some methodologies mix observed implied volatilities with historical price data. Still others choose to combine fundamental assessments of market conditions with historical price data.

In the case of options, there is another problem in that changes in the levels of implied volatility can have substantial, if not catastrophic, implications for portfolio risk. This problem has several dimensions. The first is that option sensitivity to changes in implied volatility (kappa) is a function of time to expiration, option delta, and other factors. In particular, long-dated options are the most sensitive to implied volatility. This is complicated because movements in implied volatility are greater for the near dates on the implied curve. Also clouding the issue is the fact that no simple relationship exists between actual price movements and implied volatility. Sometimes volatility and price movements are positively correlated, sometimes they are negatively correlated, and sometimes no relationship exists at all. There is also the issue, however secondary it may seem, of option price sensitivity to movements in interest rates. In fact, long-dated currency options can have substantial risk exposure to interest rates that can outweigh the risk of spot exchange rate movements.

On a higher level, the dollars-at-risk approach looks only at market risk. A short, but not exhaustive, list of other types of risk would include:

Credit risk: The risk of a potential inability of a counterparty to meet its obligations.

Operational risk: Risk derived from errors in the execution or booking of trades or from mistakes in instructing payments or settling transactions.

Liquidity risk: Refers to the inability of a firm to fund positions in illiquid assets.

Intellectual risk: The risk of a material misunderstanding of a risk exposure or the risk associated with the loss of the key personnel responsible for monitoring and managing the portfolio.

Finally, monitoring risk and managing risk are two separate things. A well-managed process has established risk limits in place for every trading unit. Enforcement of limits must be taken seriously because no risk-monitoring system, however sophisticated, can avert a catastrophe if the risk-management process is faulty.

NOTES

1. The Newton or Newton–Raphson method is discussed in Press et al. (1986).

2. At-the-money forward deltas are near to but not necessarily equal to 0.50. Setting the strike equal to the forward outright makes the delta equal to

$$\delta_{\text{ATMF}} = e^{-R_f \tau} N\left(\frac{1}{2}\sigma\sqrt{\tau}\right)$$

3. In special circumstances, interbank dealers have been known to require that option trades be accompanied by forward outright hedges rather than the usual spot hedges. This was manifest during the 1993 ERM crisis when there were concerns about the viability of rolling positions in EMS currencies in the spot/next and tom/next swap market.

4. Bates (1994a) proposes an alternative measure of the skew

$$\text{Skew}(x) = \frac{C(F,\tau;K_C)}{P(F,\tau;K_P)} - 1$$

where F is the forward rate, $C(F, \tau; K_C)$ and $P(F, \tau; K_P)$ are the values of a call and a put valued at the forward rate with time to expiration τ and strikes K_C and K_P, respectively. The strikes are given by

$$K_P = \frac{F}{(1+x)} < F < K_C = F(1+x), \qquad x > 0$$

and x can be regarded as the "moneyness" parameter.

CHAPTER 8

American Exercise
Currency Options and
Futures Options

American currency options can be exercised at any time before expiration, unlike European options, which can be exercised only at expiration. In all other respects, American options and European options are identical. Only a small portion of the inter-bank currency option market is American exercise. However, American exercise currency options are abundant in the form of exchange-traded currency options and currency futures options.

AMERICAN CURRENCY OPTIONS
AND EARLY EXERCISE

Early exercise implies two basic principles of option valuation. First, the value of an American option should never be less than a like-specified European option because early exercise is a privilege, not an obligation

$$C' \geq C$$

$$P' \geq P$$

where the prime symbol denotes American exercise. A call option refers to a call on one unit of foreign currency; likewise, a put refers to a put option on one unit of foreign currency. Spot is quoted in the American convention.

Secondly, an in-the-money American option should never trade for less than intrinsic value:

$$C' \geq S - K$$

$$P' \geq K - S$$

This follows because intrinsic value can be extracted at any time by exercising the American option.

Why would early exercise be optimal? Consider Exhibit 8–1, which displays a one-year USD put/DEM call. By assumption, the interest rate on the U.S. dollar is 5 percent, the interest rate on the German mark is 9 percent, and the implied volatility is 13 percent. The intrinsic value, which is the value of immediate early exercise, is the asymptote of the American

EXHIBIT 8–1

American and European USD Put/DEM Call
At-the-Money Spot; $R_d = 5\%$; $R_f = 9\%$; Vol = 13%; 365 Days

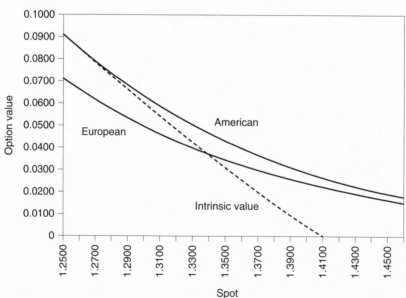

option. As an American option moves deeper into-the-money, it converges on the intrinsic value line. The value of the European option lies directly below the value of the American option. In certain circumstances, the value of a European option can be worth less than intrinsic value. In the exhibit, the intrinsic value intersects the value of the European option at the spot level of 1.3340. At spot levels below 1.3340, which are further into the in-the-money range, early exercise of the European option would be optimal if that were permitted.[1] The reason this particular option can be worth less than intrinsic value is because it is a European call on a discount currency. The absence of an early exercise privilege imposes an opportunity cost on the holder of the option because there is no immediate access to the higher-interest rate currency.

The spread between the domestic and foreign interest rates is an important determinant of the relative valuation of American and European currency options. This is because American exercise grants immediate delivery or receipt of the foreign currency. Exhibit 8–2 shows the value for American and European USD puts/DEM calls at varying levels of interest rate spread. American and European calls on foreign currency converge at a sufficiently high interest rate spread, meaning in the range where the foreign currency is at premium (its interest rate is below the domestic rate). Likewise, the value of an American put on a premium foreign currency converges on its European counterpart in the case of a discount currency. The delta of an American option is greater than or equal to the delta of a European option, as a function of spot in relation to the strike (Exhibit 8–3) as well as to the interest rate spread (Exhibit 8–4).

American exercise currency options are far more complex in use than are European options. A portion of their demand derives simply from the fact that a large part of the exchange-traded market happens to be American exercise. Some traders prefer American exercise because they have a strategic need for early exercise. Sophisticated traders use American options in strategies that combine views on exchange rates and interest rate spreads.

American and European USD Put/DEM Call versus Interest Spread
At-the-Money Spot; Vol = 13%; 365 Days

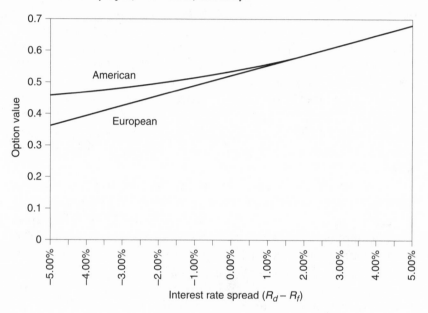

THE VALUATION OF AMERICAN EXERCISE CURRENCY OPTIONS

American options must obey the BSGK partial differential equation, early exercise notwithstanding, provided the model's assumptions are in force. This equation for American call option on foreign currency is as follows.

BSGK Partial Differential Equation for American Calls

$$\frac{1}{2}\sigma^2 S^2 \frac{\partial^2 C'}{\partial S^2} - R_d C' + \left(R_d S - R_f S\right)\frac{\partial C'}{\partial S} - \frac{\partial C'}{\partial \tau} = 0$$

Early exercise makes it impossible to impose the expiration day payoff function as a boundary constraint for the purpose of

EXHIBIT 8-3

Deltas of American and European USD Put/DEM Call
At-the-Money Spot; R_d = 5%; R_f = 9%; Vol = 13%; 365 Days

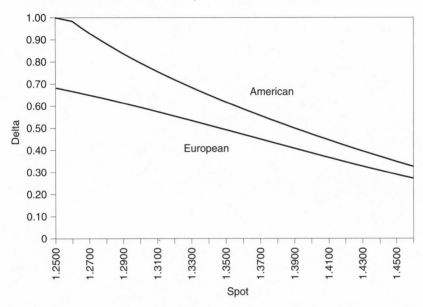

solving the partial differential equation, as it was possible to do for European exercise options. Consequently, no analytical solution (or closed form solution) for American options is known to exist. This has led option theorists to turn to different classes of models. Two such models will be discussed in this chapter: the binomial model of Cox, Ross, and Rubinstein (1979) and the quadratic approximation model of Barone-Adesi and Whaley (1987) and MacMillan (1986).

THE BINOMIAL MODEL
FOR AMERICAN CURRENCY OPTIONS

The binomial option model proposed by Cox, Ross, and Rubinstein (1979) values American options on dividend-paying common stocks with explicit recognition of early exercise. The

E X H I B I T   8–4

Deltas of USD Put/DEM Call versus Interest Rate Spread
At-the-Money Spot; Vol = 13%; 365 Days

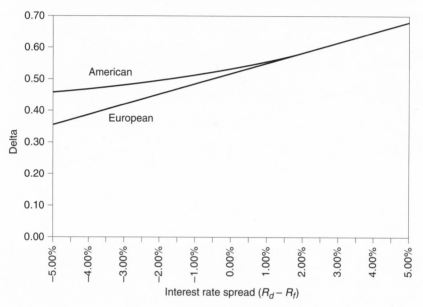

binomial model can be readily modified to work on currency options (Bodurtha and Courtadon 1987).

The Binomial Approach

In the binomial model, the spot exchange rate at a point in time is constrained to move (or jump) in one of two mutually exclusive paths. One is upwards, and the other is downwards. During the remaining time before expiration, designated as τ, the spot exchange rate must make a fixed number, N, of such jumps. N is a parameter. A greater value for N implies greater precision but slower speed of calculation. The size of each jump is a function of the domestic and foreign currency interest rates, the assumed volatility, and the number of jumps in the remaining time to expiration. The sizes of an up jump, u, and a down jump, d, are given by

$$u = e^{\left(R_d - R_f\right)\tau/N + \sigma\sqrt{\tau/N}}$$

$$d = e^{\left(R_d - R_f\right)\tau/N - \sigma\sqrt{\tau/N}}$$

After the first jump, the spot rate will either be up, ^1S_u, or down, ^1S_d

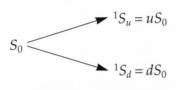

$$^1S_u = uS_0$$

$$S_0$$

$$^1S_d = dS_0$$

where S_0 is the spot exchange rate at time zero. The pre-superscript, which is 1 in this case, denotes the number of realized jumps.

Consider a one-year American exercise USD put/DEM call struck at-the-money spot (1.4100) with the dollar interest rate equal to 5 percent, the mark interest rate equal to 9 percent, and implied volatility equal to 13 percent. If the spot rate is constrained to make only one jump (i.e., $\tau = N = 1$) during the one-year span of time before expiration, u and d would be equal to

$$u = e^{(5.00\% - 9.00\%) + 13\%} = 1.09417$$

$$d = e^{(5.00\% - 9.00\%) - 13\%} = 0.84366$$

The spot rate S_0 expressed in American quotation is equal to .70922 (equivalent to 1.4100 European). The spot rate S_T at expiration will be either

$$S_T = {}^1S_u = uS_0 = 1.09417 \times .70922 = .77601$$

or

$$S_T = {}^1S_d = dS_0 = .84366 \times .70922 = .59834$$

The expiration value of the call option is a function of the spot binomial tree. Specifically, the value of the option depends on whether the spot moves up or down.

Up

$$^1C_u = \text{Max } \{0, {}^1S_u - K\} = .06679$$

Down

$$^1C_d = \text{Max } \{0, {}^1S_d - K\} = 0$$

where expiration values are denominated in dollars per one unit of mark face.

The value at time zero of this option can be calculated using an insight introduced by Cox, Ross, and Rubinstein. The idea is that the value at expiration of the option can be replicated with a portfolio that consists of borrowing a sum of dollars, B, and lending a sum of marks, D, to be repaid at option expiration, T. The future value at time T of the dollars is equal to

$$Be^{R_d(\tau/N)}$$

The value at time zero of the spot marks is

$$S_0D$$

Interest would accrue at the rate R_f on the marks until expiration. Thereupon, the dollar value of the marks would be a function of the spot rate. It would be equal to either

$$^1S_uDe^{R_f(\tau/N)} = uS_0De^{R_f(\tau/N)}$$

or

$$^1S_dDe^{R_f(\tau/N)} = dS_0De^{R_f(\tau/N)}$$

The option's payoff at expiration can be replicated by choosing B and D as follows:

$$B = \frac{u^1C_d - d^1C_u}{(u-d)e^{R_d(\tau/N)}} = -.21396$$

$$D = \frac{^1C_u - {}^1C_d}{(u-d)S_0e^{R_f(\tau/N)}} = .34358$$

It can be demonstrated that the value of the replication portfolio and the value of the call are equal on expiration day:

Call (^1C_u and ^1C_d)		Portfolio	
Up	.06679	Dollar loan	−.22494
		Marks	.29173
		Total	.06679
Down	0	Dollar loan	−.22494
		Marks	.22494
		Total	0

To preclude profitable, riskless arbitrage, the value of the call must be equal to the value of the replication portfolio at time zero. The value of the call at time zero is equal to

$$C = B + S_0 D = .02970$$

This equation can be written as

$$C_0 = e^{-R_d(\tau/N)}\left[p\,^1C_u - (1-p)\,^1C_d\right]$$

where

$$p = \frac{e^{(R_d - R_f)(\tau/N)} - d}{(u - d)}$$

In the context of the risk-neutral approach, p is the probability of an upwards move and $(1 - p)$ is the probability of a downwards move. The risk-neutral expected value of the spot rate is given by

$$pS_u + (1-p)S_d = e^{(R_d - R_f)(\tau/N)}S_0$$

which is equal to the forward exchange rate under interest points.

Expanding the Binomial Tree

The next step is to expand the binomial tree by increasing the number of jumps. If there are two jumps in the remaining time to expiration, then u and d corresponding to a single jump are

$$u = e^{(5.00\%-9.00\%)\times\frac{1}{2}+13\%\times\sqrt{\frac{1}{2}}} = 1.07457$$

$$d = e^{(5.00\%-9.00\%)\times\frac{1}{2}-13\%\times\sqrt{\frac{1}{2}}} = .89411$$

The spot tree structure becomes

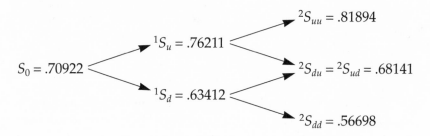

which implies the payoff pattern for the European call

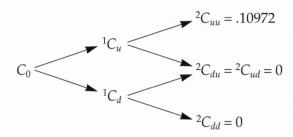

The binomial model starts with the expiration values and moves backwards in time, calculating the value of each node based on one pair of binomial outcomes. For example, at the ^1C_u node in the $N = 2$ case, the option will advance according to

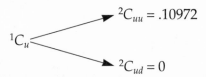

The payoff at this node can be replicated using $B = -.53021$ and $D = .762695$. For an American exercise option, the value of $^1C_u'$ is the greatest of zero, the replication portfolio, or the immediate exercise value

$$^1C_u' = \text{Max}[0, B + {}^1S_u D, {}^1S_u - K)$$
$$= \text{Max}(0, .051049, .05289) = .05289$$

Note that early exercise is optimal at the $^1C_u'$ node. This is because the value of early exercise

$$^1S_u - K = .762109 - .70922 = .05289$$

is worth more than .051049, which is the value of the replication portfolio.

The same procedure is used to calculate the value of the $^1C_d'$ node, but by inspection it must be equal to zero. The value of the final binomial pair gives the value of C_0'

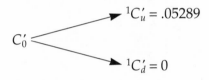

C_0' is equal to .02461 (using $B = -.25557$ and $D = 0.39506$).

The binomial $N = 4$ case is displayed in Exhibit 8–5. Early exercise is optimal in the $^3C_{uuu}'$ and $^2C_{uu}'$ nodes.

In the general case, precision can be increased by choosing a greater value for N. But no matter how large N is, the procedure is always the same. First, evaluate the expiration values. Next, move back one jump to calculate the option values at the $(N-1)^{\text{th}}$ node, checking for the possibility that early exercise might be optimal for American options. Continue until the entire binomial tree has been evaluated, which in the end produces the value of C_0'. Using $N = 50$, the binomial model calculates the value of the option to be .02596.

THE BINOMIAL MODEL
FOR EUROPEAN CURRENCY OPTIONS

The binomial model can also be used to value European currency options. Here the risk-neutrality approach provides a shortcut. The option's value can be derived directly from the final set of

E X H I B I T   8–5

Binomial Currency Option Pricing Model

Parameters

Sigma	13.00%	N	4	K	0.70922
R_f	9.00%	Time	365 days	u	1.0565
R_d	5.00%	S_0	0.70922	d	0.9277

N=0	N=1	N=2	N=3	N=4
				$S_{4uuuu} = 0.8837$
			$S_{3uuu} = 0.8364$	
		$S_{2uu} = 0.7917$		$S_{4uuud} = 0.7760$
	$S_{1u} = 0.7493$		$S_{3uud} = 0.7345$	
$S_0 = 0.7092$		$S_{2ud} = 0.6952$		$S_{4uudd} = 0.6814$
	$S_{1d} = 0.6580$		$S_{3udd} = 0.6449$	
		$S_{2dd} = 0.6104$		$S_{4uddd} = 0.5983$
			$S_{3ddd} = 0.5663$	
				$S_{4dddd} = 0.5254$

American Option

N=0	N=1	N=2	N=3	N=4
				$C_{4uuuu} = 0.1745$
			$C_{3uuu} = 0.1272^*$	
		$C_{2uu} = 0.0825^*$		$C_{4uuud} = 0.0668$
	$C_{1u} = 0.0472$		$C_{3uud} = 0.0319$	
$C_0 = 0.0262$		$C_{2ud} = 0.0152$		$C_{4uudd} = 0.0000$
	$C_{1d} = 0.0073$		$C_{3udd} = 0.0000$	
		$C_{2dd} = 0.0000$		$C_{4uddd} = 0.0000$
			$C_{3ddd} = 0.0000$	
				$C_{4dddd} = 0.0000$

European Option

N=0	N=1	N=2	N=3	N=4
				$C_{4uuuu} = 0.1745$
			$C_{3uuu} = 0.1174$	
		$C_{2uu} = 0.0724$		$C_{4uuud} = 0.0668$
	$C_{1u} = 0.0423$		$C_{3uud} = 0.0319$	
$C_0 = 0.0239$		$C_{2ud} = 0.0152$		$C_{4uudd} = 0.0000$
	$C_{1d} = 0.0073$		$C_{3udd} = 0.0000$	
		$C_{2dd} = 0.0000$		$C_{4uddd} = 0.0000$
			$C_{3ddd} = 0.0000$	
				$C_{4dddd} = 0.0000$

Note: * Denotes early exercise.

nodes and their associated binomial risk-neutral probabilities of occurrence. The value of the call is equal to the expected present value of the payoff at expiration, as is given by

$$C_0 = e^{-R_d T} \sum (C_T \times P_T)$$

where the C_T terms represent the payoff at expiration for each binomial path and the P_T terms are their probabilities of occurrence as can be derived from the binomial distribution. The risk-neutral probability of an up move is denoted as p; $(1 - p)$ is the probability of a down move. Each potential expiration day payoff might have been the result of any of a predictable number of paths. For example, where $N = 4$, the payoff from one up and three down moves could have been achieved by four possible paths (*uddd, dudd, ddud,* and *dddu*). For a given number j of up moves, there are exactly

$$\frac{N!}{[j!(N-j)!]}$$

paths to any one expiration payoff, where $N!$ represents N factorial. The probability of any one particular such path materializing is

$$p^j (1-p)^{N-j}$$

The risk-neutral value of all of the potential expiration payoffs is the present value of

$$\sum \frac{N!}{j!(N-j)!} p^j (1-p)^{N-j} \mathrm{MAX}[0, u^j d^{N-j} S_0 - K]$$

This equation completes the binomial model for European currency options.

As the number of nodes grows large, the binomial distribution converges on the lognormal distribution. This implies that the binomial model converges on the BSGK model in the limit for European options.

IMPLIED VOLATILITY
AND THE IMPLIED BINOMIAL TREE

The binomial model prices options on the basis of an assumed underlying tree structure of future spot exchange rates. The binomial tree is predicated on constant volatility in the first log differences in spot exchange rates. The evidence of a smile and skew in the observed implied volatility of currency options suggests that the binomial tree structure and its associated risk-neutral probabilities might not be compatible with market-clearing option prices.

Recent theoretical work by Derman and Kani (1994), Rubinstein (1993), and Dupire (1994) introduce a concept called the implied binomial tree. The general idea is to manufacture a spot binomial tree that implicitly reflects the smile and skew information that is observed in quoted option prices. Derman and Kani form the implied binomial tree by a process of mathematical induction. Consider the state of the tree after N jumps have been realized. There would then be N number of known spot prices, denoted $s_1,...,s_N$. Each of these will transit to a higher or lower level with the next jump, which is the $(N + 1)^{th}$ move in the course of unit of time Δt. The generalized value, s_i, represents the ith node in the tree at the nth level. s_i will either become S_{i+1} after an up move or S_i after a down move:

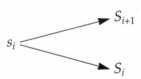

Denote the risk-neutral probability of an up move as p_i and the risk-neutral probability of a down move as $(1 - p_i)$. In sum, there are $2N + 1$ parameters that govern the movement from the Nth to the $(N + 1)^{th}$ levels. There are $(N + 1)$ values of S associated with the $(N + 1)^{th}$ level plus N transition probability parameters, $p_1,...,p_N$.

In the Derman and Kani methodology, the implied binomial tree is risk-neutral, which makes the forward exchange rate associated with any spot level equal to

$$F_i = p_i S_{i+1} + (1 - p_i) S_i = e^{(R_d - R_f)\Delta t} s_i$$

where the right-hand final expression guarantees covered interest rate parity. It is possible to imagine that there are N number of one-transition period calls, C_i, each with a strike equal to the known exchange rate s_i. The expiration value of C_i is either

$$\text{Max}(0, S_{i+1} - s_i)$$

or

$$\text{Max}(0, S_i - s_i)$$

Prices for the call options can be interpolated from the observable market prices of options. This totals to $2N$ equations, N from the forward rates and N from the option prices. The final equation centers the spine of the implied binomial tree on top of the constant volatility tree. Solving for the $(2N + 1)$ unknowns produces the $(N + 1)$[th] level of the implied binomial tree along with the associated probabilities of transition. By method of induction, the entire implied tree can be produced.

The implied binomial approach is a potentially important new piece of financial engineering. It provides a closer empirical fit with how options are actually priced in the market by comparison to the constant volatility binomial model. It has been shown to be useful in practice, especially in the case of American exercise options and exotic options.

THE QUADRATIC APPROXIMATION MODEL

Barone-Adesi and Whaley (1987) and MacMillan (1986) discovered an efficient method of approximation for the value of an American option. The approach involves locating a critical value, S^*, at which early exercise would be optimal. The value of an American call option would then be either

$$C' = (S - K), \ S \geq S^*$$

or

$$C' = C + A_2 \left(\frac{S}{S^*} \right)^{q_2}, \quad S < S^*$$

where

$$A_2 = \frac{S^*}{q_2}\left[1 - e^{-R_d\tau}N\big(d_1(S^*)\big)\right]$$

$$q_2 = \frac{1}{2}\left[-(N-1) + \sqrt{(N-1)^2 + 4\frac{M}{B}}\right]$$

$$N = 2\frac{(R_d - R_f)}{\sigma^2}$$

$$M = 2\frac{R_d}{\sigma^2}$$

$$B = 1 - e^{-R_d\tau}$$

$$d_1(S^*) = \frac{\ln\left(\dfrac{S^*}{K}\right) + \left(R_d - R_f + \dfrac{1}{2}\sigma^2\right)\tau}{\sigma\sqrt{\tau}}$$

$N()$ is the cumulative normal density function. The only variable that is an unknown is S^*, the critical level of spot that triggers early exercise. Barone-Adesi and Whaley provide an algorithm that iteratively converges on S^* within an acceptable level of tolerance for error. The procedure values the one-year USD put/DEM call from the binomial example above at .02615, and S^* equals .7960 (1.2563, European convention).

CURRENCY FUTURES OPTIONS

Currency futures options are traded on the International Monetary Market division of the Chicago Mercantile Exchange. A currency futures option exercises into a currency futures contract, whereupon the in-the-money spread between the strike and futures price becomes an immediate credit or debit to long or short positions. The mechanics of trading these options were discussed in Chapter 3.

Put–Call Parity

Stoll and Whaley (1986) provided put–call parity relationships for European and American futures options.

Put–Call Parity for European Currency Futures Options

$$C^f - P^f = e^{-R_d\tau}(f - K)$$

The proof of this relationship depends on the Margrabe and Cox, Ingersoll, and Ross proof that a rollover futures hedge is a perfect substitute for a forward contract (discussed in Chapter 4). This proof implies that the futures price must be equal to the forward outright for value at option expiration. A long position in a European futures call combined with a short position in a European futures put will result in a cumulative cash flow equal to the futures price minus the strike $(f - K)$ as of expiration. The present value of this is the right-hand-side of the futures option put–call parity equation. Put–call parity for American exercise is an inequality.

Put–Call Parity for American Currency Futures Options

$$e^{-R_d\tau}f - K \le C^{f\prime} - P^{f\prime} \le f - Ke^{-R_d\tau}$$

where $C^{f\prime}$ and $P^{f\prime}$ are American exercise currency futures options.

Black's Model for European Futures Options

Black (1976) adapted the Black–Scholes common stock option pricing model to work on a generic class of European commodity futures options that includes currency futures options. Once again there are three familiar assumptions:

1. There are no taxes or transactions costs, and all foreign exchange, futures, and option market participants are price-takers.
2. The domestic interest rate is riskless and constant over the life of the futures option.

3. Instantaneous proportional changes in the futures price
    are generated by a diffusion process of the form

$$\frac{d\tilde{f}}{f} = \alpha dt + \sigma d\tilde{z}$$

where α is the drift term, dt is an instant in time, σ is the
standard deviation of the process, and $d\tilde{z}$ is a stochastic
variable that is independent and identically distributed ·
normally with zero mean and standard deviation equal
to the square root of dt.

Under these assumptions, it is possible to construct a local
hedge for a long position in a currency futures option using positions in currency futures contracts. As before, the no-arbitrage
rule forces the rate of return on the perfectly hedged theoretical
position to be equal to the risk-free interest rate R_d.

Given the above assumptions, Black showed that a European futures option must obey a partial differential equation
similar to the Black–Scholes equation. Black solved this equation
under the constraint of the expiration payoff functions

$$C^f_T = \text{Max}[0, f_T - K]$$

$$P^f_T = \text{Max}[0, K - f_T]$$

where C^f_T and P^f_T are the values of a futures option call and put
at expiration time T, f_T is the futures price at time T, and K is the
strike. Black's solution for the values of a futures option call and
put is

$$C^f = e^{-R_d\tau}\left[fN\left(h + \sigma\sqrt{\tau}\right) - KN(h)\right]$$

$$P^f = e^{-R_d\tau}\left[f\left(N\left(h + \sigma\sqrt{\tau}\right) - 1\right) - K\left(N(h) - 1\right)\right]$$

$$h = \frac{\ln\left(\dfrac{f}{K}\right) - \dfrac{\sigma^2}{2}\tau}{\sigma\sqrt{\tau}}$$

Models for American Futures Options

The futures options listed on the International Monetary Market division of the Chicago Mercantile Exchange have American exercise convention. Early exercise is sometimes optimal for American futures options. This is likely to be true for a deep-in-the-money option trading at low implied volatility. As such, the Black model may not be a good approximation for American futures options. Hull (1991) showed that the binomial model can be adapted with little modification to work on American futures options. The u and d terms and the probability of an up move are defined as follows:

$$u = e^{\sigma\sqrt{\tau/N}}$$

$$d = e^{-\sigma\sqrt{\tau/N}}$$

$$p = \frac{1-d}{u-d}$$

Whaley (1986) adapted the Barone-Adesi and Whaley quadratic approximation method to handle American futures options (see DeRosa 1992).

NOTES

1. See DeRosa (1992) for a discussion of the conditions under which early exercise is optimal and for an analysis of the early exercise premium.

CHAPTER 9

Exotic Currency Options and Equity Structures with Currency Features

New varieties of currency derivatives appear in the marketplace with regular frequency. One of the fastest-growing areas is exotic currency options. An exotic currency option has at least one nonstandard feature that distinguishes it from a standard option. For example, a knock-out option can extinguish at any time before normal expiration if it falls sufficiently out-of-the-money. The exotic feature of an average rate option is that the payoff rule is based upon an average of spot exchange rates over a period of time. A basket option is exotic because it is struck on a weighted average of exchange rates rather than on a single exchange rate. Cross-currency warrants are put and call currency options that are exotic in the sense that they are priced in a third currency. An example is a mark put/yen call that has a payoff structure in dollars and is traded in U.S. dollars. Two other new derivative structures that are discussed in this chapter are equity index–linked warrants with special currency features, of which the quantos option is a special case, and cross-currency index–linked swaps.

EXOTIC CURRENCY OPTIONS

Three types of exotic currency options will be considered in detail: barrier options, average rate options, and basket options.

Barrier Options

A barrier option has a defined spot level that when traded determines the state of existence of the option. "Out" options extinguish immediately when the spot exchange rate trades at or through the "outstrike." "In" options become live standard options immediately when the spot exchange rate trades at or through the barrier "in-strike." "Knock" options have barriers placed in the out-of-the-money range; "kick" options have barriers placed in the in-the-money-range.

Barrier options are cheap in absolute terms compared to standard options, which is the reason behind their popularity. The reason barrier options are less expensive is that the option holder is exposed to some form of path dependent–related risk that would not be the case with a standard option. The term path dependent refers to the fact that the ultimate value to the option holder is a function not only of whether the option is in-the-money at expiration but also upon the price path of the underlying spot exchange rate throughout the course of the option's life. Path dependent–related risk in the case of a knock-out or kick-out option is the chance that the spot rate will cross the out-strike and trigger the immediate extinction of the option. Kick-in and knock-in options have path dependent–related risk because the in-strike must be breached in order for the option to come to life; unless the in-strike is crossed, the option will be worthless at expiration even if it is in-the-money.

The knock-out option is the most popular type of exotic currency option. An example is a European knock-out USD put/DEM call transacted at a spot level of 1.4100, strike set at 1.4100 and out-strike at 1.4300 (Exhibit 9–1). This option grants the right, but not the obligation, to exercise to deliver U.S. dollars in exchange for German marks at the exchange rate of 1.4100 at expiration. However, if at any time before expiration spot USD/DEM were to trade at or through 1.4300, the option would immediately expire worthless. This example is an "up-and-out" knock-out dollar put. An example of a "down-and-out" knock-out dollar call would be a European USD call/DEM put transacted at spot level 1.4100, strike set at 1.4100 and out-strike at 1.3900.

E X H I B I T 9–1

Knock-Out USD Put/DEM Call, 32 Days to Expiration
Strike 1.41; Out-Strike 1.43; Vol 14.75%; R_f 4.46%; R_d 6.00%

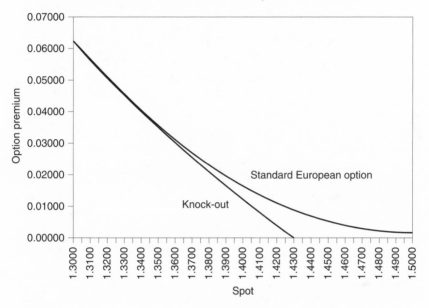

When the spot exchange rate is far from the out-strike, the knock-out behaves in a similar manner to and has a value almost equal to a standard option. Differences emerge when the spot exchange rate approaches the out-strike. The closer spot is to the out-strike, the greater the probability of immediate expiration. In the region near to the out-strike, the knock-out has little sensitivity to volatility and to interest rates. Delta is generally greater than the equivalent standard option (Exhibit 9–2). Gamma is generally smaller because there is less curvature in the option's theoretical value. The knock-out is a favorite with directional traders because it provides a cheap, high-delta bet.

Rubinstein (1990) offered the following model for European knock-out options, based on earlier work by Merton (1973) and Black and Cox (1976):[1]

$$C_{\text{down-and-out}} = e^{-R_f \tau} S N(x) - e^{-R_d \tau} K N\left(x - \sigma\sqrt{\tau}\right)$$

$$- e^{-R_f \tau} S \left(\frac{H}{S}\right)^{2\lambda} N(y) + e^{-R_d \tau} K \left(\frac{H}{S}\right)^{2\lambda-2} N\left(y - \sigma\sqrt{\tau}\right)$$

$$P_{\text{up-and-out}} = -e^{-R_f \tau} S \left(1 - N(x)\right) + e^{-R_d \tau} K \left(1 - N\left(x - \sigma\sqrt{\tau}\right)\right)$$

$$+ e^{-R_f \tau} S \left(\frac{H}{S}\right)^{2\lambda} \left(1 - N(y)\right)$$

$$- e^{-R_d \tau} K \left(\frac{H}{S}\right)^{2\lambda-2} \left(1 - N\left(y - \sigma\sqrt{\tau}\right)\right)$$

$$x = \frac{\ln\left(\dfrac{S}{K}\right)}{\sigma\sqrt{\tau}} + \lambda\sigma\sqrt{\tau}$$

E X H I B I T   9–2

Delta of Knock-Out USD Put/DEM Call, 32 Days to Expiration
Strike 1.41; Out-Strike 1.43; Vol 14.75%; R_f 4.46%; R_d 6.00%

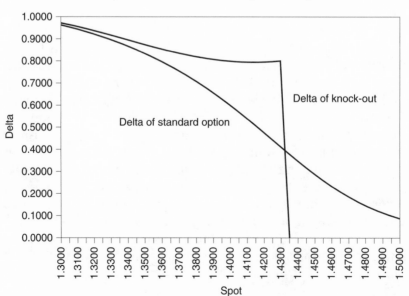

$$y = \frac{\ln\left(\dfrac{H^2}{SK}\right)}{\sigma\sqrt{\tau}} + \lambda\sigma\sqrt{\tau}$$

$$\lambda = \frac{\mu}{\sigma^2} + 1$$

$$\mu = \ln\left(\frac{1+R_d}{1+R_f}\right) - .5\sigma^2$$

where H is the out-strike, and other terms are as were previously defined.

The knock-in option is closely related to the knock-out option. The knock-in option is "born" dead but can come to life when the in-strike is crossed. The European knock-in option is related to the knock-out option and standard option as follows:

$$C_{\text{standard}} = C_{\text{down-and-out}} + C_{\text{down-and-in}}$$

$$P_{\text{standard}} = P_{\text{up-and-out}} + P_{\text{up-and-in}}$$

Another type of barrier option is the kick-out option. The difference between the kick-out and the knock-out option is that the kick-out strike is in-the-money while the knock-out strike is out-of-the-money. An example of a kick-out dollar put would be a USD put/DEM call transacted at spot level 1.4100 with strike set at 1.4100 and out-strike at 1.3600. The kick-out option tends to be cheap because its maximum payoff is capped to the range between the strike and out-strike (equal to five big figures (1.4100 – 1.3600) in the example), and because it can be extinguished before expiration. The kick-out has negligible delta early on but can have substantial sensitivity to spot later in its life.

Barrier options are useful in expressing views on volatility. A trader can be long volatility by selling structures that have one or more out-strikes. Similarly, a short volatility play can be created by buying structures with barriers. Consider the knock-out strangle. There are two out-strikes. Breaching either out-strike knocks out the entire strangle. For example, with spot dollar/ mark reference 1.4100, the knock-out strangle could have strikes at 1.3900 and 1.4200 and out-strikes at 1.3700 and 1.4400. The maximum gross payout at expiration is equal to 200 DEM pips. The buyer of this option is short volatility in the sense that he has the view that spot volatility will not be sufficiently large so as to push through either of the out-strikes. The seller of the knock-out strangle is long volatility because he hopes for a large movement that pushes spot through either of the out-strikes to terminate the life of the option structure.

Average Rate Options

The average rate option is also called the Asian option. The basic idea is that the payoff function is based upon an average of observed spot prices over some defined time period. The averaging period typically spans the entire life of the option but shorter periods are possible. In the case of currency options, the average is usually calculated across some officially reported exchange rate, examples being the Bundesbank's daily fixing and the New York Federal Reserve Bank's 10 A.M. fixing.

Intuition suggests that an average rate option should be less expensive than a standard option because the standard deviation of an average is less than or equal to the standard deviation of its individual constituents. This is the appeal of average options, but there is also the built-in antifraud feature. The average option is popular in commodity markets where it is conceivable that the spot price at expiration could be subject to manipulation. This is less of a threat if the option depends not on the spot price on one day but on the spot price for a number of days or for the entire life of the option.

An average rate option is relatively easy to model if the average is the geometric mean. The geometric mean of a series is given by

$$G = \left[\prod_{i=1}^{n} S_i \right]^{\frac{1}{n}}$$

The value of a geometric mean average currency call, assuming that the averaging is conducted over the entire life of the option, has a closed-form solution, which is given by[2,3]

$$C_{\text{gmaro}} = e^{-R_d \tau} e^{d^*} S(d_1) - e^{-R_d \tau} K N(d_2)$$

where

$$d_1 = \frac{\left[\ln\left(\dfrac{S}{K} \right) + \dfrac{1}{2}\left(R_d - R_f + \dfrac{1}{6}\sigma^2 \right)\tau \right]}{\sigma \sqrt{\dfrac{\tau}{3}}}$$

$$d^* = \frac{1}{2}\left(R_d - R_f - \frac{1}{6}\sigma^2 \right)\tau$$

$$d_2 = d_1 - \sigma \sqrt{\frac{\tau}{3}}$$

Deriving a model for arithmetic mean average options is problematic. Kemna and Vorst (1990) proposed an efficient control variate Monte Carlo simulation procedure. In this approach, the value of a geometric mean average option, which is known from the closed-form solution, is used as the lower bound for the arithmetic mean average option. A different tact is taken by Levy (1990 and 1991), who developed an analytical closed-form solution that proves to be reasonably precise.

Basket Options

A basket currency option is a put or a call on a collection of currencies taken together as a portfolio. By definition, a basket option is an all-or-none exercise—there is no allowance for exercise of some but not all currencies in the basket. Basket options can be cash settled or physically settled. One-way baskets are either long all of the foreign currencies or short all of the foreign currencies in the basket. Mixed cash flow baskets combine long and short positions in various foreign currencies. European one-way baskets can be valued with the BSGK model.

Exhibit 9–3 shows an example of a basket consisting of exposures to roughly equal proportions of marks, pounds, and yen from the perspective of a U.S. dollar–based investor. The spot value of the total exposure as of June 19, 1995, is $36,976,851. The forward value is higher, $37,527,821, because the yen was at significant premium to the dollar. Consider a one-year at-the-money put on the basket. By convention, strike is set relative to the forward value of the basket. If the option is physically settled, the owner of the put has the right to exercise and deliver 17.5 million marks, 8 million pounds, and 1 billion yen in exchange for $37,527,821. If the option is cash settled, the seller of the option upon exercise will be obligated to pay dollars to the buyer of the option in an amount equal to the strike value, $37,527,821, less the spot value of the basket at expiration.

Basket options are favored by portfolio managers and corporate treasurers who seek to hedge a collection of currency exposures with a single option. Motivation comes from a savings in option premium with the basket option by comparison to the cost of purchasing a strip of options, one for each separate currency. This savings results from the fact that the implied volatility of the basket is less than the average of the separate currency implied volatilities. This is demonstrated in Exhibit 9–4, which is taken from Hsu (1995). Said another way, the value of the basket option must be less than the value of a strip of standard currency options because there is a possibility that the basket option could expire out-of-the-money whereas one or more of the options in the strip could expire in-the-money.

The calculation of the implied volatility of a basket option requires knowledge of the implied volatilities of each currency in the basket with respect to the base currency, which are called the leg volatilities, as well as the implied volatilities of each of the associated cross exchange rates, which are called the cross volatilities. There are a total of $N(N + 1)/2$ such terms for a basket that is comprised of N currencies. There are N leg volatilities and $N(N - 1)/2$ are cross volatilities. For example, there are three currencies in the basket in Exhibit 9–3: marks, pounds, and yen.

EXHIBIT 9–3

Currency Basket Options

	Spot	Forward Points	Forward Outright	Currency Amount	Spot Value	Forward Value	Weights
USD/DEM	1.4100	−0.0169	1.3931	17,500,000	$12,411,348	$12,561,912	33.47%
GBP/USD	1.5975	−0.0194	1.5781	8,000,000	$12,780,000	$12,624,800	33.64%
USD/JPY	84.85	−3.82	81.03	1,000,000,000	$11,785,504	$12,341,108	32.89%
					$36,976,851	$37,527,821	100.00%

Leg Volatilities

USD/DEM	13.00%
GBP/USD	11.05%
USD/JPY	14.00%

Cross Volatilities

GBP/DEM	9.70%
GBP/JPY	15.00%
DEM/JPY	10.50%

Implied Correlations

USD/DEM, GBP/USD	68.57%
GBP/USD, USD/JPY	30.09%
USD/DEM, USD/JPY	69.99%

Option Parameters

Face amount	$37,527,821
Forward index level	100.00
Strike index level	95.00
Expiry (days)	365
Interest rate (USD)	6.00%
Basket volatility	10.70%

Basket Options

	Call	Put
Total cost	$ 2,519,299	$ 752,181
Percent of forward	6.713%	2.004%

EXHIBIT 9–4

Implied Volatility: Basket Option Compared to Put Strip
40% DEM, 30% JPY, 20% ITL, 10% AUD
January 1993–April 1995

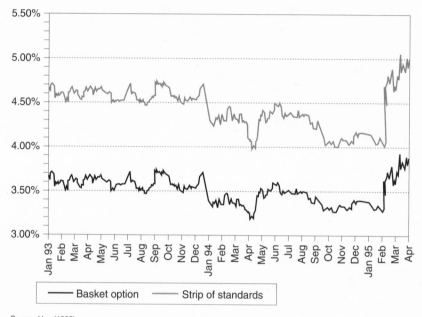

Source: Hsu (1995).

What is needed to calculate the basket implied volatility are the implieds for the legs USD/DEM, GBP/USD, and USD/JPY plus the implieds for the crosses GBP/DEM, GBP/JPY, and DEM/JPY. It is possible to derive a set of implied correlations from these volatilities. The implied correlation between currencies 1 and 2 is given by

$$\rho_{1,2} = \frac{\sigma_1^2 + \sigma_2^2 - \sigma_{1/2}^2}{2\sigma_1\sigma_2}$$

where σ_1^2 and σ_2^2 are the variances of exchange rates 1 and 2, and $\sigma_{1/2}^2$ is the variance of the cross rate of exchange between currencies 1 and 2. For example, the correlation between dollar/mark and dollar/yen is given by

$$\rho(USD/DEM, USD/JPY) = \frac{\sigma_{USD \atop DEM}^2 + \sigma_{USD \atop JPY}^2 - \sigma_{DEM \atop JPY}^2}{2\sigma_{USD \atop DEM}\sigma_{USD \atop JPY}}$$

The implied correlations can be used to create a set of co-variance terms

$$Cov(1,2) \equiv \sigma_{12} = \rho_{12}\sigma_1\sigma_2$$

that complete the variance–covariance matrix, **V**.

$$\mathbf{V} = \begin{bmatrix} \sigma_1^2 & \sigma_{12} & \sigma_{13} \\ \sigma_{21} & \sigma_2^2 & \sigma_{23} \\ \sigma_{31} & \sigma_{32} & \sigma_3^2 \end{bmatrix}$$

The implied variance of the basket is equal to the variance–covariance matrix pre-multiplied by the row vector of the currency weights and post-multiplied by the column vector of the currency weights. The weight of each currency is defined as its percentage component in the basket. The implied volatility of the basket is equal to the square root of the implied variance.

The value of a European basket option can be found directly from the forward exchange rate version of the BSGK model, as discussed in Chapter 6. The value of the put or the call is equal to

$$C = e^{-R_d\tau}\left(FN(y + \sigma\sqrt{\tau}) - KN(y)\right)$$

$$P = e^{-R_d\tau}\left(F(N(y + \sigma\sqrt{\tau}) - 1) - K(N(y) - 1)\right)$$

$$y = \frac{\ln\left(\frac{F}{K}\right) - \frac{\sigma^2}{2}\tau}{\sigma\sqrt{\tau}}$$

Exhibit 9–3 demonstrates the valuation of the basket option.

Examples of Other Exotic Options

The barrier, average, and basket options are the most common exotic options used to manage foreign exchange risk. However, there are a great number of other exotic currency options; financial engineers and academicians are constantly inventing new varieties of exotics. A few of them are as follows.

Compound Currency Option

A compound option delivers a standard currency option upon exercise (see Geske 1979, Rubinstein 1990, or DeRosa 1992 for valuation of compound options). A "ca-call" is a call option that delivers a standard call option upon exercise. A "ca-put" is a call that delivers a standard put option.

The Digital Option

A digital option has a payoff function that delivers a lump sum at exercise. It is not linearly related to the in-the-moneyness of the option (see Rubinstein and Reiner 1991b).

Lock Option

The lock option is a barrier digital option. A lock-in option releases a digital payoff at expiration provided that at some time in the life of the option one or more of its in-strikes have been triggered. The lock-in is a long volatility play. A lock-out option releases a digital payoff provided that no in-strike has been triggered, which makes it a short volatility bet.

Exploding Option

An exploding option automatically exercises at once when the spot exchange rate crosses the preset, in-the-money explode strike price.

Range Accumulation Option

The range accumulation option, also known as a range accrual option, makes a digital payout at expiration for each day in the option life that the spot exchange rate is located inside a certain preset range.

The Chooser Option

A chooser option, or "as-you-like-it" option, gives the holder the right to purchase before expiration either a call or a put with a certain strike (see Rubinstein 1991a).

Lookback Option

A lookback option has a payoff that depends not only on the asset price at expiry but also on the maximum or the minimum of the asset price over some time prior to expiry (see Garman 1989). The purpose of a lookback is to give the holder the most favorable price attained over some interval of time. Strictly speaking, a lookback really isn't an option in that there is no chance that it will not be exercised.

Perpetual American Currency Option

A perpetual American currency option has no expiration date. The value of this option derives from the early exercise privilege (see Garman 1986).

CROSS-CURRENCY WARRANTS

A cross-currency warrant is an option to buy (call warrant) or to sell (put warrant) one currency for another where the payoff function as well as option price are defined in a third currency. This warrant should not be confused with a cross-rate option. A cross-rate option is a standard option on a cross exchange rate, such as mark/yen, where the price of the option is quoted in either marks or yen. The presence of a third currency is what distinguishes a cross-currency warrant from a cross-rate option.

The first publicly traded cross-currency warrant in the United States was issued by AT&T Capital Corporation in October 1990. This warrant was a dollar-payoff option on the mark/yen cross rate (i.e., mark put/yen call). It was American exercise with expiration on October 31, 1992. The payoff function was

$$\text{Max}\left[0, \$50 \times \frac{85.20 - S}{85.20}\right]$$

Exercise of the warrant at DEM/JPY equal to 80.00 would have paid $3.05. Many cross-currency warrants since have had payoff functions similar in structure to the AT&T warrant, so it is possible to speak of a generalized payoff function. The generalized payoff function for a cross-currency put warrant is

$$\text{Max}\left[0, A \times \frac{K-S}{K}\right]$$

The generalized payoff function for a cross-currency call warrant is

$$\text{Max}\left[0, A \times \frac{S-K}{K}\right]$$

where A is a scaling factor, K is the strike, and S is the spot-cross exchange rate.

Margrabe (see DeRosa 1992) demonstrated that a cross-currency option can be valued in either of two ways. The more direct method is to value the option as though it were a cross-rate option and then simply convert the premium to the third currency at the prevailing spot exchange rate. In the example of the AT&T warrant, the procedure would be to value the option as an ordinary mark put/yen call, working with the premium in marks or yen. Next, that premium would be converted to dollars at the spot exchange rate (dollar/mark or dollar/yen).

In the second approach, the cross-currency option is treated as a Margrabe option. A Margrabe option (Margrabe 1978) is an option to exchange one risky asset for another risky asset. Seen as a Margrabe option, the cross-currency mark/yen option is an option to exchange one risky asset, dollar/yen, for another risky asset, dollar/mark. Dravid, Richardson, and Sun (1994) apply Margrabe's method to value European cross-currency warrants. They assumed that the dollar-exchange rates follow diffusion processes

$$d\tilde{S}_{\text{dem}} = \left(R_{\text{usd}} - R_{\text{dem}}\right)\tilde{S}_{\text{dem}} dt + \sigma_m \tilde{S}_{\text{dem}} d\tilde{z}$$

$$d\tilde{S}_{\text{jpy}} = \left(R_{\text{usd}} - R_{\text{jpy}}\right)\tilde{S}_{\text{jpy}} dt + \sigma_y \tilde{S}_{\text{jpy}} d\tilde{z}_2$$

where

$\tilde{S}_{dem}$ and $\tilde{S}_{jpy}$ are the spot dollar exchange rates for marks and yen, quoted American convention.

R_{usd}, R_{dem}, and R_{jpy} are the risk-free interest rates for dollar, marks, and yen.

σ_m and σ_y are the standard deviations for marks and yen.

$\tilde{z}_1$ and $\tilde{z}_2$ are two white noise processes with correlation ρ.

The cross-rate itself (i.e., mark/yen) at time t will be denoted as S_t

$$\tilde{S}_t = \frac{\tilde{S}_{dem}}{\tilde{S}_{jpy}}$$

Under the perfect-market, risk-neutral conditions, Dravid, Richardson, and Sun show that the values of call and put warrants with time to expiration τ are given by

$$c(S_t, K, \tau) = \frac{A}{K}\left[S_t e^{-\left(R_{usd} - R_{jpy} + R_{dem} - \sigma_y^2 + \rho\sigma_m\sigma_y\right)\tau} N(d_1)\right.$$
$$\left. - Ke^{-R_{usd}\tau} N\left(d_1 - \sigma\sqrt{\tau}\right)\right]$$

$$p(S_t, K, \tau) = \frac{A}{K}\left[-S_t e^{-\left(R_{usd} - R_{jpy} + R_{dem} - \sigma_y^2 + \rho\sigma_m\sigma_y\right)\tau} N(-d_1)\right.$$
$$\left. + Ke^{-R_{usd}\tau} N\left(-d_1 + \sigma\sqrt{\tau}\right)\right]$$

where

$$d_1 = \frac{\ln\left(\dfrac{S_t}{K}\right) + \left(R_{jpy} - R_{dem} + \sigma_y^2 - \rho\sigma_m\sigma_y\right)\tau}{\sigma\sqrt{\tau}} + \frac{1}{2}\sigma\sqrt{\tau}$$

$$\sigma^2 \equiv \sigma_m^2 + \sigma_y^2 - 2\rho\sigma_m\sigma_y$$

Exhibit 9–5A shows the value of a one-year, at-the-money spot European call warrant on the mark/yen cross rate.

The interesting thing about the Margrabe option formulation is that the value of the cross-currency warrant on mark/yen is a function of the correlation between dollar/mark and dollar/yen. The value of the cross-currency warrant is inversely related to the correlation (Exhibit 9–5B). This is intuitively plausible because the lower the correlation between dollar/mark and dollar/yen, the higher the likelihood of a large move in mark/yen.

Cross-currency warrants are issued on a fairly regular basis. Whether they offer an advantage over standard cross-rate options that actively trade in the interbank market is a matter of consumer preference and price. At least some of their appeal stems from the fact that they bring options on cross rates—normally exclusive to the domain of the interbank currency option market—to a wide spectrum of investors.

QUANTOS OPTIONS AND EQUITY INDEX–LINKED WARRANTS WITH SPECIAL CURRENCY FEATURES

An index-linked warrant is a call or put option on a stock market index.[4] The warrant may be exchange-listed or over-the-counter. At expiration, the holder of the warrant is promised the maximum of zero and a payment based on the level of some stock market index in relation to the warrant strike price. The S&P 500, Nikkei 225 and 300 (Japan), CAC 40 (France), FTSE 100 (U.K.), and DAX 30 (Germany) are some examples of popular stock market indices.

There are two general types of index-linked warrants. One has a "floating" exchange rate and the other a "fixed" exchange rate. The fixed exchange rate version is popularly known as a quantos option. The floater works as follows, using the example of a now-expired PaineWebber Nikkei call warrant.

Nikkei strike	29,249.06
Exchange rate	Floating
Divisor	10
Expiration	April 8, 1993
Exercise	American

EXHIBIT 9–5A

Cross-Currency Call Warrant
One-Year, At-the-Money Spot Call Warrant on DEM/JPY
R_{USD} 5%; R_{DEM} 4%; R_{JPY} 2%; $\sigma_{USD/DEM}$ 14%; $\sigma_{USD/JPY}$ 12%; ρ 65%

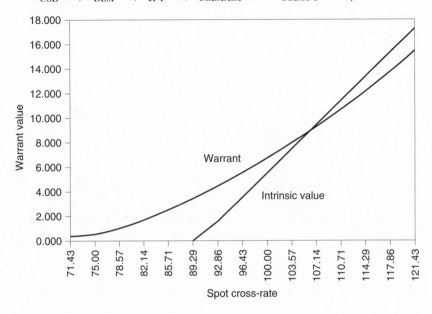

EXHIBIT 9–5B

Cross-Currency Call Warrant versus Correlation
One-Year, At-the-Money Spot Call Warrant on DEM/JPY

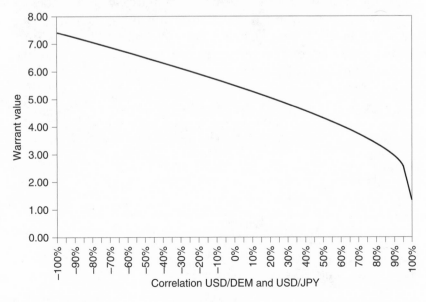

The divisor scales the index down to a level where the warrant can be comfortably traded by retail investors. The payoff function at expiration of this call warrant is

$$\text{Max}\begin{bmatrix} 0, \text{Nikkei} \leq 29,249.06 \\ x, \text{if Nikkei} > 29,249.06 \end{bmatrix}$$

where

$$x = \frac{1}{\text{divisor}}[\text{Nikkei} - \text{strike}]\frac{1 \text{ yen}}{\text{USD/JPY}}$$

If the Nikkei had been at 35,000 at expiration and the exchange rate had been 150, the warrant would have paid the holder

$$\frac{1}{10}[35,000 - 29,249.06]\frac{1}{150} = \$3.83$$

Dravid, Richardson, and Sun (1993) show that the value of the European exercise floater is equal to the value of an otherwise identical option that is quoted in and pays in the foreign currency converted into dollars at the prevailing exchange rate.[5] In other words, the value of the PaineWebber Nikkei call European exercise is equal to the product of (a) the value of a similar call warrant that pays in yen

$$\text{Max}\begin{bmatrix} 0, \text{Nikkei} \leq 29,249.06 \\ w, \text{Nikkei} > 29,249,06 \end{bmatrix}$$

where

$$w = \frac{1}{\text{divisor}}[\text{Nikkei} - \text{strike}]$$

and (b) the current exchange rate of yen for dollars. The value of floater calls and puts is given by

$$C_t^{\text{floater}} = S_t \left[Z_t e^{-D\tau} N(d_1) - K e^{-R_f \tau} N(d_2) \right]$$

$$P_t^{\text{floater}} = S_t \left[K e^{-R_f \tau} N(-d_2) - Z_t e^{-D\tau} N(-d_1) \right]$$

where

$$d_1 = \frac{\ln\left(\dfrac{Z_t}{K}\right) + \left(R_f - D + \dfrac{\sigma_z^2}{2}\right)\tau}{\sigma_z \sqrt{\tau}}$$

$$d_2 = d_1 - \sigma_z \sqrt{\tau}$$

and

- S_t is the exchange rate at time t quoted American convention.
- D is the continuously compounded dividend rate on the foreign stock index.
- Z_t is the level of the foreign stock market index at time t.
- K is the strike in foreign currency.
- τ is the time remaining until expiration.
- R_f is the risk-free rate in the foreign currency.
- σ_z is the volatility of the foreign stock market.

The deltas of the call and put warrants are, respectively

$$\delta_{\text{call}} = S_t e^{-D\tau} N(d_1)$$

and

$$\delta_{\text{put}} = -S_t e^{-D\tau} N(-d_1)$$

The second class of warrants has a fixed exchange rate and is therefore more interesting from a currency-risk perspective. This type of warrant is equivalent to an option on a hypothetical foreign stock index, such as the Nikkei, that is denominated in an alternative currency, such as the U.S. dollar. The value of these warrants is dependent upon the level of the foreign stock market index but not upon the exchange rate. The fixed exchange rate warrant is an example of a "quantos option" (also referred to as a "guaranteed exchange rate option").

An example of a fixed exchange rate warrant is the now-expired PaineWebber Nikkei put. The terms were as follows:

Nikkei strike	29,249.06
Exchange rate	159.08
Divisor	5
Expiration	April 8, 1993
Exercise	American

The payoff at expiration of this call warrant was

$$\text{Max}\begin{bmatrix} 0, \text{Nikkei} \geq 29,249.06 \\ x, \text{if Nikkei} < 29,249.06 \end{bmatrix}$$

where

$$x = \frac{1}{\text{divisor}}[\text{strike} - \text{Nikkei}]\frac{1 \text{ yen}}{159.80}$$

If the Nikkei had been at 25,000 at expiration, the warrant would have paid the holder

$$\frac{1}{5}[29,249.06 - 25,000]\frac{1}{159.80} = \$5.32$$

The payoff function for calls and puts can be written in the general form

$$\text{Call} = \text{Max}[\bar{S}Z_T - \bar{S}K, 0]$$

and

$$\text{Put} = \text{Max}[\bar{S}K - \bar{S}Z_T, 0]$$

where $\bar{S}$ is the fixed level of the exchange rate.

Derman, Karasinski, and Wecker (1990) and Dravid, Richardson, and Sun (1993) solve for the value of this option given European exercise. The value of a call and a put are, respectively[6]

$$C_t^{\text{fixed}} = \left[Z_t e^{(R_f - D')\tau} N(d_1) - KN(d_2) \right] \overline{S} e^{-R_d \tau}$$

and

$$P_t^{\text{fixed}} = \left[KN(-d_2) - Z_t e^{(R_f - D')\tau} N(-d_1) \right] \overline{S} e^{-R_d \tau}$$

where

$$d_1 = \frac{\ln\left(\dfrac{Z_t}{K}\right) + \left(R_f - D' + \dfrac{\sigma_z^2}{2} \right)\tau}{\sigma_z \sqrt{\tau}}$$

$$d_2 = d_1 - \sigma_z \sqrt{\tau}$$

$$D' = D + \sigma_{zs}$$

σ_s and σ_{zs} are the standard deviation of the exchange rate (in rates of return form) and the covariance between the stock market index and the exchange rate, respectively.

The deltas for the call and put are given by

$$\delta_{\text{call}} = \overline{S} e^{-(R_d - R_f + D')\tau} N(d_1)$$

and

$$\delta_{\text{put}} = -\overline{S} e^{-(R_d - R_f + D')\tau} N(-d_1)$$

The role of the covariance term σ_{SZ} is interesting. To place things in the more familiar context of correlation

$$\sigma_{zs} = \rho_{zs} \sigma_z \sigma_s$$

where ρ_{zs} is the correlation coefficient between the stock market index and exchange rate. Exhibit 9–6 displays sample theoretical

EXHIBIT 9–6

Fixed and Floating Exchange Rate Equity Warrants

	Fixed Exchange Rate Warrants					
	USD Interest = 6% JPY Interest = 8%		USD Interest = 8% JPY Interest = 8%		USD Interest = 8% JPY Interest = 6%	
Correlation	Call	Put	Call	Put	Call	Put
−100%	15.95	5.53	15.64	5.42	14.23	6.04
−50%	15.05	5.92	14.75	5.80	13.39	6.45
0%	14.17	6.33	13.89	6.20	12.59	6.88
50%	13.33	6.76	13.07	6.62	11.82	7.33
100%	12.53	7.20	12.28	7.06	11.08	7.79
	Floating Exchange Rate Warrants					
	13.89	6.20	13.89	6.20	12.85	7.02

Assumptions: One-year warrants. Spot exchange rate = 1. Stock index level = 100. Strike = 100. Volatility of stock index = 25%. Volatility of exchange rate = 10%. No dividends.

values for call and put fixed exchange rate options at various levels of assumed correlation. Calls are inversely related and puts positively related to the level of correlation between the stock market index and the exchange rate.

Aside from listed fixed exchange rate warrants, quantos options are generally found in the domain of the over-the-counter market. Usually they are created by option dealers at the request of end-user clients. Dealers almost always hedge an exposure to a quantos option that they take onto their book. This can be costly if there are substantial transactions costs in the underlying instruments. In addition to the normal transactions costs, it will also be more expensive for the dealer to create a quantos option on an underlying stock market index that tends to make discontinuous price movements. The dealer also must consider the possibility that the correlation between the stock market index and the exchange rate might be sufficiently unstable so as to create the risk of under- or overhedging. The advantage of the quantos option is that it provides a perfect exchange rate hedge, no matter that the future level of the stock index is an unknown when the option is transacted. But as Piros (1996) points out, the investor probably should expect to pay for this convenience.

CROSS-CURRENCY EQUITY-LINKED SWAPS

Equity derivative instruments offer investors a variety of ways to take exposure, hedge, or go short stock markets apart from assuming long or short positions in actual common stocks. All of the major stock markets now have actively traded stock-index futures contracts. There are also listed options contracts on stock indices as well as options on stock index futures. In the over-the-counter market, there is a large market for stock-index swaps, some of which have interesting currency features (see DeRosa and Nehro 1992).

An equity-linked swap is a contractual agreement between two counterparties, one of whom is an investor, whereby one counterparty pays or receives the equity index return. This return can either be the equity composite return or the equity index total return. The counterparty who pays the equity return receives another floating rate (usually LIBOR) interest payment. The LIBOR term—usually three or six months—matches the swap reset frequency. In this fashion, the investor (a counterparty) can use the equity index swap to gain or add exposure (receive index return and pay LIBOR), hedge exposure (pay index return and receive LIBOR), or short exposure (pay index return and receive LIBOR). Equity index-linked swaps are based on a notional amount of principal that is not exchanged with the counterparty. At the end of each LIBOR term, the notional value of the swap is adjusted upwards or downwards according to the performance of the stock index. The actual principal is invested in what is called an operant portfolio, which is held by the investor's custodian bank or trust company. The operant portfolio is invested in securities with the intention of outperforming the investor's liability payment in the swap agreement—in other words, LIBOR or an equity index—without exceeding the investor's tolerance for risk. The most basic operant portfolio to gain exposure to an equity market is composed of LIBOR-based floating rate notes, a natural for index-linked swaps because they also have periodic reset dates when their coupons are adjusted to market LIBOR conditions. This portfolio would cover the LIBOR liability that the investor would periodically be required to pay when receiving the equity index payment.

For example, the mechanics of an S&P 500 index–linked swap is shown in Exhibit 9–7. The investor's objective is to gain exposure to the S&P index and outperform the index. The terms are as follows:

S&P 500 Index–Linked Swap

Investor pays: six-month USD LIBOR – 15 basis points.

Counterparty pays: S&P 500 Index total return.

Notional amount: $100 million.

Reset: semiannual.

Swap maturity: three years.

Note that this swap is supposed to have been negotiated at LIBOR minus 15 basis points. In the exhibit, the S&P 500 total

E X H I B I T   9-7

S&P 500 Index–Linked Swap
Investor to Pay Six-Month LIBOR minus 15 Basis Points
Counterparty to Pay S&P 500 Total Return

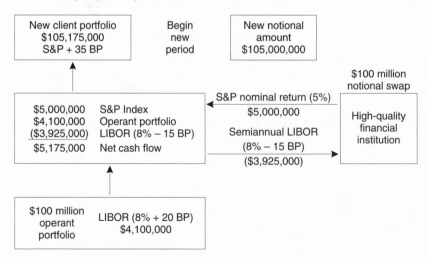

return over the first six months is 5 percent, and the annualized return on the operant portfolio is LIBOR (8 percent for the period) plus 20 basis points. The operant portfolio could just as easily be a portfolio of S&P stocks. The investor could pay the return of the S&P 500 and receive LIBOR as a means to hedge in a declining market.

Index-linked swaps offer institutional portfolio managers advantages over the alternative of investing directly in common shares. Swaps are efficient because they avoid cash market transaction costs and administrative costs. They deliver the exact index return with no tracking error. Moreover, the configuration of the swap with the operant portfolio allows for potential enhancement of the index return. Any performance above LIBOR in the operant portfolio translates into an overperformance above the equity index when combined with the swap. One disadvantage with the swap vis-à-vis common shares is that the swap is less liquid, should the investor wish to arrange for an early termination, although an opposite and canceling cash trade can always be executed in the operant portfolio. Also, the swap involves a single counterparty credit exposure, whereas stocks diversify credit exposure. However, raising the counterparty to AA or AAA quality can provide sufficient credit protection. The extent of the counterparty risk should not be exaggerated as it does not pertain to the notional value but rather to the net accrued difference between the equity index and the LIBOR interest payment in between swap reset dates. Moreover, in any given reset period, the investor's payment could exceed the S&P index return. In the event of counterparty bankruptcy, the investor would not remit payment, and the next positive difference would accrue to the investor.

Index-linked swaps are more interesting when they involve foreign stock indices. In the basic sense, they may be more efficient than direct equity investments because the counterparty, presumably a multinational financial institution, may be in an advantaged position to collect dividend payments by virtue of not being subject to full tax withholding in some countries. Therefore, the investor might receive a higher return than could be received by investing in the cash instrument as there would not be a withholding tax.

More interesting yet, swaps can be structured to include currency risk–management features. Swaps may be currency hedged with respect to principal or interest or both. Generally, if the index swap payment and LIBOR payment are unhedged and in the same currency, the cost of the index-linked swap is unchanged. But if the investor wishes to make the interest rate payments in one currency and receive a currency-hedged return on the foreign stock market index, the swap pricing must be different. Consider the following swap:

Cross-Currency Hedged S&P 500 Index Swap

Investor pays: six-month USD LIBOR + 170 basis points.

Counterparty pays: S&P 500 Index total return in Canadian dollars hedged.

Notional amount: $100 million.

Reset: semiannual.

Currency: USD.

Swap maturity: three years.

Exchange rate: fixed at beginning of swap (1.400).

The mechanics of this swap are displayed in Exhibit 9–8. Two factors complicate the pricing of this swap. One is the interest differential between Canada and the United States. The second has to do with the counterparty having to deliver a hedged return on unknown, future performance of the stock market index—which is the same problem addressed earlier in this chapter, concerning equity-index warrants with a fixed exchange rate (the "quantos" option).

Macro-index equity index–linked swaps are also traded on popular global benchmarks such as the MSCI EAFE Index (i.e., Europe, Australia, and the Far East) and FT-Actuaries Index. These swaps also have been known to include currency hedging.

SOME WORDS OF ENCOURAGEMENT AND SOME WORDS OF CAUTION

Exotic currency options and equity derivatives with complex currency features are alluring on an intellectual level. Some of

EXHIBIT 9-8

Cross-Currency Hedged S&P 500 Index Swap
Investor to Pay Six-Month LIBOR plus 170 Basis Points
Counterparty to Pay S&P 500 Total Return in CAD
Hedged (1 USD = 1.40 CAD)

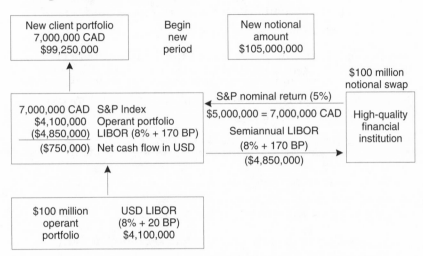

them offer practical solutions to the currency hedging dilemma. Practitioners of finance are well advised to pay serious attention to these new financial products. Most exotic derivatives, like the ones discussed in this chapter, are designed to reduce or at least cope with foreign exchange risk. Others may have a similarly stated purpose but include incidental exposure to what might be an obscure set of risks. A familiar paradigm should never be forgotten—where there is the prospect of great benefit there is also the possibility of great risk. This is not to say that there is anything wrong with taking risk but simply to point out that it is always essential to clearly understand the risk embedded in any structure before making an investment decision.

NOTES

1. Also see Cox and Rubinstein (1985), Rubinstein and Reiner (1991a), Benson and Daniel (1991), and Hudson (1991).

2. See Kemna and Vorst (1990), Margrabe (1978 and 1990), and Ruttiens (1990).

3. See Boyle and Emanuel (1985) and Rubinstein (1990).

4. The author wishes to acknowledge useful discussions with Dr. William Margrabe on this result and others concerning index-linked warrants.

5. Also see Reiner (1992) and Babbel and Isenberg (1993).

6. Dravid, Richardson, and Sun postulate that risk-neutral probability conditions prevail and that spot prices obey the following differential equations

$$d\tilde{Z}_{usd} = (R_d - D)Z_{usd}dt + \sigma_z\tilde{Z}_{usd}dV^z + \sigma_s Z_{usd}dV^s$$

$$d\tilde{S} = (R_d - R_f)S'dt + \sigma_s S dV^s$$

$$d\tilde{Z} = (R_f - D - \rho_{zs}\sigma_z\sigma_s)Z dt + \sigma_z Z dV^z$$

where Z is the foreign stock market index in the local currency, Z_{usd} is the index in U.S. dollars ($Z_{usd} \equiv ZS_t$), and V^z and V^s are two Brownian motion processes with correlation ρ_{zs}.

CHAPTER 10

Currency Overlay Programs

The objective of a currency overlay program is to manage the foreign exchange exposure that derives from holding international assets. By definition, an overlay program addresses currency risk apart from the investment process that determines portfolio composition. Equity portfolio managers traditionally apply their talents to country, sector, and stock selection. This leaves open the possibility that an independent currency manager can add value in an overlay framework. In fixed-income investing, however, many but not all believe that international yield curve decisions are coupled with and imply currency decisions. Having an independent overlay program, it is feared, might create accidental currency exposures that magnify or nullify the intended strategy of the portfolio manager. While this point is debatable, there is no doubt that overlay is more popular in combination with international equity portfolios than with international fixed-income portfolios. Some portfolio managers, meaning the person or persons responsible for making country and security selection in the underlying portfolio, run overlay programs themselves, but it has become commonplace to engage specialized currency risk managers. The mandate for overlay managers runs the full gamut from passive hedging to active management of currency exposure as an asset class to option replication and other forms of dynamic hedging.

THE SEPARATION RULE

It is necessary to be precise about the definition of currency risk because movements in foreign exchange rates can affect international investments in many ways. In the context of overlay, currency risk is usually taken to mean the risk of currency translation gains or losses on the conversion from the local currency of the investment back to the home currency of the investor. In this paradigm, all other ways that exchange rates affect international investments are classified as local market risks. Local market risks include but are not limited to strikes, changes in the cost of raw materials, shifts in world demand, technological change, and revision of government policies. Consider the following cases:

1. A dollar-based investor buys a French Government bond. The price of the bond, quoted in French francs, remains stable, but the value of the franc falls by 10 percent against the dollar. This is an example of exchange rate risk as it applies to currency overlay.

2. A dollar-based investor buys shares in a French pharmaceutical company that exports a major portion of its output to Australia. The French franc is stable against the dollar but rises in value by 10 percent against the Australian dollar. This might adversely affect the competitive position of the company and depress the value of the shares. Although this is an exchange rate phenomenon, this risk is classified as a local market risk.

The distinction between currency risk and local market risk as it pertains to overlay leads to a useful decomposition of investment returns. Define the local currency holding period return on an investment bought at the end of period 1 and held until the end of period 2 as

$$R_2^{local} = \frac{(P_2 + d_2)}{P_1} - 1$$

where P_1 and P_2 are the prices of the investment at the end of two successive periods (1 and 2), respectively, as observed in the currency of the local market, and d_2 is the amount of any dividends or other cash distributions paid to the investor at the end of the second period. Calculation of the total return in the investor's home currency requires that local prices and dividends be converted at prevailing spot exchange rates. The total return in the domestic currency ("home") is

$$R_2^{\text{home}} = \frac{P_2 S_2 + d_2 S_2}{P_1 S_1} - 1$$

which equals

$$R_2^{\text{home}} = \left[\frac{S_2}{S_1}\right] \times \left[\frac{P_2 + d_2}{P_1}\right] - 1$$

where S_1 and S_2 are the spot exchange rates at the ends of periods 1 and 2, quoted in American terms (i.e., the number of units of domestic currency equal to one unit of foreign currency). The first term in brackets, on the right-hand side of the second equation, is the portion of the total return generated by exchange rate movements. The second term in brackets is the local market performance.

For example, suppose that the shares of a hypothetical Japanese company sell for 1,000 yen today and that the exchange rate is 100 yen to one U.S. dollar. Over the next year, the stock pays no dividends but rises to 1,200 yen. At the end of the year, the exchange rate is 95 yen per dollar. Then

$$R^{\text{local}} = \frac{1200}{1000} - 1 = 20.00\%$$

$$R^{\text{home}} = \left[\frac{\frac{1}{95}}{\frac{1}{100}}\right] \times \left[\frac{1200}{1000}\right] - 1 = 26.32\%$$

Some overlay managers infer from this decomposition that there is a natural division of labor in the investment management process by which currency risk can or even should be managed separately from local market risk. The idea has become known as the separation rule. Taken to its logical end, the separation rule means it is possible to think about whether an exposure to the pound sterling should or should not be hedged independent of the consideration of whether to continue holding the investment. Furthermore, the foreign exchange implications to an investor of owning a share in a British bank should be no different from those of owning a gilt-edged bond or of holding any other investment that happens to be denominated in sterling.

SOME PRACTICAL MATTERS RELATING TO OVERLAY

Determination of Currency Exposure

The first step in the implementation of an overlay program is the determination of what currency exposures are going to be managed. A convenient demarcation of the responsibilities of the portfolio manager and the overlay manager is to have the overlay managers work only with the currency exposure of the portfolio benchmark. For example, the overlay manager might manage the risk of the FT-Actuaries World non-USA Index (Exhibit 5–5). By implication, the portfolio manager would be responsible for any currency exposures that deviate from the benchmark. Continuing with the example of the FT-Actuaries Index, the sterling weight of 14.86 percent would be the responsibility of the overlay manager. If the actual portfolio had an exposure of 20 percent to sterling-denominated assets, the portfolio manager would have responsibility for a "long" position in sterling equal to the residual 5.14 percent. To take a case to the contrary, if the exposure to U.K. assets were 10 percent, the portfolio manager would be "short" sterling equal to 4.86 percent.

Another arrangement is to have the overlay manager work with the actual currency exposure of the portfolio. This requires open lines of communication between the currency overlay manager and the portfolio manager, especially whenever any significant shifts in currency exposure occur, such as after portfolio rebalancing or by market revaluation. Many institutional investors engage the services of more than one portfolio manager. One prevalent configuration among large U.S. pension fund trusts allocates the largest portion of total assets to passive index fund managers while reserving smaller pieces for active managers who have specialized skills in local markets (see Exhibit 5–9). Having multiple managers may reflect a desire to diversify management style or might be an attempt to select superior investment talent. In this case, the exposure to each currency must be summed across all of the independently managed portfolios.

Investments can take the form of any number of derivative instruments, which can complicate the assessment of currency exposure. Some forms of derivatives give investors a choice of whether to assume currency exposure. Take the instance of the Nikkei index futures contract as it is traded on the Osaka Stock Exchange. This contract has no exposure to the Japanese yen except for unconverted profits and losses from variation margin and initial margin deposits that are yen-denominated. A similar investment could be structured with an equity-index–linked swap, as was described in Chapter 9. In an equity-index–linked swap, the investor receives from the counterparty periodic payments based on the performance of a stock market index and makes payments to the counterparty based on some floating interest rate, usually in the investor's base currency. This structure produces no currency exposure apart from accrued interim net swap payments. Equity stock options, equity index options, and warrants can have exceedingly complex exposure to exchange rate risk. If the option premium and payoff at expiration are denominated in foreign currency, the currency exposure is equal to the market value of the option. But other options have no foreign currency exposure at all, for instance, any equity-related option with a payoff denominated in the investor's base currency. An example is the JPN options listed on the American Stock Exchange, which have no yen exposure; the JPNs are options on the Nikkei index as though it were denominated in U.S. dollars. Then there are structured notes. A structured note is a debt instrument where the coupon and possibly the face value are linked mathematically to asset prices, interest rates, or foreign exchange rates. Practically any exposure imaginable can be embedded in a structured note, so the question as to exchange rate risk must be approached analytically on a case-by-case basis.

Management of the Cash Flow Generated
by an Overlay Program

All currency overlay programs ultimately produce cash flow, whether positive or negative in sign. Any program that hedges with spot or forward foreign exchange contracts generates cash flow at the time that contracts are rolled or closed. Programs that use currency options move cash around when puts or calls are bought or sold, or in the event of exercise. The question of how to handle the overlay cash flow does not have an obvious answer. Whether or not to mix the overlay cash flow with the portfolio assets and whether to include it in the investment process are tough questions.

One possibility is to run a noninvasive overlay program. A noninvasive overlay program isolates its cash flow from the underlying portfolio. This requires that a pool of assets be reserved to pay out or receive funds from the overlay program. If the pool is sufficiently large relative to the size of the cash flows from the overlay program, there never will be a need to invade the assets of the underlying portfolio. This convenience is at the cost of added administrative costs and at the sacrifice of having the assets in the reserve pool not participate in the returns of the underlying portfolio.

Why go to the trouble to set up a noninvasive program? The obvious reason is that portfolio managers rightfully object to having to buy or liquidate securities upon demand, especially at times and prices not of their choosing, to meet the cash flow needs of a currency hedging program. Allowing the overlay program to invade the underlying securities portfolio can create ambiguities about the portfolio manager's performance. The problem is the same one faced by an open-end mutual fund when shareholders add and subtract from the portfolio by purchasing or redeeming shares. The best solution for performance analysis is to use the time-weighted rate of return method (Lorie 1968).

ACTIVE PROGRAMS: CURRENCY
AS AN ASSET CLASS

Currency overlay managers have various styles and risk appetites. At the far end of the risk spectrum are the actively managed programs. In an active program, the overlay manager has authority to radically alter the currency exposure of the portfolio by taking long and short positions in spot and forward contracts and in currency options with the intent of expressing directional views on exchange rates. Leverage may or may not be permitted. Less aggressive active managers set out with the more modest objective of exploiting some alleged market anomalies, such as price trends (Levitch and Thomas 1993) or biases in the forward exchange rate (Kritzman 1993).

Some form of risk control must be specified to the active manager, because it is rarely the intent to give any manager an open-ended speculative mandate. Yet popular risk constraints tend to be quite arbitrary. The overlay manager might be prohibited from taking any position larger than double that of the index weighting in a currency. Or the program might be limited to selective hedging within the range of 0 to 100 percent of the index exposure. While constraints like these can have some limited effectiveness in risk control, more sophisticated measures can be imagined. One idea is to proceed along the lines of the dollars-at-risk methodology and enforce sensible shock-loss protective measures (as described in Chapter 7).

Performance measurement for an active manager is measured relative to the size of the actual security portfolio. For example, a $100 million overlay that generates $8 million of trading profits (including the currency returns on the portfolio's foreign exchange exposures) can report a performance of 8 percent. It has become standard practice in the industry to report performance in absolute terms as well as in risk-adjusted form. The standard for the latter has become the Sharpe ratio (AIMR 1993)

$$\frac{\overline{R}_p - R_d}{\sigma}$$

where $\overline{R}_P$ is the portfolio currency performance, R_d is the risk-free domestic interest rate, and σ is the standard deviation of currency performance returns. Among the very few sources of historical performance statistics for active currency managers is the Ferrell Capital Management survey (Exhibit 10–1). The sample is sorted into "systematic traders," which refers to traders who primarily rely on technical analysis, and "discretionary" managers, which means traders who use fundamental analysis. The data in Exhibit 10-1 show that there have been a few periods of outstanding performance but also a substantial degree of variability in the returns for the active managers taken as a group.

Active overlay programs are typically undertaken upon the belief that currency management should be regarded as an asset class separate from equities, bonds, or any other assets that comprise the securities portfolio. In the same vein, some institutional investors have embraced the somewhat controversial idea that commodities trading strategies are a legitimate asset class. However, the notion of what should constitute an asset class is somewhat vague. The case for active currency management is often made with the support of the finding that rates of return on managed accounts are relatively uncorrelated with returns on other

E X H I B I T   10–1

Ferrell Capital Management Foreign Exchange Manager Universe, Total Returns

	Systematic Traders	Discretionary Traders	FX Index All Traders
1987	51.23%	31.15%	46.17%
1988	42.95%	−3.55%	17.39%
1989	24.69%	7.61%	17.83%
1990	50.57%	21.59%	56.38%
1991	24.29%	25.47%	21.51%
1992	17.38%	6.63%	10.62%
1993	−4.98%	15.50%	1.08%
1994	−10.60%	1.67%	−6.36%
Summary Statistics			
Geometric mean	22.38%	12.69%	19.00%
Standard deviation	23.56%	12.17%	21.25%
Percent of periods with gain	54.64%	61.64%	51.55%
Average gain in gain period	7.13%	2.60%	5.57%
Average loss in loss period	−4.28%	1.44%	−2.68%
Maximum drawdown (peak to valley)	22.49%	8.03%	14.78%
Sharpe ratio (5% risk-free rate)	0.74	0.63	0.66

asset categories. There is a subtle issue here. The lack of correlation suggests that active currency programs are good diversifiers, but that may not be sufficient to prove they are a desirable addition to an investment portfolio. In a theoretical context, any proposed asset class should be Pareto optimal in the risk-expected return plane: Adding the candidate asset class should advance the portfolio to a superior efficient frontier. The question turns on whether there exists a group of specialized investment managers who can demonstrate ability to add value relative to risk. This remains an open question that is under more or less ongoing evaluation by the investment community.

OPTION REPLICATION PROGRAMS

Currency option replication programs are undertaken by investors who believe that a desired option can be replicated by dynamic hedging at a cheaper cost than what would have to be paid to buy the actual option. A replication program takes a position in foreign exchange (either spot or forward) to match the delta of the target option. To take a concrete example, suppose that an investor wishes to replicate a one-year USD call/DEM put with 10 million USD of face that is struck 5 percent below the at-the-money forward. Assume the following conditions hold:

Exchange Rates	American Quotation
Spot exchange rate (1.4100 USD/DEM)	0.70922
Forward exchange rate (1.3915 USD/DEM)	0.71865
95% strike (1.4647 USD/DEM)	0.68273
Option Parameters	
Expiration	1 year
Implied volatility	13%
Option face	$10,000,000 USD
Option delta	$ 3,092,000 USD

Replication begins by taking a long spot position equal to $3,092,000 USD/DEM. Because the delta of the target option changes as a function of many factors, including the spot exchange rate, implied volatility, time to expiration, and the foreign and domestic interest rates, it is necessary to adjust the size of the spot position regularly. This is why replication is sometimes called dynamic hedging. For example, if spot were to advance to 1.4200, the correct delta hedge then would be $3,281,000, all other things constant. The problem with replication programs is that a large move in the spot rate might occur so suddenly that it would be impossible to speedily rebalance the hedge.

The justification for option replication is a belief that a desired option is expensive as it is priced in the market. To say that an option is expensive could have several meanings. A put on a discount currency will usually appear expensive because the option price must reflect the forward discount. Replication cannot get around this problem because some form of discount may be paid in the form of spot/next or tom/next points in the process of rolling the dynamic hedge. Another argument for replication is the assertion that buying an option is expensive because of the option bid–offer spread. The problem with this is that replication itself encounters another bid–offer spread, namely the one in the spot market, every time position is adjusted. Any substantive argument that an option is expensive must involve a statement about implied volatility. Taken by itself, a high level of implied volatility may mean that an option is expensive but it does not necessarily mean that option replication can save money. The reason comes from basic option pricing theory. Recall from the discussion in Chapter 6 that the BSGK model was founded on the notion that a perfectly executed, frictionless cash hedge could be combined with an option to create a riskless position. By extension, it can be said that a perfectly executed replication program should be able to produce the same experience as owning an option. The question is whether the subsequent actual volatility in exchange rates is greater than, equal to, or less than the implied volatility of the option at the time of the commencement of the replication program. If the subsequent actual volatility is greater than the original implied volatility, the experience of the replication program can be inferior to the foregone opportunity of owning the actual option. On the other hand, if the subsequent actual volatility is less than the original implied, the replication program may be able to achieve actual cost savings.

Exhibit 10–2 shows implied volatility and subsequently observed actual volatility for one-month USD/DEM options for the period October 9, 1993, to October 9, 1995. There is no tendency for implied volatility to be above or below actual spot volatility, and this is consistent with the history of the foreign exchange option market. This is why it is difficult to claim that there is any clear advantage to replication over owning an actual option.

Beyond the question of implied and actual volatility, replication has considerable operational risks. Running an option replication program in lieu of buying an option is no different from assuming a short gamma position. Even a perfectly executed, error-free program can be the victim of large spot movements, as any option dealer will attest. A large gapping move in spot may be nearly impossible to match by adjusting the cash position in a timely fashion.

E X H I B I T   10–2

USD/DEM Actual and Implied Volatilities, One-Month Options
October 9, 1993–October 9, 1995

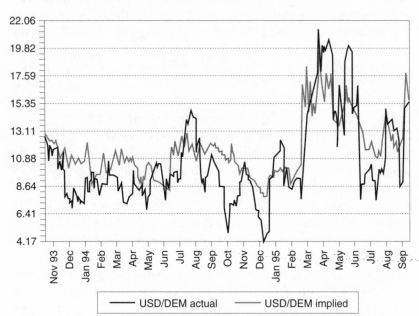

Nonetheless, option replication can provide substantial benefit when used correctly and in the right circumstances. Unfortunately, experience shows that the best time to replicate has proven to be under the most dangerous conditions, specifically in the course of a panic, when implied volatility gaps to unrealistically high levels. Under these conditions, value can be added by choosing replication to avoid having to pay an exorbitant implied volatility, provided actual volatility comes in at lower levels. But if actual volatility exceeds implied volatility, the option that formerly looked expensive may come to be regarded as having been a bargain.

The ultimate test for any replication program is how well it does relative to the alternative of buying the option. Still other questions may be addressed with respect to the efficiency of the rebalancing rule and to whether the replication program was executed with any trading finesse.

THE CPPI ALTERNATIVE

Black and Jones (1986) and Perold (1986) independently discovered a clever mathematical algorithm that is capable of producing option-like return patterns without using the option-theoretic replication presented in the previous section (also see Black and Perold 1989). The idea has come to be called constant proportion portfolio insurance (CPPI), the reason for which will soon become apparent. CPPI was developed as an alternative to option-theoretic portfolio insurance on the stock market, but the concept has been extended to currencies (DeRosa 1991).

In CPPI theory, there are two assets, one risky and the other riskless. At the start of a program, the investor decides on the maximum acceptable loss that could be tolerated, thereby establishing a floor level to the portfolio. The difference between the actual market value of the portfolio and the floor is called the cushion. The idea is to set the exposure to the risky asset in constant proportion to the size of the cushion. The balance of the portfolio is put into the riskless asset.

This simple strategy can be effective in maintaining the market value of the portfolio above the floor, without precluding participation in up markets. A simple demonstration is shown with

50 simulations of CPPI in Exhibit 10–3. The floor in this experiment was set to 90 percent (a maximum loss of 10 percent). The stochastic shocks were sampled from a normal white noise population with zero mean and standard deviation of 9.5 percent. Each of the 50 observations represents the total rate of return on the "insured portfolio" after experiencing 10 shocks. The overall pattern is decidedly option-like. The floor is preserved in all cases.

The CPPI equation can be written:

$$E = k[MV - \text{Floor}]$$

where

E	is the exposure to the risky asset.
MV	is the market value of the portfolio.
$[MV - \text{Floor}]$	is the cushion.
k	is the constant proportion.

EXHIBIT 10–3

CPPI—50 Random Simulations (Floor 90%; $k = 5$)

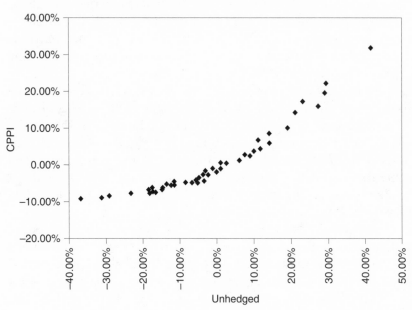

The constant k is the speed with which the program moves in reaction to changes in the value of the portfolio. When the risky asset declines, it lowers the market value of the portfolio and the cushion. In this circumstance, CPPI reduces the exposure to the risky asset fast enough to protect the portfolio's value and keep it above the chosen floor. When the risky asset rises, it raises the portfolio and the cushion. The CPPI algorithm increases the exposure to the risky asset. The speed at which the exposure to the risky asset is increased or decreased is the constant k. A k between 2.0 and 7.5 seems to work well in currency applications. k was set to 5.0 in the random simulations depicted in Exhibit 10–3.

CPPI will preserve the market value of the portfolio above the floor so long as the market does not drop by more than the fraction $(1/k)$ before rebalancing is done. Herein lie the seeds of the program's possible failure. If exchange rates make a large, discontinuous move, as did stock prices in October 1987, the program might break through the floor. As discussed in the previous section, option-theoretic replication has the same problem. This is why any dynamic program, including CPPI, is much better suited to major currencies, where large discontinuous jumps are less likely. Minor currencies, especially those whose values are artificially supported by government stabilization programs, are the most likely to experience extreme market shocks and as such are poor candidates for dynamic replication strategies.

To modify CPPI to work for currency risk, think of the portfolio as being partially hedged with currency forward contracts. The portion of the portfolio that is not hedged is the "risky asset"; and the other portion, which is hedged, is the "risk-free asset." In usual practice, the program is constrained not to sell more than 100 percent of the currency exposure forward and not to allow new currency exposure to be taken by adding long forward positions.

Rebalancing or trigger rules have to be established. Some practitioners follow the simple rule of rebalancing once or twice per month. This may be sufficient but it is probably wise to rebalance before too large of a cumulative move in exchange rates has occurred. This is an important consideration because the CPPI algorithm cannot maintain the floor if exchange rates move adversely by more than $(1/k)$ before rebalancing takes place.

How does CPPI compare to option-theoretic replication? Black and Rouhani (1987) reported that CPPI is superior to option-theoretic put replication in both calm and turbulent markets. The opposite was true in markets with intermediate levels of volatility. This may give an important edge to CPPI, given the leptokurtic nature of currency returns.

There are other reasons for favoring the CPPI strategy. It is relatively simple to use compared with the option-theoretic approach. Unlike option-theoretic programs, CPPI has no fixed horizon date. An option-theoretic program usually sets out to replicate European exercise puts. This means it can guarantee the floor only as of the expiration date. CPPI, on the other hand, is always in force. The floor is never broken, provided there is timely rebalancing. This is particularly important if there is no defined investment horizon.

AN OPTION-BASED APPROACH TO MULTICURRENCY OVERLAY

A simple, dynamic option-based strategy can be used as a part of an overlay program for the purpose of replicating a basket option to protect a multicurrency portfolio exposure (DeRosa 1993).

Consider a portfolio exposure implied by the three currencies in Exhibit 10–4. The exposures are the same ones used in discussion on basket options in Chapter 9 (Exhibit 9–3). Suppose the investor seeks protection equal to 95 percent of the one-year forward dollar value of the portfolio, or $37,527,821. This would equate to a floor value of $35,798,869. In the first instance, the investor could purchase a strip of three currency puts (USD call/DEM put; USD call/GBP put; USD call/JPY put), each struck at 95 percent of the forward outright level. The portfolio now would be protected from exchange rate movements at 95 percent of its forward value less the cost of the puts.

Note that the cost of the strip of the three separate puts is $1,055,324, or 2.8 percent, compared to $752,181, or 2.00 percent, for the basket put shown in Exhibit 9–3. The difference in price

EXHIBIT 10-4

Option-Based Approach to Multicurrency Overlay

One-Year Program
Floor   95.00%
Interest USD   6.00%

Currency Exposures

	Spot	Foreign Interest Rate	1-Year Forward Points	Forward Outright	Currency Amount	Spot Equivalent	Forward Equivalent	Weight
USD/DEM	1.4100	4.78%	−0.0169	1.3931	17,500,000	$12,411,348	$12,561,912	33.47%
GBP/USD	1.5975	7.22%	−0.0194	1.5781	8,000,000	$12,780,000	$12,624,800	33.64%
USD/JPY	84.85	1.38%	−3.82	81.03	1,000,000,000	$11,785,504	$12,341,108	32.89%
						$36,976,851	$37,527,821	100.00%

Step 1 Initial Basket of Puts

	Spot	Initial Strike	Implied Vol	Currency Put	Option Cost	Protected Value
USD/DEM	1.4100	1.4664	14.00%	0.02234	$391,001	$11,933,817
GBP/USD	1.5975	1.5176	11.05%	0.03982	$318,553	$12,141,000
USD/JPY	84.85	85.29	13.00%	0.00035	$345,770	$11,724,053
					$1,055,324	$35,798,869

(continued)

Option-Based Approach to Multicurrency Overlay (concluded)

Step 2 Restrike on Spot Movement

	Spot	Old Strike	Implied Vol	Currency Put	Option Value		New Strike	Currency Put	Option Value	Protected Value
						Restrike				
USD/DEM	1.4500	1.4664	14.00%	0.02922	$511,350		1.5500	0.01585	$277,376	$11,290,323
GBP/USD	1.5975	1.5176	11.05%	0.03982	$318,553		1.5176	0.03982	$318,553	$12,141,000
USD/JPY	81.00	85.29	13.00%	0.00020	$199,485		80.75	0.000400	$399,535	$12,383,901
					$1,029,388				$995,464	$35,815,224
								Restrike P&L	$33,924	

Step 3 Restrike on Spot Return Movement

	Spot	Old Strike	Implied Vol	Currency Put	Option Value		New Strike	Currency Put	Option Value	Protected Value
						Restrike				
USD/DEM	1.4100	1.5500	14.00%	0.01151	$201,511		1.4664	0.02234	$391,001	$11,933,817
GBP/USD	1.5975	1.5176	11.05%	0.03982	$318,553		1.5176	0.03982	$318,553	$12,141,000
USD/JPY	84.85	80.75	13.00%	0.00063	$629,930		85.29	0.000346	$345,770	$11,724,053
					$1,149,994				$1,055,324	$35,798,869
								Restrike P&L	$94,670	

arises from the fact that there can be instances of one or more of the separate puts expiring in-the-money in spite of the basket option expiring out-of-the-money. This marginal advantage, which was referred to in earlier chapters as the nonlinearity property, can be captured at least in part by periodically restriking the puts in the strip. Restriking the puts refers to replacing two or more of the puts with other puts having different strikes. The currency weights are held constant. The key concept is that there are multiple combinations of put strikes that preserve the protected forward value of the portfolio. After a movement in spot rates, it may be feasible to find a new set of puts that accomplish the same portfolio protection at a lower cost.

Exhibit 10–4 demonstrates how the restriking can capture some of the experienced economic value of the dispersion in movements in exchange rates. In the second step of the program, dollar/mark has moved up to 1.4500 from 1.4100, and dollar/yen has moved down to 81.00 from 84.85. The value of the strip of puts has changed from $1,055,324 to $1,029,388. The right-hand column shows another strip of puts that provides the same floor protection at a lower cost, $995,464. Exchanging the original basket for the new basket captures $33,924 of premium.

The proof that restriking captures dispersion is given by the simple experiment in the bottom panel of Exhibit 10–4, where the spot exchange rates are moved back to their original levels. This creates the opportunity to restrike a second time, this time recovering $94,670, by going back to the original strikes. In the course of this round trip, nothing has changed except that a total of $128,594 has been recovered by restriking the puts.

How frequently should the put strip be restruck? The manager must weigh the benefit of premium recapture against the cost of paying the option bid–ask spread. In the limit, the profits from the restriking program will be limited by the degree of correlation between exchange rates. Lower levels of correlation imply greater opportunities to extract trading profits from restriking, given a level of volatility in exchange rates. Said another way, absent transactions costs, one would expect that a perfectly executed restriking program would capture enough option premium so as to equate the cost of the program to the cost of a basket option, given the assumption that the option implied volatilities and implied correlations are realized in the subsequent actual behavior of the spot rates. On the other hand, if the actual correlation between exchange rates breaks down, the "make" over "buy" decision of going with the restriking program over buying the basket option will have been correct. The answer also depends on whether or not the overlay manager wants to express directional views on foreign exchange. For example, a skillful manager will not want to reduce the strike—and therefore the option delta—on a put on a currency that is expected to sharply deteriorate.

BENCHMARK-RELATED ISSUES AND PERFORMANCE MEASUREMENT

One topic of perennial discussion is whether there is an appropriate benchmark for a currency overlay program. Institutional investors favor an unhedged currency benchmark. The total return on an unhedged index is calculated by converting the local market returns back to the base currency using spot exchange rates. This measures the overlay manager against the alternative of having done nothing to protect the portfolio against currency risk. Any hedging the overlay manager does will look attractive in retrospect if foreign currencies deteriorate in value relative to the base currency. On the other hand, if foreign currencies appreciate, an unhedged benchmark will be particularly difficult to beat. This is because the benchmark will accrue the full upside gains with no hedging costs.

Another popular performance index is the fully hedged benchmark. Hedged benchmarks are constructed by adding the gains and losses from a rolling series of short-term forward contracts to the experienced currency translation gains or losses on the portfolio. Intellectual arguments for using a hedged benchmark were introduced by Perold and Schulman (1988), who posit that currency risk earns no risk premium in the marketplace and that hedging reduces portfolio risk. (See Chapter 1.)

The choice between hedged and unhedged benchmarks should depend on investment objectives. The fully hedged benchmark places more weight on not losing value to exchange rate fluctuations. This is because it effectively subsidizes any hedging activity by subsuming the full hedging costs, including the interest rate spread as reflected in the forward rates, into the benchmark. On the other hand, the unhedged benchmark is comparatively unforgiving of any failure on the part of the overlay manager to capture upside gains.

Performance measurement of overlay programs that utilize currency options and option replication is more complicated; traditional hedged and unhedged benchmarks are inadequate for the job. If the foreign currency has fallen in value, the question is whether the floor has been maintained. Conversely, if the foreign currency has risen, the program ought to capture a portion of the upside exchange rate movement. In the intermediate case, where the upside movement is small, the program may have a negligible or even negative capture. This is because the cost of the option may outweigh any gross gains from exercise at expiration.

Upside capture can be measured by the following method. Imagine the portfolio were run like a mutual fund with two classes of shares. All of the assets are invested in a portfolio of foreign securities. Class A shares are claims to units of the portfolio with the additional feature that a currency overlay program is functioning. A second class of hypothetical shares, B shares, are claims to units of the underlying portfolio of foreign securities with no overlay. All gains and losses from the overlay program are applied to the Class A shares exclusively.

Define A_0 and A_1 as the values of the class A shares at times 0 and 1, and B_0 and B_1 as the values of the class B shares at time 0 and 1. All are denominated in the foreign currency. Define S_0 and S_1 as the spot exchange rates at times 0 and 1, quoted American convention.

The total performance of the class A shares, measured in the investor's own currency, is given by the price relative

$$\frac{A_1 S_1}{A_0 S_0}$$

If the foreign currency were to appreciate, part of the total performance would be due to the upside capture by the currency insurance program. The remainder would be due to the performance of the foreign securities portfolio. The ratio

$$\frac{B_1}{B_0}$$

is the price relative of the Class B shares, which do not have currency overlay protection. The ratio measures the performance of the underlying portfolio of foreign securities.

The portion of the total performance of the class A shares that is due to upside capture of currency gains can be measured as

$$\left[\frac{A_1 S_1}{A_0 S_0} \div \frac{B_1}{B_0} \right] - 1$$

The upside capture ratio can be defined as

$$\frac{\left[\dfrac{A_1 S_1}{A_0 S_0} \div \dfrac{B_1}{B_0} \right] - 1}{\dfrac{S_1}{S_0} - 1}$$

The depreciation or expression in the denominator is the percentage appreciation in the foreign currency.

To consider a numerical example, consider a hypothetical mutual fund that invests in U.S. dollar securities on behalf of yen-based investors and has the following U.S. dollar NAV (net asset value).

	$t = 0$	$t = 1$
A shares	$1,000	$1,025
B shares	$1,000	$1,050
USD/JPY	100	110

Between time 0 and time 1, the dollar appreciated

$$\frac{S_1}{S_0} - 1 = \frac{110}{100} - 1 = 10.00\%$$

Class B shares accrued all of this appreciation. How much of the appreciation did class A enjoy? The amount of upside capture is

$$\left[\frac{A_1 S_1}{A_0 S_0} \div \frac{B_1}{B_0}\right] - 1 = \frac{1025 \times 110}{1000 \times 100} \div \frac{1050}{1000} - 1 = 7.38\%$$

This means that the upside capture ratio is

$$\frac{7.38\%}{10.00\%} = 73.80\%$$

BIBLIOGRAPHY

Abramowitz, Milton, and Irene A. Stegun, eds. *Handbook of Mathematical Functions with Formulas, Graphs, and Mathematical Tables.* Washington, DC: National Bureau of Standards, Applied Mathematics Series 55, December 1972.

Adler, Michael, and Bernard Dumas. "Exposure to Currency Risk: Definition and Measurement." *Financial Management*, Summer 1984, pp. 41–50.

Association Cambiste Internationale. *Code of Conduct.* Paris: Dremer-Muller & Cie, Foetz, 1991.

Association for Investment Management and Research (AIMR). *Performance Presentation Standards*, Charlottesville, VA, 1993.

Babbel, David F., and Laurence K. Isenberg. "Quantity-Adjusting Options and Forward Contacts." *The Journal of Financial Engineering* 2, no. 2 (June 1993), pp. 89–126.

Bachelier, Louis. *Theorie de la Speculation.* Paris: Gauthier-Villars, 1900. Reprinted in *The Random Character of Stock Market Prices*. Edited by Paul H. Cootner. Cambridge, MA: MIT Press, 1967.

Ball, Clifford A., and Antonio Roma. "Stochastic Volatility Option Pricing." *The Journal of Financial and Quantitative Analysis* 29, no. 4 (December 1994), pp. 589–607.

Bank for International Settlements. "Survey of Foreign Exchange Market Activity." Basle, 1993.

Barone-Adesi, Giovanni, and Robert E. Whaley. "Efficient Analytic Approximation of American Option Values." *Journal of Finance* 42 (June 1987), pp. 301–20.

Bates, David S. "The Skewness Premium: Option Pricing under Asymmetric Processes." Manuscript. The Wharton School, May 1994a.

———. "Jumps and Stochastic Volatility: Exchange Rate Processes Implicit in Deutschemark Options." Manuscript. The Wharton School, December 1994b. (Forthcoming, *Review of Financial Studies*).

Benson, Robert, and Nicholas Daniel. "Up, Over and Out." *Risk* 4 (June 1991), pp. 17–19.

Bilson, John F. O. "The Speculative Efficiency Hypothesis." *Journal of Business* 54, no. 3 (1981), pp. 435–51.

Black, Fischer. "The Pricing of Commodity Contracts." *Journal of Financial Economics* 3 (January–March 1976), pp. 167–79.

———. "Universal Hedging: How to Optimize Currency Risk and Reward in International Equity Portfolios." *Financial Analysts Journal* 45 (July/August 1989), pp. 16–22.

———. "Equilibrium Exchange Rate Hedging." *The Journal of Finance* 45, no. 3 (July 1990), pp. 899–907.

Black, Fischer, and John Cox. "Valuing Corporate Securities: Some Effects of Bond Indenture Provisions." *Journal of Finance* 31 (May 1976), pp. 351–68.

Black, Fischer, and Robert Jones. "Simplifying Portfolio Insurance for Corporate Pension Plans." New York: Goldman Sachs, 1986.

———. "Simplifying Portfolio Insurance." *Journal of Portfolio Management*, Fall 1987, pp. 48–51.

Black, Fischer, and Andre F. Perold. "Theory of Constant Proportion Portfolio Insurance." Working Paper #90-028. Harvard Business School, 1989.

Black, Fischer, and Ramine Rouhani. "Constant Proportion Portfolio Insurance and the Synthetic Put Option: A Comparison." New York: Goldman Sachs, 1987.

———. "Constant Proportion Portfolio Insurance: Volatility and the Soft-Floor Strategy." New York: Goldman Sachs, 1988.

Black, Fischer, and Myron Scholes. "The Pricing of Options and Corporate Liabilities." *Journal of Political Economy* 81 (May–June 1973), pp. 637–59.

Bodurtha, James N. Jr., and Georges R. Courtadon. "Tests of an American Option Pricing Model on the Foreign Currency Options Market." *Journal of Financial and Quantitative Analysis* 22 (June 1987), pp. 153–67.

Boyle, Phelim P., and David Emanuel. "Mean Dependent Options." Working Paper. University of Waterloo, 1985.

Brock, William A., David A. Hsieh, and Blake LeBaron. *Nonlinear Dynamics, Chaos, and Instability.* Cambridge, MA: MIT Press, 1992.

Cavaglia, Stefano M. F. G., Willem F. C. Verschoor, and Christian C. P. Wolff. "On the Biasedness of Forward Foreign Exchange Rates: Irrationality or Risk Premia?" *Journal of Business* 67, no. 3 (1994), pp. 321–43.

Chesney, M., and L. Scott. "Pricing European Currency Options: A Comparison of the Modified Black–Scholes Model and a Random Variance Model." *Journal of Financial and Quantitative Analysis* 24 (September 1989), pp. 267–84.

Cornell, Bradford, and Marc R. Reinganum. "Forward and Futures Prices: Evidence from the Foreign Exchange Markets." *Journal of Finance* 36, no. 12 (December 1981), pp. 1035–45.

Cox, John C., Jonathon E. Ingersoll, and Stephen A. Ross. "The Relationship Between Forward and Futures Prices," *Journal of Financial Economics* 9 (December 1981), pp. 321–46.

Cox, John C., and Stephen A. Ross. "The Valuation of Options for Alternative Stochastic Processes." *Journal of Financial Economics* 3 (January–March 1976), pp. 145–66.

Cox, John C., Stephen A. Ross, and Mark Rubinstein. "Option Pricing: A Simplified Approach." *Journal of Financial Economics* 7 (September 1979), pp. 229–63.

Cox, John C., and Mark Rubinstein. *Options Markets.* Englewood Cliffs, NJ: Prentice-Hall, 1985.

Derman, Emanuel, and Iraj Kani. "The Volatility Smile and Its Implied Tree." New York: Goldman Sachs, January 1994.

Derman, Emanuel, Piotr Karasinski, and Jeffrey S. Wecker. "Understanding Guaranteed Exchange-Rate Contracts in Foreign Stock Investments." New York: Goldman Sachs, 1990.

DeRosa, David F. "An Introduction to Currency Insurance." In *Global Portfolios—Quantitative Tools for Maximum Performance,* edited by Robert Aliber and Brian Bruce. Homewood, IL: Dow Jones-Irwin, 1991.

———. *Options on Foreign Exchange.* Chicago: Probus Publishing, 1992.

———. "An Option-Based Approach to Currency Risk Management." In *Strategic Currency Investing,* edited by Andrew W. Gitlin. Chicago: Probus Publishing, 1993.

DeRosa, David F., and Philip G. Nehro. "Equity-Linked Cross Currency Swaps." In *Cross Currency Swaps,* edited by Carl R. Beidleman. Homewood, IL: Business-One Irwin, 1992.

Deutsche Bundesbank. *Exchange Rate Statistics,* 1994.

Dominguez, Kathryn M., and Jeffrey A. Frankel. *Does Foreign Exchange Intervention Work?* Washington, DC: Institute for International Economics, 1993.

Dravid, Ajay, Mathew Richardson, and Tong-sheng Sun. "Pricing Foreign Index Contingent Claims: An Application to Nikkei Index Warrants." *The Journal of Derivatives* 1 (1993), pp. 33–51.

———. "The Pricing of Dollar-Denominated Yen/DM Warrants." *Journal of International Money and Finance* 13, no. 5 (1994), pp. 517–36.

Dupire, Bruno. "Pricing with a Smile." *Risk,* January 1994, pp. 18–20.

Fama, Eugene F. "Forward and Spot Exchange Rates." *Journal of Monetary Economics* 14 (1984), pp. 319–38.

Fama, Eugene F., and Merton Miller. *The Theory of Finance.* New York: Holt, Rinehart and Winston, 1972.

Francis, Jack Clark, and Stephen A. Archer. *Portfolio Analysis.* 2d ed. Englewood Cliffs, NJ: Prentice-Hall, 1979.

Frankel, Jeffrey A., and Kenneth A. Froot. "Using Survey Data to Test Standard Propositions on Exchange Rate Expectations." *American Economic Review* 77 (March 1987), pp. 133–53.

Freidman, Daniel, and Stoddard Vandersteel. "Short-Run Fluctuations in Foreign Exchange Rates: Evidence from the Data 1973–79." *Journal of International Economics* 13 (1982), pp. 171–86.

Froot, Kenneth A. "Currency Hedging over Long Horizons." Working Paper No. 4355. National Bureau of Economic Research, May 1993.

Froot, Kenneth A., and Jeffrey A. Frankel. "Forward Discount Bias: Is It an Exchange Risk Premium?" *Quarterly Journal of Economics* 416 (February 1989), pp. 139–61.

Froot, Kenneth A., and Richard A. Thaler. "Anomalies—Foreign Exchange." *Journal of Economic Perspectives* 4, no. 3 (Summer 1990), pp. 179–92.

Funabashi, Yoichi. *Managing the Dollar: From the Plaza to the Louvre.* 2d ed. Revised. Washington, DC: Institute for International Economics, 1989.

Garman, Mark B. "A General Theory of Asset Valuation under Diffusion State Processes." Working Paper No. 50. The University of California, Berkeley, 1976.

———. "Perpetual Currency Options." Manuscript. Department of Business Administration, University of California, Berkeley, 1986.

———. "Recollection in Tranquillity." *Risk* 2 (March 1989), pp. 16–19.

Garman, Mark B., and Steven W. Kohlhagen. "Foreign Currency Option Values." *Journal of International Money and Finance* 2 (December 1983), pp. 231–37.

Gastineau, Gary L. "The Currency Hedging Decision: A Search for Synthesis in Asset Allocation." Forthcoming, *Financial Analysts Journal.*

Gemmill, Gordon. *Options Pricing.* Berkshire, England: McGraw-Hill, 1993.

Geske, Robert. "The Valuation of Compound Options." *Journal of Financial Economics* 7 (March 1979), pp. 63–81.

Giavazzi, Francesco, and Alberto Giovanninni. *Limiting Exchange Rate Flexibility: The European Monetary System.* Cambridge, MA: MIT Press 1989.

Gibson, Rajna. *Option Valuation.* New York: McGraw-Hill, 1991.

Goodhart, Charles A. E., and Thomas Hesse. "Central Bank Forex Intervention Assessed in Continuous Time." *Journal of International Money and Finance* 12 (1993), pp. 368–89.

Grabbe, J. Orlin. "The Pricing of Call and Put Options on Foreign Exchange." *Journal of International Money and Finance* 2 (1983), pp. 239–53.

Hazuka, Thomas B., and Lex C. Huberts. "A Valuation Approach to Currency Hedging." *Financial Analysts Journal,* March–April 1994, pp. 55–59.

Heston, Steven L. "A Closed Form Solution for Options with Stochastic Volatility with Applications to Bond and Currency Options." *Review of Financial Studies* 6, no. 2 (1993), pp. 327–43.

Hodrick, Robert J. *The Empirical Evidence of the Efficiency of Forward and Futures Foreign Exchange Markets.* New York: Harwood Academic Publishers, 1987.

Hodrick, Robert J., and Sanjay Srivastava. "An Investigation of Risk and Return in Forward Foreign Exchange." *Journal of International Money and Finance* 3 (April 1984), pp. 315–29.

Hsieh, David. "Testing for Nonlinear Dependence in Daily Foreign Exchange Rates." *Journal of Business* 62 (1989), pp. 339–68.

Hsu, Hans. "Practical Pointers on Basket Options." *International Treasurer*, May 15, 1995, pp. 4–7.

Hudson, Mike. "The Value of Going Out." *Risk* 4, no. 3 (March 1991), pp. 29–33.

Hull, John C. *Options, Futures, and Other Derivative Securities.* 2d ed. Englewood Cliffs, NJ: Prentice-Hall, 1993.

Hull, John, and Alan White. "The Pricing of Options on Assets with Stochastic Volatilities." *Journal of Finance* 42 (June 1987), pp. 281–300.

International Monetary Fund. *Exchange Arrangements and Exchange Restrictions 1994.* Washington, DC.

J.P. Morgan. "RiskMetrics™—Technical Document." New York, November 1994.

Jacquier, Eric, Nicholas G. Polson, and Peter E. Rossi. "Baysian Analysis of Stochastic Volatility Models." *Journal of Business and Statistics* 12, no. 4 (October 1994), pp. 371–417.

Jarrow, Robert A., and Andrew Rudd. *Option Pricing.* Homewood, IL: Dow Jones-Irwin, 1983.

Jorion, Philippe. "On Jump Processes in the Foreign Exchange and Stock Markets." *Review of Financial Studies* 1, no. 4 (1988), pp. 427–45.

Kemna, A. G. Z., and C. F. Vorst. "A Pricing Method for Options Based on Average Asset Values." *Journal of Banking and Finance* 14 (1990), pp. 113–29.

Keynes, John Maynard. *A Tract on Monetary Reform.* London: Macmillan, 1923.

Kritzman, Mark. "Serial Dependence in Currency Returns: Investment Implications." *Journal of Portfolio Management*, Fall 1989, pp. 96–101.

———. "The Optimal Currency Hedging Policy with Biased Forward Rates." *Journal of Portfolio Management*, Summer 1993, pp. 94–100.

Levitch, Richard, M. "Empirical Studies of Exchange Rates: Price Determination and Market Efficiency." In *Handbook of International Economics*, edited by R. Jones and P. Kenen. Amsterdam: North-Holland Publishing, 1985.

Levitch, Richard M., and Lee R. Thomas. "The Merits of Active Currency Risk Management: Evidence from International Bond Portfolios." *Financial Analysts Journal.* September/October 1993, pp. 63–70.

Levy, Edmond. "Asian Arithmetic." *Risk* 3 (May 1990), pp. 7–8.

———. "Pricing of European Average Rate Currency Options." *Journal of International Money and Finance* 11 (1992), pp. 474–91.

Liu, Christina, and Jia He. "A Variance-Ratio Test of Random Walks in Foreign Exchange Rates." *The Journal of Finance* 46, no. 2 (June 1991), pp. 773–85.

Ljung, G. M., and G. E. P. Box. "On a Measure of Lack of Fit in Time Series Models." *Biometrika* 65 (1978), pp. 297–303.

Lorie, James H., et al. *Measuring the Investment Performance of Pension Funds for the Purpose of Inter-Fund Comparison*. Park Ridge, IL: Bank Administration Institute, 1968.

Macaulay, Frederick R. *The Movements of Interest Rates, Bond Yields, and Stock Prices in the United States Since 1856*. New York: National Bureau of Economic Research, 1938.

MacMillan, Lionel W. "Analytic Approximation for the American Put Option." *Advances in Futures and Options Research*. Vol. 1. Greenwich, CT: JAI Press, 1986, pp. 119–40.

Margrabe, William. "A Theory of Forward and Futures Prices." Working Paper. The Wharton School, University of Pennsylvania, 1976.

————. "The Value of an Option to Exchange One Asset for Another." *Journal of Finance* 33 (March 1978), pp. 177–86.

————. "Average Options." Working Paper. Bankers Trust Company, 1990.

McFarland, James W., R. Richardson Pettit, and Sam K. Sung. "The Distribution of Foreign Exchange Price Changes: Trading Day Effects and Risk Measurement." *Journal of Finance* 37, no. 3 (June 1982), pp. 693–715.

Merton, Robert C. "Theory of Rational Option Pricing." *Bell Journal of Economics and Management Science* 4 (Spring 1973), pp. 141–83.

————. "Option Pricing when Underlying Stock Returns Are Discontinuous." *Journal of Financial Economics* 3 (January/March 1976), pp. 99–118.

Perold, Andre F. "Constant Proportion Portfolio Insurance." Cambridge, MA: Harvard Business School, 1986.

Perold, Andre F., and Evan C. Schulman. "The Free Lunch in Currency Hedging: Implications for Investment Policy and Performance Standards." *Financial Analysts Journal*, May/June 1988, pp. 45–50.

Piros, Christopher D. "The Perfect Hedge: To Quanto or Not to Quanto." Working Paper. Massachusetts Financial Services. Forthcoming in *Currency Derivatives*, edited by David DeRosa. Burr Ridge, IL: Irwin Professional Publishing: 1996.

Press, William H., Brian P. Flannery, Saul A. Teukolsky, and William T. Vetterling. *Numerical Recipes*. Cambridge, MA: Cambridge University Press, 1986.

Reiner, Eric. "Quanto Mechanics." *Risk* 5 (March 1992), pp. 59–63.

Roberts, Harry V., and Robert Ling. *Conversational Statistics with IDA*. New York: The Scientific Press, 1982.

Rogalski, Richard J., and Joseph D. Vinso. "Empirical Properties of Foreign Exchange Rates." *Journal of International Studies*, Fall 1978, pp. 69–79.

Rubinstein, Mark. "Exotic Options." Manuscript. University of California at Berkeley, 1990.

————. "Options for the Undecided." *Risk* 4 (April 1991a), p. 43.

———. "Implied Binomial Trees." *The Journal of Finance* 69, no. 3 (July 1994), pp. 771–818.

Rubinstein, Mark, and Eric Reiner. "Breaking Down the Barriers." *Risk* 4 (September 1991a), pp. 29–35.

———."Unscrambling the Binary Code." *Risk* 4 (October 1991b), pp. 75–83.

Ruttiens, Allain. "Classical Replica." *Risk* 3 (February 1990), pp. 33–36.

Schwartz, Anna J. *Money in Historical Perspective.* Chicago: University of Chicago Press, 1987.

Scott, L. O. "Option Pricing when the Variance Changes Randomly: Theory, Estimation and an Application." *Journal of Financial and Quantitative Analysis* 22 (December 1987), pp. 419–38.

Stein, E. M., and C. J. Stein. "Stock Price Distributions with Stochastic Volatility: An Analytic Approach." *Review of Financial Studies* 4 (1991), pp. 727–52.

Stoll, Hans R., and Robert E. Whaley. "New Options Instruments: Arbitrageable Linkages and Valuation." *Advances in Futures and Options Research.* Vol. 1. Greenwich, CT: JAI Press, 1986, pp. 25–62.

Taylor, Stephen J., and Xinzhong Xu. "The Magnitude of Implied Volatility Smiles: Theory and Empirical Evidence for Exchange Rates." *Review of Futures Markets* 13 (1994), pp. 355–80.

Wasserfallen, Walter. "Flexible Exchange Rates: A Closer Look." *Journal of Monetary Economics* 23 (1989), pp. 511–21.

Wasserfallen, Walter, and Heinz Zimmermann. "The Behavior of Intra-Daily Exchange Rates." *Journal of Banking and Finance* 9 (1985), pp. 55–72.

Weinrib, Bruce, H., Thomas J. Discoll, and Peter J. Connors. "Final and Proposed Regulations Expand Available Foreign Currency Hedging Opportunities." *Journal of Taxation*, August 1992, pp. 110–18.

Westerfield, Janice M. "Empirical Properties of Foreign Exchange Rates under Fixed and Floating Rate Regimes." *Journal of International Economics* 7 (June 1977), pp. 181–200.

Whaley, Robert E. "On Valuing American Futures Options." *The Financial Analyst Journal* 42 (May/June 1986), pp. 194–204.

Xu, Xinzhong, and Stephen J. Taylor. "The Term Structure of Volatility Implied by Foreign Exchange Options." *Journal of Financial and Quantitative Analysis* 29, no. 1 (March 1994), pp. 57–73.

INDEX

Other books of interest to you from Irwin Professional Publishing . . .

CURRENCY FORECASTING

A Guide to Fundamental and Technical Models of Exchange Rate Determination

Michael R. Rosenberg

Explains every major method and aspect of exchange rate forecasting, from purchasing power, to parity, to interest rate differentials, to technical analysis. Gives guidelines for reducing risk with forecasting strategies.

1-55738-918-7   350 pages

EXCHANGE RATES AND CORPORATE PERFORMANCE

Yakov Amihud and Richard M. Levich

Describes the impact of the exchange rate on the global financial environment. Includes the views of practitioners and investment managers who are concerned about exchange rate volatility and the macroeconomic environment.

1-55623-596-8   432 pages